EX LIBRIS

VINTAGE **CLASSICS**

LOVE LETTERS

VIRGINIA WOOLF AND VITA SACKVILLE-WEST

WITH AN INTRODUCTION BY

Alison Bechdel

VINTAGE

7 9 10 8

Vintage Classics is part of the Penguin Random House group
of companies whose addresses can be found at
global.penguinrandomhouse.com

Penguin
Random House
UK

Selection by Lily Lindon, Vintage Classics 2021

This edition first published in Vintage Classics in 2021

penguin.co.uk/vintage-classics

A CIP catalogue record for this book is available from
the British Library

ISBN 9781784876722

Typeset in 10.75/13.25 pt Perpetua Std
by Integra Software Services Pvt. Ltd, Pondicherry

Printed and bound in Great Britain by Clays Ltd, Elcograf S.p.A.

The authorised representative in the EEA is Penguin Random House Ireland,
Morrison Chambers, 32 Nassau Street, Dublin D02 YH68.

Penguin Random House is committed to a sustainable future for
our business, our readers and our planet. This book is made from
Forest Stewardship Council® certified paper.

MIX
Paper from
responsible sources
FSC® C018179
FSC
www.fsc.org

CONTENTS

INTRODUCTION BY ALISON BECHDEL

When I was an undergraduate and just coming out as a lesbian, I slunk to a dimly lit, out-of-the-way place where I knew I would find other people like me – the stacks of the library. Vita Sackville-West was not the first companion I encountered there, but she was certainly the most indelible one.

I found her in *Portrait of a Marriage*, her son Nigel Nicolson's 1973 book about his parents' enduring and open relationship. I learned that both Vita and her husband, the diplomat Harold Nicolson, had numerous affairs, mostly with people of their own sex, while remaining otherwise devoted to one another, their children and their famous garden. The book also includes Vita's own account of her obsessive love affair with Violet Keppel in the early days of her marriage to Harold. I was spellbound by the image of Vita in Paris, passing as a man by wrapping her head with a khaki bandage – not an unusual sight just at the end of World War I – and strolling the streets with her lover. Who *was* this woman?

Towards the end of the book, the author provides a brief account of his mother's affair with Virginia Woolf. I hadn't yet read any of her books, but many of my friends had a postcard of her on their walls – the ethereal Beresford portrait taken when she was twenty. Her fragile beauty fit the narrative of tragic and doomed feminist heroine that was cohering at this time: she was a genius; she'd been molested by her step-brother; she struggled with some kind of mental illness; and in the end, after writing a few of the greatest books of the twentieth century, she had drowned herself. In some circles, more controversially, she was said to be a lesbian – a bold claim in those days.

Lesbian or not, she was quite a character too. I was touched by the fact that as children, Nigel Nicolson and his brother instinctively liked Virginia. 'We knew that she would notice us, that there would come a moment when she would pay no attention to my mother ("Vita, go away! Can't you see I'm talking to Ben and Nigel")' I learned a bit in *Portrait of a Marriage* about how Vita and Harold weathered Vita's relationship with Virginia, but I found myself longing for more of a window into what had gone on between these two redoubtable women. I wanted the details.

My wish was granted a few years later, when an edition of Vita's letters to Virginia was published. I had read some of Virginia's books by then, so it was all the more rewarding to observe these two writers pushing and pulling their way to a profound intimacy – the kind of intimacy I hoped to have with someone one day. Their passion for one another felt bound up for me with the new ground they were staking out for all women: Virginia in her work, and Vita in the world. I was in my twenties then, and despite how vividly this love story sprang from the page, it felt as if it had happened quite a long time ago, in the ancient past.

In middle age, I read the letters again. If I had had any doubt as to their continuing relevance, it would have been dispelled during one thorny patch of my own intimate life, when I found myself having passages quoted to me by two different women. This time though, the thing that impressed me most was how Vita and Virginia juggled all the elements of their fantastically busy lives – public demands, creative work, family and social obligations, other relationships, including those with their husbands – while still maintaining their own intimate connection.

Now at age sixty, a year older than Virginia was at her death, and ten years short of Vita's age when she died from cancer, I am struck by another aspect of the letters: the dogged fortitude of these women as they kept on going in the face of loss, illness, disillusionment and change. After a period of drifting apart, the two grow closer again as fascism spreads across Europe and the threat to their personal and intellectual freedom comes closer and closer to home. It has now been almost a century since Virginia and Vita fell in love, and strangely, that time feels much closer than it did when I was younger. Perhaps that's the perspective of age, perhaps it's because the world seems once again to be approaching an inflection point. But it's also a tribute to how intrepidly Vita and Virginia cast off the old forms and traditions of relationships to improvise something new.

The edition of the letters that I read in my youth consisted primarily of Vita's to Virginia, but included some extracts of Virginia's to Vita. The collection you hold in your hands, while not a complete compendium of their correspondence, focuses on a more gratifying exchange of letters between the two. And even better, it includes diary entries from both women, as well as letters from Vita to Harold. These occasional shifts in point of view provide a fuller picture of the relationship, and add momentum to a narrative that's already as gripping as a well-plotted novel.

If the correspondence between Vita and Virginia *were* a novel, it would be criticised for the too-obvious names of its protagonists. One surging with life force as she strides halfway across the world and back, the other living primarily in the wild reaches of her own imagination. Virginia's marriage to her husband Leonard was a chaste one, despite her brave attempt in the beginning at 'copulation'. ('Which,' Vita relays to Harold, 'was a terrible failure, and was abandoned quite soon.') But Virginia and Leonard had their own kind of intimacy. He was her first reader, and nursed her through her collapses. They had no children, but their joint enterprise, the Hogarth Press, brought many important books into the world.

When Vita and Virginia met at the end of 1922, Vita was thirty and already a famous writer. Virginia was forty, and just beginning to get recognition for her novels and essays. Vita was an aristocrat and a socialite, Virginia was a shabby inhabitant of Bloomsbury – that den of socialists, homosexuals, artists and conscientious objectors. Vita is better known now, of course, for her lovers and her garden than for her books, while Virginia has entered the canon. But at the time, Virginia was thrilled to learn that Vita had even heard of her. As the two women progress from 'Mrs Nicolson' and 'Mrs Woolf' to 'darling' and 'dearest', and thence to a menagerie of nicknames and avatars, one of the great literary love affairs of all time unfolds.

Although their early letters contain sparks of flirtation, it takes a while for things to heat up. Vita became entangled soon after they met in an affair with a man – an unusual change of pace for her. And Virginia was wary of this 'Sapphist' who 'may have an eye on me, old though I am.' But once Virginia invites Vita to submit a novel to the Hogarth Press, and Vita dedicates *Seducers in Ecuador* to her, the pace of the mutual seduction picks up. In 1925, Virginia is exhausted in the wake of *The Common Reader* and *Mrs Dalloway* – books which dazzled Vita and intensified the mystique Virginia held for her. But it's only when Virginia learns that Vita will be heading off to join Harold in Teheran for several months that the prospect of her absence seems to galvanise them both.

The letters they exchange when Vita is off on her travels are master-pieces of longing. Letters from the train – a brief one from Virginia that says only, 'Yes yes yes I do like you. I am afraid to write the stronger word.' Vita calculating the seconds until they will see each other (480,000). These letters are so intoxicating that when Vita finally returns to England, it's anticlimactic. But of course that's the nature of an epistolary narrative. The thing the reader most wants – for the protagonists to hook up at last – is the thing the reader never gets. That's where the writing stops.

From the outset, there's complete clarity on each woman's part about what she desires in the other. Virginia loves Vita's body, and Vita loves Virginia's mind. Virginia writes in her diary, 'She is stag like or race horse like… and has no very sharp brain. But as a body hers is perfection.' By 'body' Virginia means not just Vita's actual body, but, as she will later articulate, 'her capacity I mean to take the floor in any company, to represent her country, to visit Chatsworth, to control silver, servants, chow dogs; her motherhood (but she is a little cold and offhand with her boys), her being in short (what I have never been) a real woman.'

Vita records her first impression of Virginia in a letter to Harold. 'At first you think she is plain; then a sort of spiritual beauty imposes itself on you…' Vita will remain at great pains to convince Harold that her love for Virginia is 'a mental thing, a spiritual thing if you like, an intellectual thing…' She reports delightedly to him that conversation with Virginia made her feel 'as though the edge of my mind were being held against a grindstone.' While Virginia makes a few private digs about Vita's writing in her diary, Vita has nothing but admiration for Virginia's work, and one of her more laudable traits is her ability to appreciate Virginia's superior talent without envy. In fact, she would devote herself, along with Leonard, to protecting and nurturing it. She writes to Harold that Virginia 'inspires a feeling of tenderness, which is, I suppose, owing to her funny mixture of hardness and softness – the hardness of her mind, and her terror of going mad again.'

It's this dynamic of tenderness and the need to be cared for that is the real core of Vita's and Virginia's connection. As they approach the point where their relationship becomes physical, Virginia describes in her diary how Vita 'so lavishes on me the maternal protection which, for some reason, is what I have always most wished from everyone.' Virginia's actual mother was famously absent from her childhood, even before she died when Virginia was thirteen. Vita's narcissistic mother, a formidable presence in the letters, perhaps has something to do with the way Vita uses her caretaking to keep people from coming too close. Both women are expert, actually, at calibrating just the right amount of distance to maintain. When Vita makes an offhand remark about Virginia using people for copy, Virginia takes great exception, and it's only after a few letters that Vita manages to smooth her down again. Yet using Vita for copy is precisely what Virginia would proceed to do, in the most flagrant and fantastical way imaginable.

'... a biography beginning the year 1500 and continuing to the present day, called *Orlando*: Vita; only with a change about from one sex to another. I think, for a treat, I shall let myself dash this in for a week.' Although Virginia began writing *Orlando* in an intense, almost automatic burst in the autumn of 1927 after Vita had taken up with another woman, the book seems to have begun gestating the moment the two of them met five years earlier. Fascinated by Vita's aristocratic lineage, Virginia had requested from her a copy of *Knole and the Sackvilles*, a history of her ancestral home. A few weeks later, after Vita and Harold dined for the first time with Virginia and Leonard, the bohemian Virginia writes in her diary, 'Snob as I am, I trace her passions five hundred years back, and they become romantic to me, like old yellow wine.' By the time Virginia visited Knole in 1924, *Orlando* was an embryo. 'You perambulate miles of galleries; skip endless treasures

– chairs that Shakespeare might have sat on – tapestries, pictures, floors made of the halves of oaks…'

The phantasmagorical portrait that is *Orlando*, the romp through English history and literature in the form of a biography that is fictional, yet true, and whose subject is fixed in neither time nor gender, defied categorization. It was Virginia's best-selling book to date, no doubt due in part to the gossip factor – Virginia dedicated it to Vita and even included photographs of her, so there was no secret as to who it was modelled on. But also due to the fact that it was so good, so different, so new. It's hard to fathom how Virginia could play so freely with sexual identity in that much more conservative era, but play she did, inventing her way into the future. Orlando's fluid morphing from male to female both anticipated and had a part in generating the later theoretical shifts that are still unfolding in how we think about sex and gender.

Orlando can be read as a lesbian love story, but one so ingeniously involute that it escaped the fate of *The Well of Loneliness* – which, published in the same year, was tried and found obscene. Perhaps Virginia's biggest triumph with *Orlando*, though, was the fact that Vita loved it. Despite the fact that it was motivated to a certain extent by jealousy, and that it ruthlessly penetrates to the heart of Vita's personality, it also reflects her as the heroic nobleman Vita had always felt herself, on some level, to be. If she'd been born male, she would have inherited Knole. With her father's recent death, the house and title had officially passed to her uncle. But in the pages of *Orlando*, Virginia gloriously restored them to her.

Film and television portrayals of Virginia and of Vita have proliferated over the years, each capturing certain attributes of their models. Janet McTeer in BBC Two's *Portrait of a Marriage* embodies Vita's Wildean androgyny. Tilda Swinton in Sally Potter's *Orlando*, her magnetism. Nicole Kidman with her prosthetic proboscis in *The Hours* is a tormented Virginia, while Elizabeth Debicki in Chanya Button's recent *Vita & Virginia* is a fey, otherworldly one. But of course even the most brilliant performance can't convey the minds and souls of these remarkable women the way their own words do.

It would be remiss of me in this introduction to a book of letters not to observe that letter writing, with its friction of nib on paper, its pace slow enough to allow for the formation of actual thoughts, has fallen out of fashion. If Virginia and Vita had had smartphones, what a stream of sexting acronyms, obscure emoji (Scissors? A Bosman's potto?), Twitter links to *TLS* reviews, and endless snapshots of Alsatians and spaniels would sift through our fingers in lieu of this magnificent paper trail. But fortunately for all of us, they wrote, and wrote, and wrote, even as their feelings shifted over the years from passion to something quieter. Their letters are ardent, erudite, moving and playful. They are filled with gossip, desire, jealousy and tips on craft. And perhaps most delightfully, they are frequently laugh-out-loud hilarious. Virginia wonders in her diary, 'Am I in love with her? But what is love?' In these letters, both those questions are answered in dazzling, digressive detail.

EDITORIAL NOTE

This selection of letters and diaries is presented chronologically. Where the date was unmarked on the original letter, this edition has followed the date established by previous editors, including Nigel Nicolson, Joanne Trautmann Banks, Quentin Bell, Louise DeSalvo and Mitchell A. Leaska. Annotations and notes have been provided to clarify references that may be unfamiliar to the general reader. If there is an omission within the body of an extract, this has been marked with ellipses – […] – but omissions at the beginning or end of an extract are unmarked. Errors in spelling and punctuation have been silently corrected.

1922

Virginia's Diary

I am too muzzy headed to make out anything. This is partly the result of dining to meet the lovely gifted aristocratic Sackville-West last night at Clive's.[1] Not much to my severer taste – florid, moustached, parakeet coloured, with all the supple ease of aristocracy, but not the wit of the artist. She writes fifteen pages a day – has finished another book – publishes with Heinemanns – knows everyone. But could I ever know her? I am to dine there on Tuesday. The aristocratic manner is something like an actress's – no false shyness or modesty – makes me feel virgin, shy, and schoolgirlish. Yet after dinner I rapped out opinions. She is a grenadier; hard; handsome; manly; inclined to double chin.

Letter from Vita to Harold

Long Barn, Sevenoaks
19 December

I simply adore Virginia Woolf, and so would you. You would fall quite flat before her charm and personality. It was a good party. They asked a lot about your

---

1 Clive Bell, the art critic, was married to Virginia's sister Vanessa Bell.

Tennyson. *Mrs Woolf is so simple: she does give the impression of something big. She is utterly unaffected: there is no outward adornments — she dresses quite atrociously. At first you think she is plain; then a sort of spiritual beauty imposes itself on you, and you find a fascination in watching her. She was smarter last night; that is to say, the woollen orange stockings were replaced by yellow silk ones, but she still wore the pumps. She is both detached and human, silent till she wants to say something, and then says it supremely well. She is quite old.* I've rarely taken such a fancy to anyone, and I think she likes me. At least, she's asked me to Richmond where she lives. Darling, I have quite lost my heart.

1923

Letter from Virginia

Hogarth House, Surrey
3 January

Dear Mrs Nicolson,

I should never have dared to dun you if I had known the magnificence of the book.[1] Really, I am ashamed, and would like to say that copies of all my books are at your service if you raise a finger – but they look stout and sloppy and shabby. There is nothing I enjoy more than family histories, so I am falling upon Knole the first moment I get [...]

I wonder if you would come and dine with us? We don't dine so much as picnic, as the Press has got into the larder and into the dining room, and we never dress.

I would look up a train and give you directions if you can come, as I hope.

Yours very sincerely,

Virginia Woolf

---

1 Virginia had requested to see *Knole and the Sackvilles*, and Vita sent her a copy.

Letter from Vita to Harold

182 Ebury Street, London
10 January

Tomorrow I dine with my darling Mrs Woolf at Richmond [...] I love Mrs Woolf
with a sick passion. So will you. In fact I don't think I will let you know her.

Virginia's Diary

19 February

We had a surprise visit from the Nicolsons. She is a pronounced
Sapphist, and may, thinks Ethel Sands, have an eye on me, old though
I am. Snob as I am, I trace her passions five hundred years back, and
they become romantic to me, like old yellow wine. Harold is simple
downright bluff; wears short black coat and check trousers; wishes to
be a writer, but is not, I'm told and can believe, adapted by nature.
Soul, you see, is framing all these judgements, and saying, this is not
my liking, this is second rate, this vulgar; this nice, sincere, and so on.
My soul diminished, alas, as the evening wore on.

Vita's Diary

22 February

Dined with Virginia at Richmond. She is as delicious as ever. How right she is
when she says that love makes everyone a bore, but the excitement of life lies in
'the little moves' nearer to people. But perhaps she feels this because she is an
experimentalist in humanity, and has no grande passion in her life.

Virginia's Diary

17 March

46 [Gordon Square] has been very pleasant to me this winter. Two nights
ago the Nicolsons dined there. Exposed to electric light eggs show dark
patches. I mean, we judged them both incurably stupid. He is bluff,

but oh so obvious; she, Duncan[2] thought, took the cue from him, and had nothing free to say. There was Lytton,[3] supple and subtle as an old leather glove, to emphasise their stiffness. It was a rocky steep evening.

Vita's Diary

19 March

Lunched with Virginia in Tavistock Square, where she has just arrived. The first time that I have been alone with her for long. Went on to see Mama, my head swimming with Virginia.

Letter from Vita

182 Ebury Street
26 March

Dear Mrs Woolf
I write this tonight, because I think you said you were going to Spain on the 27th and I want it to catch you before you go. The PEN club committee are very anxious for you to join the club, and at their request I proposed you, — now will you be nice and let them make you a member? For my sake if for no other reason. It is only a guinea a year, and they would be so pleased. They dine once a month; it is quite amusing. Do, please, and come to the May dinner when they are entertaining distinguished foreign writers. There was a little shout of excitement from the Committee about you, and [John] Galsworthy[4] (so to speak) got up and made a curtsey.

---

2 Duncan Grant, a British painter, member of the Bloomsbury Group, who lived with Vanessa Bell.
3 Lytton Strachey, a British writer, critic and founding member of the Bloomsbury Group.
4 PEN's first president.

I hope you will have fun in Spain. It is the best country I know. Please let me know when you come back, as I do want you both to come and stay at Long Barn, and come up to Knole with me. And I shan't know when you are back unless you tell me.

Yours very sincerely
Vita Nicolson

Letter from Virginia

Hotel Ingles, Madrid
30 March

Dear Mrs Nicolson,
(But I wish you could be induced to call me Virginia.) I got your letter as we left Richmond. I am much flattered that the PEN should ask me to become a member.

I would do so with pleasure, except that I don't know what being a member means. Does it commit one to make speeches, or to come regularly, or to read papers or what? Living so far out, dinners are apt to be difficult, and I can't speak.

Letter from Vita

Long Barn, Sevenoaks
8 April

My dear Virginia
(You see I don't take much inducing. Could you be induced likewise, do you think?)

It is nice of you to say you will join the PEN club provided you don't have to make speeches. I can guarantee that, as by one of the club rules they are forbidden. The most you ever get is a statement from the chairman. Nor need you go to any dinners unless you want to. Nor does anyone read papers. You just go to a dinner when the spirit moves you, and take your chance of sitting next to Mr H. G. Wells or an obscure and spotty young journalist.

I don't suppose this letter will ever reach you. It always seems to be quite incredible anyway that any letter should ever reach its destination. But I seem to remember that you have already said – or, rather, written – all that there is to be said about letters. So I won't compete.

I am envying you Spain more than I can say. I wish I were with you – But the lady's smocks are very nice, along the hedges, and my tulips are coming out.

Yours very sincerely

Vita Nicolson

[Written in pencil] This paper is like blotting paper to write on in ink.

Letter from Virginia

Murcia, Spain

15 April

Dear Mrs Nicolson

The secretary of the PEN club has written to me to say that I have been elected a member. Very regretfully I have had to decline – since I see from the club papers that it is wholly a dining club, and my experience is that I can't, living at Richmond, belong to dining clubs. I've tried two dining clubs, with complete disaster. But I'm very sorry, as I should like to know the members, and see you also.

But this last I hope can be managed in other ways.

1924

There was then a hiatus in their correspondence, but when in March 1924 Virginia and her husband Leonard moved to Bloomsbury's Tavistock Square, Vita was among their first visitors. Virginia invited her to publish a book with the Woolfs' Hogarth Press. In response, Vita wrote *Seducers in Ecuador* while on her walking tour of the Dolomites with her husband, Harold Nicolson.

Virginia's Diary

5 July

Just back, not from the 1917 Club, but from Knole, where indeed I was invited to lunch alone with his Lordship. His Lordship lives in the kernel of a vast nut. You perambulate miles of galleries; skip endless treasures – chairs that Shakespeare might have sat on – tapestries, pictures, floors made of the halves of oaks; and penetrate at length to a round shiny table with a cover laid for one. [...] But the extremities and indeed the inward parts are gone dead. Ropes fence off half the rooms; the chairs and the pictures look preserved; life has left them. Not for a hundred years have the retainers sat down to dinner in the great hall. Then there is Mary Stuart's altar, where she prayed before execution. 'An ancestor of ours took her the death warrant,' said Vita. All these ancestors and centuries, and silver and gold, have bred a perfect body. She is stag like, or race horse like, save for the face, which pouts, and has no very sharp brain. But as a body hers is perfection. So many rare and curious objects hit one's brain like pellets which perhaps unfold later. But it's the breeding of Vita's that I took away with me as an impression, carrying her and Knole in my eye as I travelled up with the lower middle classes, through slums. There is Knole, capable of housing all the desperate poor of Judd Street, and with only that one solitary earl in the kernel.

Letter from Vita

Tre Croci, Cadore, Italy
16 July

I hope that no one has ever yet, or ever will, throw down a glove I was not ready to pick up. You asked me to write a story for you. On the peaks of mountains, and beside green lakes, I am writing it for you. I shut my eyes to the blue of gentians, to the coral of androsace; I shut my ears to the brawling rivers; I shut my nose to the scent of pines; I concentrate on my story. Perhaps you will be the Polite Publisher, and I shall get my story back – 'The Hogarth Press regrets that the accompanying manuscript,' etc. – or whatever your formula may be. Still, I shall remain without resentment. The peaks and the green lakes and the challenge will have made it worthwhile, and to you alone shall it be dedicated. But of course the real challenge wasn't the story (which was after all merely a 'commercial proposition'), but the letter. You said I wrote letters of impersonal frigidity. Well, it is difficult, perhaps, to do otherwise, in a country where two rocky peaks of uncompromising majesty soar into the sky immediately outside one's window, and where an amphitheatre of mountains encloses one's horizons and one's footsteps. Today I climbed up to the eternal snows, and there found bright yellow poppies braving alike the glacier and the storm; and was ashamed before their courage. Consequently, you see, one is made to feel extremely impersonal and extremely insignificant. I can't tell you how many Dolomitic miles and altitudes I have by now in my legs. I feel as though all intellect has been swallowed up into sheer physical energy and well-being. This is how one ought to feel, I am convinced. I contemplate young mountaineers hung with ropes and ice-axes, and think that they alone have understood how to live life — Will you ever play truant to Bloomsbury and culture, I wonder, and come travelling with me? No, of course you won't. I told you once I would rather go to Spain with you than anyone, and you looked confused, and I felt I had made a gaffe — been too personal, in fact — but still the statement remains a true one, and I shan't be really satisfied till I have enticed you away. Will you come next year to the place where the gipsies of all nations make an annual pilgrimage to some Madonna or other? I forget its name. But it is a place somewhere near the Basque provinces, that I have always wanted to go to, and next year I AM GOING. I think you had much better come too. Look on it, if you like, as copy, — as I believe you look upon everything, human relationships included. Oh yes, you like people through the brain better than through the heart, — forgive me if I am wrong. Of course there must be exceptions; there always are. But generally speaking [...]

And then, I don't believe one ever knows people in their own surroundings; one only knows them away, divorced from all the little strings and cobwebs of habit. Long Barn, Knole, Richmond, and Bloomsbury. All too familiar and entrapping. Either I am at home, and you are strange; or you are at home, and I am strange; so neither is the real essential person, and confusion results. But in the Basque provinces, among a horde of zingaros, we should both be equally strange and equally real.

On the whole, I think you had much better make up your mind to take a holiday and come.

Letter from Virginia

Monk's House, Lewes
19 August

Have you come back, and have you finished your book – when will you let us have it? Here I am, being a nuisance with all these questions.

I enjoyed your intimate letter from the Dolomites. It gave me a great deal of pain – which is I've no doubt the first stage of intimacy – no friends, no heart, only an indifferent head. Never mind: I enjoyed your abuse very much [...]

But I will not go on else I should write you a really intimate letter, and then you would dislike me, more, even more, than you do.

But please let me know about the book.

Letter from Vita

Long Barn
22 August

Aren't you a pig, to make me feel like one? I have searched my brain to remember what on earth in my letter could have given you 'a great deal of pain'. Or was it just one of your phrases, poked at me? Anyhow, that wasn't my intention, as you probably know. Do you ever mean what you say, or say what you mean? Or do you just enjoy baffling the people who try to creep a little nearer?

My story I fear is but a crazy affair. If you gave me a severe date by which it must reach you, typed and tidy, I should obey, being very tractable. If you say you must have it next week I will sit up all night and finish it. If you say 'any time will do' I shall continue to glance at it disgustedly once a day and shove it back into its drawer with no word added. Three-quarters of it exist at present and your letter gave it a fillip. Please issue an irrevocable command.

'Dislike you even more.' Dear Virginia (said she, putting her cards on the table), you know very well that I like you a fabulous lot; and any of my friends *could tell you that. But I expect you are blasé about people liking you, — no you aren't, though, — I take that back.*

I nearly came to see you last Sunday, as I was coming back from my mother at Brighton, but I thought you mightn't like it. And it was such a horrible day of gale and rain.

Now I had better go on with that story.

Letter from Virginia

Monk's House

26 August

My position about your story is this: if you could let us have it by Sept. 14th, we should make an effort to bring it out this autumn; if later, it is highly improbable that we could bring it out before early next year [...]

But really and truly you did say — I can't remember exactly what, but to the effect that I made copy out of all my friends, and cared with the head, not with the heart. As I say, I forget; and so we'll consider it cancelled.

Vita spent the night of 13 September with Virginia and Leonard, her first visit to Monk's House. She brought the manuscript of her story, *Seducers in Ecuador*.

Virginia's Diary

15 September

Vita was here for Sunday, gliding down the village in her large new blue Austin car, which she manages consummately. She was dressed in ringed yellow jersey, and large hat, and had a dressing case all full of silver and nightgowns wrapped in tissue. Nelly [Boxall][1] said 'If only

---

1 Nelly Boxall, the Woolfs' live-in housekeeper.

she weren't an honourable!' and couldn't take her hot water. But I like her being honourable, and she is it; a perfect lady, with all the dash and courage of the aristocracy, and less of its childishness than I expected. She is like an over ripe grape in features, moustached, pouting, will be a little heavy; meanwhile, she strides on fine legs,[2] in a well cut skirt, and though embarrassing at breakfast, has a manly good sense and simplicity about her which both L. and I find satisfactory. Oh yes, I like her; could tack her on to my equipage for all time; and suppose if life allowed, this might be a friendship of a sort. [She] took us to Charleston[3] – and how one's world spins round – it looked all very grey and shabby and loosely cut in the light of her presence. As for Monk's House, it became a ruined barn, and we picnicking in the rubbish heap.

Letter from Virginia

Monk's House
15 September

I like the story very very much – in fact, I began reading it after you left, was interrupted by Clive, went for a walk, thinking of it all the time, and came back and finished it, being full of a particular kind of interest which I daresay has something to do with its being the sort of thing I should like to write myself. I don't know whether this fact should make you discount my praises, but I'm certain that you have

---

2 In a letter to Jacques Raverat from the same period, Virginia described Vita's legs: 'her real claim to consideration is, if I may be so coarse, her legs. Oh they are exquisite – running like slender pillars up into her trunk, which is that of a breastless cuirassier (yet she has 2 children) but all about her is virginal, savage, patrician; and why she writes, which she does with complete competency and a pen of brass, is a puzzle to me. If I were she, I would merely stride, with 11 Elk hounds behind me, through my ancestral woods.'
3 The Sussex home of Vanessa Bell and Duncan Grant.

done something much more interesting (to me at least) than you've yet done. It is not, of course, altogether thrust through; I think it could be tightened up, aimed straighter, but there is nothing to spoil it in this. This is all quite sincere, though not well expressed.

I am very glad we are going to publish it, and extremely proud and indeed touched, with my childlike dazzled affection for you, that you should dedicate it to me.

Letter from Vita

Long Barn
17 September

I have walked on air all day since getting your letter. I am more pleased than I can tell you at your approval, and if I can tighten I will, – I felt myself that it needed this. Any suggestion would be welcomed?

How charming of you to sit on the millstones and say nice things. Altogether after reading your letter I felt like a stroked cat. You see, I appreciate the fact that neither of you are easy-going critics [...] whether of work or persons.

Letter from Virginia

52 Tavistock Square, London
4 October

We are just back; what did I find on the drawing room table, but a letter from which (to justify myself and utterly shame you) I make this quotation:

'Look on it, if you like, as copy, – I believe you look upon everything, human relationships included. Oh yes, you like people through the brain, rather than through the heart' etc.: So there. Come and be forgiven. *Seducers in Ecuador* looks very pretty, rather like a lady bird. The title however slightly alarms the old gentlemen in Bumpuses.

Letter from Vita

66 Mount Street, London
6 November

I came to Tavistock Square today. I went upstairs and rang your bell — I went downstairs and rang your bell. Nothing but dark inhospitable stairs confronted me. So I went away disconsolate. I wanted

a) *To see you.*
b) *To ask you whether any copies of our joint progeny had been sold, and if so how many.*
c) *To ask for some more circulars.*
d) *To ask you to sign two of your books which my mother had just been out to buy.*
e) *To be forgiven.*

I came away with all these wants unappeased.

Now I am going back to my mud till December 1st when I remove to Knole.

I await reviews in some trepidation.

Letter from Virginia

52 Tavistock Square
9 November

You have added to your sins by coming here without telephoning — I was only rambling the streets to get a breath of fresh air — could easily have stayed in, wanted very much to see you […]

I will sign as many books as Lady Sackville wants. No: I will not forgive you. Won't you be coming up for a day later, and won't you let me know beforehand?

Letter from Vita

Long Barn
13 November

This in haste.

I shan't be up till December now, but will then take the precaution of telephoning! Only I hate bothering people on the telephone.

I was grateful for the little bulletin — I hope the 430 copies will increase in splendour.

SINS:

1. Saying V.W. looked on friends as copy.

2. Coming without telephoning.

What else?

I will try to make up by passing on some remarks I got in a letter today, 'I am reading Jacob's Room *again. I think it is one of the first [rate] books of the day. It terrifies me. It is a book that leaves every other book both commonplace and common. One's own stuff seems horrible and vulgar.'*

There now: incense to your censer.

Virginia's Diary

21 December

Really it is a disgrace — the number of blank pages in this book! The effect of London on diaries is decidedly bad. This I fancy is the leanest of them all [...]

How sharply society brings one out — or rather others out! Roger[4] the other night with Vita for instance [...] The effect on Vita was disastrous [...] His Quaker blood protests against Vita's rich winy fluid; and

---

4 Roger Fry, English painter, critic, and member of the Bloomsbury Group.

she has a habit of praising & talking indiscriminately about art, which goes down in her set, but not in ours. It was all very thorny until that good fellow Clive came in, and addressed himself to conciliate dear old obtuse, aristocratic, passionate, Grenadier-like Vita.

1925

At the start of the year, Vita and Virginia occasionally met in London. Vita began to write her long poem *The Land*, and between bouts of illness Virginia started to write *To the Lighthouse*.

Letter from Vita

Long Barn
26 May

I have been horribly remiss in writing to thank you for Mrs Dalloway, *but as I didn't want to write you the 'How-charming-of-you-to-send-me-your-book-I-am-looking-forward-to-reading-so-much' sort of letter, I thought I would wait until I had read both it and* The Common Reader, *which I am sorry to say I have now done. Sorry, because although I may and shall read them again, the first excitement of following you along an unknown road is over, and nothing gives way so quickly as surprise to familiarity. I feel however that there are passages of* The Common Reader *that I should like to know by heart; it is superb; there is no more to be said. I can't think of any book I like better or will read more often.* Mrs Dalloway *is different; it is a novel; its beauty is in its brilliance chiefly; it bewilders, illuminates, and reveals;* The Common Reader *grows into a guide, philosopher and friend, while* Mrs Dalloway *remains a will-of-the-wisp, a dazzling and lovely acquaintance. One thing she has done for me for ever: made it unnecessary ever to go to London again, for the whole of London in June is in your first score of pages. (Couldn't you do a winter London now? With fogs and flares at the street corners, blue twilights, lamps, and polished streets?)*

How I envy you your English — How do you manage to make it as limpid as French, and yet preserve all the depth of its own peculiar genius?

When will you come here? For a weekend or in the week? And who am I to ask to meet you? You did promise to come in the summer, you know, — if a promise given on your area steps can bind you. I am going away for Whitsun, but apart from that I propose to be here immovably for several months. I cannot write, so I am keeping chickens instead.

Please come. I shan't think you 'nice' any longer if you don't.

Letter from Virginia

52 Tavistock Square
27 May

Hah ha! I thought you wouldn't like *Mrs Dalloway*.

On the other hand, I thought you might like *The Common Reader*, and I'm very glad that you do [...] I'm trying to bury my head in the sand, or play a game of racing my novel against my criticism according to the opinions of my friends. Sometimes *Mrs D.* gets ahead, sometimes the *C. R.*

Virginia's Diary

5 June

And we have had Vita, Edith Sitwell, Morgan,[1] Dadie[2] — old Vita presenting me with a whole tree of blue Lupins, and being very uncouth

---

1 E. M. Forster, the English writer and critic.
2 George Rylands, scholar and theatre director.

and clumsy, while Edith was like a Roman Empress, so definite, clear cut, magisterial, and yet with something of the humour of a fishwife [...] tremendously pleased by Morgan's compliments (and he never praised Vita, who sat hurt, modest, silent, like a snubbed schoolboy).

Letter from Virginia

52 Tavistock Square

24 August

I have a perfectly romantic and no doubt untrue vision of you in my mind – stamping out the hops in a great vat in Kent – stark naked, brown as a satyr, and very beautiful. Don't tell me this is all illusion [...]

But please tell me about your poem. Are you writing it? Is it very beautiful? I rather think I shall like it [...] What I wish is that you would deal seriously with facts. I don't want anymore accurate descriptions of buttercups, and how they're polished on one side and not on the other. What I want is the habits of earthworms; the diet given in the workhouse: anything exact about a matter of fact – milk, for instance – the hours of cooling, milking etc. From that, proceed to sunset and transparent leaves and all the rest, which, with my mind rooted upon facts, I shall then embrace with tremendous joy. Do you think there is any truth in this? Now, as you were once a farmer, surely it is all in your head ready.

Letter from Vita

Long Barn

25 August

Last Friday at midnight I stood on the top of your Downs, and, looking down over various lumps of blackness, tried to guess which valley contained Rodmell[3]

---

3 Rodmell is the Sussex village where Virginia's house, Monk's House, is located.

and you asleep therein. And now comes your letter, making me think that on the contrary you were probably awake and in pain.[4] *But knowing nothing of that at the time, I reluctantly recovered my dogs who had been galloping madly across the Downs, climbed into the motor, and drove on along deserted roads and through the sleeping villages of Sussex and Kent, with the secret knowledge in my own mind that I had paid you a visit of which you knew nothing, – more romantic, if less satisfying, than the cup of tea to which Leonard had bidden me on Saturday.*

I like extremely your corybantic picture of me [...] dancing in the vats. Please preserve it. I will not tell you the truth [...] Yet a page later you contradict yourself in your magnificent manner, and call loudly for exactitudes of the most prosaic description. Oddly enough, you have hit on the very things which my poem (which is not at all beautiful) does deal; you could run a small-holding on the information supplied [...] I have come to the conclusion that there is no longer any room for merely purple poetry; only for the prosaic (which has its own beauty), or for the intellectual. A bad definition but no doubt you will get my meaning. Purple occurs incidentally, but only with its roots ground stalworth in heavily manured soil – My interest in my own poem was dying down like an old fire, but you've fanned the embers and today there is quite a little blaze [...]

If ever you feel inclined, let me come and carry you off from Rodmell. I know that road so well, from going to see my mother at Brighton, that I can bundle along it with my eyes shut. I could devise many places to take you to.

Letter from Virginia

52 Tavistock Square
1 September

How nice it would be to get another letter from you – still better, to see you. I haven't suggested it since the headache has been an awful

---

4 Virginia had collapsed on 19 August.

nuisance this time, and I have had another week in bed. Now, however, even Leonard admits that I'm better.

My notion is that you may be motoring past and drop in and have tea, dinner, whatever you will, and a little conversation. One day next week? I'm going to be awfully quiet, and don't dare suggest what I long for – a drive to Amberley. But when I'm in robust health, as I shall be, could it really be achieved? [...]

I must stop: or I would now explain why it's all right for me to have visions but you must be exact. I write prose; you poetry. Now poetry being the simpler, cruder, more elementary of the two, furnished also with an adventitious charm, in rhyme and metre, can't carry beauty as prose can. Very little goes to its head. You will say, define beauty –

But no: I am going to sleep.

Letter from Vita

Long Barn
2 September

How much I like getting letters from you.

With what zest do they send me to meet the day.

So much do I like getting them, that I keep them as the last letter to open of my morning post, like a child keeps the bit of chocolate for the end –

But I like it less when I read that you have been ill for a week. It makes me feel guilty for every moment that I have spent, hearty and well, in such gross pursuits as gardening and playing tennis –

I shall be going to see my mother next week, one day. May I stop at Rodmell for dinner on my way back? (But not if it is a bore.) I would let you know which day. This depends on my mother. Early in the week, I expect. I shall suggest, to her, Monday or Tuesday. And Amberley any time you like – you may see in my underlining, a readiness to throw over any other engagement in order to fall in with your plans –

What nonsense you talk, though. There is 100% more poetry in one page of Mrs Dalloway *(which you thought I didn't like) than in a whole section of my damned poem [...]*

There are two people in the room, now, talking; and such fragments of their talk as reach me make me write frenziedly and-in-italics to you — out of a furnace of indignation — If my letter seems disjointed and hysterical, you must forgive it on that account [...]

I have been making a tiny garden of Alpines in an old stone trough — A real joy. It makes me long for the spring. My botanical taste tends more and more towards flowers that can hardly be seen with the naked eye — Shall I make an even tinier one for you? In a seed pan, with Lilliputian rocks? I'll bring it next week. But you must be kind to it, and not neglectful. (This all fits in with the theory that people who live in the country and like flowers are good.)

Letter from Virginia

52 Tavistock Square

7 September

Well, I don't see why you don't write to me, but perhaps it is my turn, only you are better situated for writing letters than I am. There are two people in your room, whom you can hear talking. There is one dog in my room, and nothing else but books, papers and pillows and glasses of milk and quilts that have fallen off my bed and so on. This has bred in me such a longing to hear what your two people are saying that I must implore you to tell me [...] Tell me who you've been seeing; even if I have never heard of them — that will be all the better. I try to invent you for myself, but find I really have only 2 twigs and 3 straws to do it with. I can get the sensation 'of seeing you' — hair, lips, colour, height, even, now and then, the eyes and hands, but I find you going off, to walk in the garden, to play tennis, to dig, to sit smoking and talking, and then I can't invent a thing you say — This proves, what I could write reams about – how little we know anyone, only movements and gestures, nothing connected, continuous, profound. But give me a hint I implore.

Letter from Vita

Long Barn
8 September

I am so sorry [...]

Your tale of fallen quilts really wrings my heart. And I am going to Brighton today, over your Downs, and shall leave this letter on your door step together with your garden-in-a-saucer. It looks dull at present, but in the spring it will give you flowers. You must keep it well watered.

The two people in my room were really Bulldog Drummond and Benjamin Constant. They didn't know it, and elected to go about their business under quite other names, but that's who they were. You may imagine that there were many points on which they didn't see eye to eye; and what irritated me was that I kept finding myself in agreement with both of them at the same time. My contrariness was aroused both ways at once. I disliked Drummond for his bulldoggery, and Constant for his inconstance, yet wanted to inoculate each with a dash of the faults of the other. This however appears to be an impossibility to the English character.

I went hop-picking, and have written half an article for Leonard. I'll try to finish it today or tomorrow, or all the hops will have turned into beer by the time it reaches The Nation.

My spaniel has seven puppies. My cat has five kittens. The spaniel steals the kittens, and, carrying them very carefully in her mouth, puts them into the puppies' basket. She then goes out for a stroll and the cat in search of her progeny curls up in the basket and suckles the puppies. The spaniel returns, chases out the cat, curls up in the basket, and suckles the kittens. I find myself quite unable to cope with this situation. The kittens will bark and the puppies will mew, – that's what will happen. But at present it makes a charming family party, – such a warm soft young heap.

I wish you were well and that I could see you. This is not really as selfish as it sounds, because most of all I wish that you were well, even if I were not to benefit. Is there anything you would like and that I could get you? Books, – but like the housemaid's mother, 'She's got a book.' I feel quite helpless, yet would like to please you. So you have only to say.

It will be very tantalising, stopping at your house. I shan't even ring the bell, but trust to luck that Leonard will fall over the saucer as he goes out.

Letter from Virginia

52 Tavistock Square
15 September

Oh you scandalous ruffian! To come as far as this house and make off! When the Cook came up to me with your letter, and your flowers and your garden, with the story that a lady had stopped a little boy in the village and given him them I was so furious I almost sprang after you in my nightgown.

Letter from Vita

*Long Barn
18 September*

You are a very, very remarkable person. Of course I always knew that, – it is an easy thing to know, – the Daily Xpress *knows it, – the* Dial *[Of New York] knows it, – organs so diverse, – the* Daily Herald *quotes you as an authority on the vexed question as to whether one should cross the road to dine with Wordsworth, – but I feel strongly that I have only tonight thoroughly and completely realised how remarkable you really are. You see, you accomplish so much. You are one perpetual Achievement; yet you give the impression of having infinite leisure. One comes to see you: you are prepared to spend two hours of*

Time in talk. One may not, for reasons of health, come to see you: you write divine letters, four pages long. You read bulky manuscripts. You advise grocers. You support mothers, vicariously. You produce books which occupy a permanent place on one's bedside shelf next to Gerald MANLY Hopkins and the Bible. You cast a beam across the dingy landscape of the Times Literary Supplement. *You change people's lives. You set up type. You offer to read and criticise one's poems, — criticise (in the sense which you have given to the word) meaning illumination, not the complete disheartenment which is the legacy of other critics. How is it done? I can only suppose that you don't fritter. Now here am I, alone at midnight, and I survey my day (the first that I have spent in peace for some weeks), and I ask myself what I have done with it. I finished the hops for Leonard, found an envelope and a stamp, and sent it off. I planted perhaps a hundred bulbs. I played tennis with my son. I endeavoured to amuse my other son, who has whooping-cough, and tries to crack jokes between the bouts. I read a detective story in my bath. I talked to a carpenter. I wrote five lines of poetry. Now what does all that amount to? Nothing. Just fritter. And yet it represents a better day than I have spent for a long time.*

Do you do it by concentration? Do you do it by organisation? I want a recipe so badly.

I assure you, it was misery to stop your anonymous little village boy and turn him into the Mercury who would ultimately reach your cook who would ultimately reach you. It was unselfish, wasn't it? Also, to be honest, I was frightened of Leonard. I knew he would look disapproving if I appeared at the house. He would look the more disapproving because he wouldn't know how much I approved, — of his care of you, I mean. After leaving Rodmell I took a road that wasn't a road at all; that is to say, it started by being a road and then melted away into grass, so that the last five miles of my journey were accomplished over pure Down, — very bumpy, but full of larks. A shepherd whom I met stared incredulously at the appearance of a blue motor in the middle of miles of rolling turf.

Yes I will send you my georgics when they are more consecutive; at present there is a spider here and a farrowing sow there, not tied together by an intelligible link. I will take advantage, quite unscrupulously, of your offer; but I shall continue to wonder how you fit it all in.

I like the sense of one lighted room in the house while all the rest of the house, and the world outside, is in darkness. Just one lamp falling on my paper; it gives a concentration, an intimacy. What bad mediums letters are; you will read this in daylight, and everything will look different. I think I feel night as poignantly as you feel the separateness of human beings; one of those convictions which are so personal, so sharp, that they hurt. *It seems to me that I only begin to live after the sun has gone down and the stars have come out.*

Letter from Virginia

52 Tavistock Square
23 September

Do keep it up – your belief that I achieve things. I assure you, I have need of all your illusions after 6 weeks of lying in bed, drinking milk, now and then turning over and answering a letter. We go back on Friday; what have I achieved? Nothing. Hardly a word written, masses of complete trash read, you not seen, but what was the good of asking you to come for half an hour, and then being furious to see you go? The blessed headache goes – I catch a cold or argue violently and it comes back. But now it has gone longer than ever before, so if I can resist the delights of chatter, I shall be robust for ever. But what I was going to say was to beg for more illusions. I can assure you, if you'll make me up, I'll make you […]

This is miserable scribbling, the effervescence of idleness. (I'm waiting for luncheon) but I shall rouse up in London. However, I'm going to live the life of a badger, nocturnal, secretive, no dinings out, or gallivantings, but alone in my burrow at the back. And you will

come and see me there — please say you will: if you're in London, let
me know. A little quiet talk in the basement — what fun!

Letter from Vita

Long Barn
11 October

*I wrote to you to Rodmell before I had got your letter telling me that you were
going back to London. A simple calculation leads me to the conclusion that
you will receive these two letters simultaneously, — or possible even this one
before the other [...] I will therefore conceal from you the destination of my
journeying, so that the other letter should not be deprived of its little bit of
news. (Although news is the last thing one wants or expects to find in letters.)
I will only tell you that it is not the Riviera or Italy, or even Egypt, but some
country wild, beautiful, and unsophisticated; further away in time, though not
in space, than China. The ideal travel letter should be without address, I think;
it should arrive like the Dove at the Ark, with no hint of where it has come
from, so that it may evoke a landscape romantically beautiful but geographically
vague. How I shall enjoy writing to you; how poignant it will be to feel that
ink is one's only means of communication; how ruthlessly I shall lay upon you
the burden of writing to the absent friend.*

Letter from Virginia

52 Tavistock Square
13 October

But for how long?

For ever?

I am filled with envy and despair. Think of seeing Persia — think of
never seeing you again.

The dr has sent me to bed: all writing forbidden. So this is my last
swan song. But come and see me.

Letter from Vita

Long Barn
13 October

No, not for ever. And not even immediately. Harold goes [to Teheran] next month, and I follow in January, and return in May, and then go again next October. So you see there will be a good deal of coming and going. In the meantime what concerns me much more is you and your evident un-wellbeing; I can't tell you how sorry I am. Of course I will come and see you if you are really allowed to see people. Leonard wrote me a letter which moved me almost to tears; please tell him this from me, and thank him, and tell him I wrote forty lines of georgics on the strength of it. It is nice to be told one will be missed.

I don't expect any answer to this, you know, because I know you are not allowed to write.

I wish you could see Harold's luggage, — half tropical and half arctic. Fur coats and sun-helmets; skates and khaki shorts. I dress him up to look like a game of Consequences. You soar from the desert to mountain-passes, putting on an extra garment with every thousand feet. I wish you would both come to Teheran. But it seems improbable that this wish will ever be fulfilled.

Letter from Vita

Long Barn
23 October

When I got home the other day⁵ I found that the puppet show of memory had disappeared, so I ordered it to be sent to you; I hope that it has turned up.⁶

You let fall some words to the effect that they 'wanted you to go away' presently; if you want a refuge, will you come here? I shall be all alone after

---

5 Vita had tea with Virginia on 19 October.
6 *The Puppet Show of Memory* (1922), Maurice Baring's autobiography.

Harold has gone, and I can promise you that you should be neither worried,
excited, nor disturbed — also it would be easily accessible for Leonard. You
could stay in bed all day if you wished; write if you wished, and talk if
you wished.

I've evolved some theories about friendship, but as I've got a cold in the
head I will leave their exposition for another day [...] I think, among other
things, that a set hour is full of peril; what one wants is the sudden desultory
talk, — the look-up from the book one is reading, the burst of argument between
two regions of silence. The set hour is first-cousin to being presented with an
ear-trumpet into which one has to improvise a remark.

All this is to invite your attention to the advantages of Long Barn as a
convalescent home [...] I do hope I didn't tire you — I was afraid I had. If
you came here I should leave you alone to the point of neglect. I should realise
my responsibility fully.

Letter from Virginia

52 Tavistock Square
26 October

My dear Vita — only it ought to be all execration —

I asked you to LEND me [Maurice Baring] — now you GIVE him.
Very well — I'll never ask you for so much as the loan of a boot button
again.

Nevertheless, your present was perfectly timed — All Friday I was
sick without stopping (my own fault — I refused to believe the doctor
who said it would stop if I ate a mutton chop — when I did I was cured
instantly) but by 6 p.m. I was almost extinct with the horror and then
your present came: I ate my chop, revived, and read till I fell asleep.
Nothing could have suited better [...]

You did not tire me: it was enchanting: and next time I would
arrange for some silence for you.

Letter from Vita

Long Barn
31 October

Yes, I thought I should get into a row. My intentions however were quite honourable, until I arrived home to discover that someone had made away with my Puppet Show, so I ordered one hoping that you wouldn't notice it came from a shop. I hope that this explanation may earn forgiveness for me, and restore you to that frame of mind in which you might regard my boot-buttons as yours if you stood in need of them.

I had meditated a descent upon you, but that news caused me to change my mind. If you are truly better, and no longer require chops, shall I pay you a brief visit on Tuesday next between 5 and 6? I shall be driving Harold about, while he makes his little round of farewells, and while he is in your romantic neighbourhood I could come in for a minute. But not if you are not well.

Leave it as open as you like about coming here. I shall be here till 20 December. I would love you to come, as you know; I can't say more —

Vita's Diary

7 November

Long Barn. A lovely warm golden day. Sat in the sun all the morning. Went to tea with Eddy[7] — Leonard went back to London, Virginia remained.
    ![8]

Letter from Virginia

52 Tavistock Square
16 November

I've flashed to the top of Hampstead Heath in a motor car, sat on a bench and seen three fir trees in the fog [...] And why don't I see you?

---

[7] Edward Sackville-West, a British music critic, and Vita's cousin.
[8] This ! is marked in a circle. Vita's diaries marked her most intimate encounters with Virginia as 'X' or '!'.

Owing to standing or sitting 3 minutes too long in the Press I am put back into bed – all the blame now falling on the Hogarth Press. But this is nothing very bad [...]

I am very sorry for you – really – how I should hate Leonard to be in Persia! But then, in all London, you and I alone like being married.

Virginia's Diary

27 November

Vita has been twice. She is doomed to go to Persia; and I mind the thought so much (thinking to lose sight of her for five years) that I conclude I am genuinely fond of her.

Virginia's Diary

7 December

Now, to write a list of Christmas presents. Ethel Sands comes to tea. But no Vita.

Letter from Vita

Long Barn
8 December

I have been doing something so odd, so queer, – or rather, something which though perhaps neither odd nor queer in itself, has filled me with such odd and queer sensations, – that I must write to you. (The thing, by the way, was entirely connected with you, and wild horses won't drag from me what it was.) And high time, too, that I did write. I meant to come and see you last Friday, but the fog and a variety of complaints prevented me. I was furious [...]

May I come and see you on Monday 21st? Which is my nearest London date.

I never said you were cruel. You must have been answering someone else's letter when you wrote to me. (I suspect you of dozens of correspondents.) I did

say 'esteem'. But I meant 'love'. Only I was afraid of getting snubbed. You see
you have only to be a little testy with me to get the truth.

I contrast my illiterate writing with your scholarly one, and am ashamed.

So dull, I am; dull outwardly, at least; all oafish and muddy; but not dull
inside. A week's solitude restores me to the sense that I am a person and not a
rag-heap for other people to pick over [...]

I have become a planet-snob — drunk with journeying. This makes me savour
my last days here all the more keenly.

May I, too, like the school girls, be told how to read a book?[9] *I am in such*
a temper with Proust.

Letter from Virginia

52 Tavistock Square
9 December

The dr says I may go away. Would you like me to come to you for a
day or two, if you are alone, before the 20th? I expect this is too late
and too difficult; I only suggest it on the off chance.

Letter from Virginia

52 Tavistock Square
10 December

Would Tuesday afternoon suit you?
Should I stay till Friday or Saturday?
Should Leonard come and fetch me back?
Should you mind if I only brought one dressing gown?
Should I be a nuisance if I had breakfast in bed?

---

9 Virginia's lecture, given to a girls' school at Hayes Common on 30 January 1926, was
published as 'How Should One Read a Book?'.

Letter from Vita

Long Barn
15 December

Yes you can have breakfast, lunch and dinner in bed if you feel like it.

Yes bring a dressing gown.

Yes let Leonard come whenever he likes.

What a pity you can't stay till Sunday — as I am going up on Sunday morning and it would have been nice to have taken you up — It will be a great joy to have you. I will look after you very well, and you shan't be bothered by anybody.

On 17 December through to 19 December, while Harold was in Teheran, Virginia went to stay with Vita at Long Barn.

Letter from Vita to Harold

Long Barn
17 December

[Virginia] is an exquisite companion, and I love her dearly. She has to stay in bed till luncheon, as she is still far from well, and she has lots of lessons to do. Leonard is coming on Saturday [...]

Please don't think that

a) I shall fall in love with Virginia

b) Virginia will fall in love with me

c) Leonard " " " " " "

d) I shall fall " " " Leonard

Because it is not so [...] I am missing you dreadfully [...] I am missing you specially because Virginia was so very sweet about you, and so understanding.

Letter from Vita to Harold

Long Barn
18 December

Virginia read the Georgics [The Land]. I won't tell you what she said. She insisted on reading them. She read them straight through. She likes you. She likes me. She says she depends on me. She is so vulnerable under all her brilliance. I do love her, but not b.s.ly.[10]

Vita's Diary

18 December

Talked to her till 3 a.m. – not a peaceful evening.

Letter from Vita to Harold

Long Barn
19 December

I think she is one of the most mentally exciting people I know. She hates the wishy-washiness of Bloomsbury young men. We have made friends by leaps and bounds, in these two days. I love her, but couldn't fall 'in love' with her, so don't be nervous!

Virginia's Diary

21 December

But no Vita! But Vita for three days at Long Barn, from which L. and I returned yesterday. These Sapphists *love* women; friendship is never untinged with amorosity. I like her and being with her, and the splendour – she shines in the grocer's shop in Sevenoaks with a candle-lit radiance, stalking on legs like beech trees, pink glowing, grape clustered, pearl

---

10 The initials 'b.s.' stood for 'back-stairs', and in Sackville shorthand meant 'homo-sexual'.

hung. Anyhow she found me incredibly dowdy, no woman cared less for personal appearance – no one put on things in the way I did. Yet so beautiful, &c. What is the effect of all this on me? Very mixed. There is her maturity and full breastedness: her being so much in full sail on the high tides, where I am coasting down backwaters; her capacity I mean to take the floor in any company, to represent her country, to visit Chatsworth, to control silver, servants, chow dogs; her motherhood (but she is a little cold and offhand with her boys), her being in short (what I have never been) a real woman. In brain and insight she is not as highly organised as I am. But then she is aware of this, and so lavishes on me the maternal protection which, for some reason, is what I have always most wished from everyone. What L. gives me, and Nessa gives me, and Vita, in her more clumsy external way, tries to give me. Anyhow, I am very glad that she is coming to tea today, and I shall ask her, whether she minds my dressing so badly? I think she does.

Letter from Virginia

52 Tavistock Square
22 December

I am dashing off to buy a pair of gloves. I am sitting up in bed: I am very very charming; and Vita is a dear old rough coated sheep dog: or alternatively, hung with grapes, pink with pearls, lustrous, candle lit, in the door of a Sevenoaks draper [...] Ah, but I like being with Vita.

Letter from Vita

Knole, Kent
24 December

I shall be oh so glad to see you again. So glad, that it makes me incapable of writing to you now. I must write you either a long letter, or else a note to say I will come to lunch. ('Damn you then, Vita, why not let it be the long letter?')

Letter from Vita to Harold

Knole

26 December

I lunched at Charleston – very plain living and high thinking. I like Virginia's sister [Vanessa] awfully. There were two huge, shaggy, rather attractive boys [Julian and Quentin Bell] who call their father and mother Clive and Vanessa. There was Clive, and Virginia and Leonard. Virginia discoursed about the Georgics [The Land] till I was shy. She does this to everyone, I find a good preliminary advertisement! I drove them over the Downs. So lovely in the mist [...] Virginia loves your mar. She really does.

1926

Vita and her children spent the New Year with Dorothy Wellesley and her family. Other guests included Virginia's brother-in-law, Clive Bell. At the New Year's Eve party, a great deal of alcohol was consumed.

Letter from Vita

Sherfield Court, Basingstoke
1 January

I write to you in a state of extreme perturbation — I'll tell you why when I see you.

I was taken off my guard.

It's early morning in the new year. I'll write you a proper letter — but I am upset now — it is Clive who is responsible.

The house is full of children and noise.

Your bewildered,

Vita

Letter from Vita to Harold

Sherfield Court
1 January

Clive with his tongue well-loosened, imagine my horror when he suddenly said, 'I wonder if I dare ask Vita a very indiscreet question?' and I, being innocent and off my guard, said yes he might, and he came out with 'Have you ever gone to bed with Virginia?' but I think my 'NEVER!' convinced him and everybody else of the truth. This will show you what the conversation was like!

Letter from Vita

Sherfield Court
3 January

It might seem strange, at first sight, that I should have talked of you so little, having thought of you so much. I had, after all, Clive at my elbow, – not merely your brother-in-law, but an authority who had loved you in his day, – yet I chose not to profit by his presence. Something kept me back; and now of course I regret the missed opportunity. No, that's not true: I don't. If I had the last three days over again, I should do the same.

I think I prefer making my own explorations. Also I don't fancy the idea of taking a false advantage.

I was rather indiscreet, all the same.

The conversation last night was free. I don't know what you would have thought, or what contributed. I wondered several times. I wondered also what report Clive would give you, if any. Can I see you on Wednesday? [...]

And it's on Wednesday fortnight that I go. Melancholy descends on me; but perhaps it's a good thing. What effect does absence have on you? Does it work like the decreasing charm of Dog Grizzle, which endears her to you the more?

I hope so, otherwise.

Letter from Virginia

52 Tavistock Square

5 January

Yes, my dear Creature, do come tomorrow, as early as possible ... But I want to know *why* you were perturbed, and wrote in such a whirl, and *what* your fire talk was about – oh and crowds of things.

But I'm in a rush – have just taken Grizzle to a vet [...] Ah, if you want my love for ever and ever you must break out into spots on your back.

Letter from Virginia

52 Tavistock Square

7 January

This is simply to ask how you are [...] Feeling very miserable, half asleep, taking a little tea and toast, and then, I daresay, towards evening becoming rather luminous and remote, and irresponsible. All this takes place in a room in the middle of Knole – What takes place in all those galleries and ballrooms, I wonder? And then, what goes on in Vita's head, lying under her arras somewhere, like a tiny kernel in a vast nut?

[...] But tell me what you are feeling? Are you aching? And if you were asked, do you like Canute,[1] Canute's wife, or Virginia best, what would you say?

I left a rain coat, a crystal ruler, a diary for the year 1905, a brooch, and a hot water bottle somewhere – either Long Barn or Charleston – and so contemplate complete nudity by the end of the year.

---

1 Vita's elk hound.

Letter from Vita

Long Barn
8 January

You angel, you have written. And I like your attitude towards illness: 'luminous and remote', where most people would have said 'hot and sticky' [...]

Please, in all this muddle of life, continue to be a bright and constant star. Just a few things remain as beacons: poetry, and you, and solitude. You see that I am extremely sentimental. Had you suspected that? [...]

Poor Canute, his feelings would be so terribly hurt if I answered your question truthfully, that loyalty forbids me.

Letter from Virginia

52 Tavistock Square
9 January

Isn't it damned? Here I am in bed with the flu, caught the moment I'd written to you about the delights of fever. Hot and sticky describes it [...]

But it is a great comfort to think of you when I'm not well – I wonder why. Still nicer – better to see you. So I hope for Tuesday [...]

A very nice dumb letter from you this morning.

Letter from Vita

Long Barn
11 January

Oh my poor dear, ill again, and the novel thwarted – How maddening for you. I have a great deal to say. Firstly that I don't care a damn, not a little row of pins, whether I catch it or not; I'd travel all the way to Egypt with the fever heavy upon me sooner than not see you – so rule that out please. Secondly that not for all the world would I tire you; so if you want to lie in a miserable heap, alone, just say so. I'll ring up at luncheon time tomorrow, and you can say 'Come' or 'Go to Hell' as you feel inclined [...]

My letters are not dumb, but vociferous: it is you who do not know how to read. And you presume to lecture schoolgirls on this subject! [...] Letters are the devil, disregarding Einstein and being subservient to so fallacious a thing as time, e.g. if you write to me in Persia and say you have got the ague it is no use my writing back to say I'm so sorry, because by the time you get it you'll have recovered, whereas if I write from the Weald you'll still be wretched when you get it and my condolence will be of some slight grain of use, but my feelings will be the same, whether in Persia or the Weald [...]

I find life altogether intoxicating, — its pain no less than its pleasure, — in which Virginia plays no mean part.

Letter from Vita

66 Mount Street, London
13 January

How are you today? I am all right — No.

Are you all right, my dear? I don't like your being ill [...]

It was nice yesterday, — wasn't it? I'll see you on Monday? And Tuesday? And then no more for months.

Letter from Virginia

52 Tavistock Square
15 January

I saw Clive yesterday, who says will you and Leonard and I dine with him on Monday at the Ivy? If you can't (as I fear) come to his rooms as soon as you can — We will come at 10.30, but I suppose I shan't be allowed to stay late.

Letter from Vita

Knole

17 January

I was dining out tomorrow, but have quite cynically chucked, so I can dine with you (with Clive I mean) at the Ivy. So you see that if my letters are dumb, my actions aren't. They are a practical demonstration of my wish to be with you [...]

I hope Clive's version didn't differ materially from mine, otherwise it is clear that one or the other is breaking the ninth commandment. And did your answer differ from mine? Alas no [...]

Oh curse, here are people and I must stop as the post goes early. I'm longing to see you. Someday I'll write and tell you all the things you mean to me in my mind. Shall I?

Virginia's Diary

19 January

Vita having this moment (twenty minutes ago) left me, what are my feelings? Of a dim November fog; the lights dulled and damped. But this will disperse; then I shall want her, clearly and distinctly. Then not – and so on. One wants that atmosphere – to me so rosy and calm. She is not clever; but abundant and fruitful; truthful too. She taps so many sources of life; repose and variety, was her own expression, sitting on the floor this evening in the gaslight. I feel a lack of stimulus, of market days, now Vita is gone; and some pathos, common to all these partings; and she has four days' journey through the snow.

Letter from Vita

21 Acacia Road, Balham[2]
20 January

No, it's no good: the train is too shaky to allow me to pretend. I am in the train, and there are sensational labels on my luggage — so there it is — and I did leave Virginia standing on her doorstep in a misty London evening — and God knows when I shall see her again. You said one thing which pleased me so much: namely, that you would try not to be in France when I came back. This gave me a real sense of counting in your life. Bless you [...]

Goodbye, my darling; and bless you.

Letter from Vita

Posted in Trieste
21 January

I am reduced to a thing that wants Virginia. I composed a beautiful letter to you in the sleepless nightmare hours of the night, and it has all gone: I just miss you, in a quite simple desperate human way. You, with all your un-dumb letters, would never write so elementary a phrase as that; perhaps you wouldn't even feel it. And yet I believe you'll be sensible of a little gap. But you'd clothe it in so exquisite a phrase that it would lose a little of its reality. Whereas with me it is quite stark: I miss you even more than I could have believed; and I was prepared to miss you a good deal. So this letter is just really a squeal of pain. It is incredible how essential to me you have become. I suppose you are accustomed to people saying these things. Damn you, spoilt creature; I shan't make you love me any the more by giving myself away like this — But oh my dear, I can't be clever and stand-offish with you: I love you too much for that. Too truly. You have no idea how stand-offish I can be with people I don't love. I have brought it to a fine art. But you have broken down my defences. And I don't really resent it.

However I won't bore you with any more.

We have re-started, and the train is shaky again. I shall have to write at the stations — which are fortunately many across the Lombard plain.

---

2 A joke address.

Venice. The stations were many, but I didn't bargain for the Orient Express not stopping at them. And here we are at Venice for ten minutes only, – a wretched time in which to try and write. No time to buy an Italian stamp even, so this will have to go from Trieste.

The waterfalls of Switzerland were frozen into solid iridescent curtains of ice, hanging over the rock; so lovely. And Italy all blanketed in snow.

We're going to start again. I shall have to wait till Trieste tomorrow morning. Please forgive me for writing such a miserable letter.

Letter from Vita

In the eastern Mediterranean
23 January

We are somewhere off the coast of Greece, and pretty beastly it is too: very rough, and the boat rolling about like an old tub. She has a deck too many, and consequently is top-heavy. There were a lot of things I wanted to ask you: whether you couldn't invent a new form of type for emphatic passages; a new system of punctuation; whether you shared my preference for the upper berth in a wagon-lit (which I believe to be atavistic), and my dislike of scraping past the stomachs of Frenchmen on the way to the wagon restaurant; and whether you would one day come on a journey with me? [...] Have you ever seen Crete? If not, you should.

My dear, I'll write you from Cairo. This is hopeless, and I must go to dinner.
PS I wrote you a frantic letter from Trieste.

Letter from Virginia

52 Tavistock Square
26 January

Your letter from Trieste came this morning – But why do you think I don't feel, or that I make phrases? 'Lovely phrases' you say which rob things of reality. Just the opposite. Always, always I try to say what I feel. Will you then believe that after you went last Tuesday – exactly a week ago – out I went into the slums of Bloomsbury, to find a barrel organ. But it did not make me cheerful … And ever since, nothing important has happened – Somehow it's dull and damp. I have been dull; I have missed you. I do miss you. I shall miss you. And if you don't believe it, you're a long-eared owl and ass. Lovely phrases?

[…] But of course (to return to your letter) I always knew about your standoffishness. Only I said to myself, I insist upon kindness. With this aim in view, I came to Long Barn. Open the top button of your jersey and you will see, nestling inside, a lively squirrel, with the most inquisitive habits, but a dear creature all the same –

Letter from Virginia

52 Tavistock Square

31 January

Shall I write the letter I made up in bed this morning? It was all about myself. I was wondering if I could explain how miserable I have been the past 4 days, and why I have been miserable. Thought about, one can gloss things over, bridge them, explain, excuse. Writing them down, they become more separate and disproportioned and so a little unreal – Only I found I had to write the lecture for the girls' school, and so had to stop writing *To the Lighthouse*. That began my misery; all my life seemed to be thwarted instantly: It was all sand and gravel; and yet I said, this is the truth, this guilty misery, and the other an illusion. […]

Yes, I miss you, I miss you. I dare not expatiate, because you will say I am not stark, and cannot feel the things dumb people feel. You know that is rather rotten rot, my dear Vita. After all, what is a lovely phrase? One that has mopped up as much Truth as it can hold.

Letter from Virginia

52 Tavistock Square

3 February

On Friday (but this will have happened weeks ago) we go to Rodmell. Dearest, how nice to have you there, in a month or two. I made £20 unexpectedly yesterday, and vowed to spend it perfecting the water closet on your behalf. But Teheran is exciting me too much. I believe, in this moment, more in Teheran than in Tavistock Square. I see you, somehow in long coat and trousers, like an Abyssinian Empress, stalking over those barren hills. But really what I want to know is how the journey went, the 4 days through the snow, the caravan. Shall you write and tell me? And the affectionate letter – when's that coming?

Letter from Vita

Luxor, Egypt
29 January

The only way I can deal with Egypt is as Molly MacCarthy did with Christmas: alphabetically.[3] Amon, Americans, alabaster, Arabs; bromides, buffaloes, beggars, Bronx; camels, crocodiles, colossi, Cook's; donkeys, dust, dahabeeahs, dragomen, dervishes, desert; Egyptians, Evian; fezzes, fellaheen, feluccas, flies, fleas; Germans, goats, granite; hotels, hieroglyphics, hoopoes, Horus, hawkes; Isis, imshi, irrigation, ignorance, jibbahs; kites, Kinemas, Kodaks; lavatories, lotus, Levantines; mummies, mud, millionaires; Nubia, Nile; ophthalmia, Osiris, obsidian, obelisks; palms, pyramids, parrokeets; quarries; Rameses, ruins; sunsets, sarcophagi, streamers, soux, sand, shadoofs, stinks, Sphinx; temples, tourists, trams, Tut-ankh-amen; Uganda; vultures, Virginia; water-bullocks, warts; Xerses, Xenophon; yaout; zest (my own).

What else? I miss you horribly, and apart from that am permanently infuriated by the thought of what you could make of this country if only you could be got here. You see, you ought to. However, that sounds too much like your own parody of my probable letters, so I'll refrain from saying it.

What fills me with dismay is the idea that I cannot hear from you till I get to Bombay, another fortnight at least. I wish I had given you an address at Cairo. You may be ill or anything. It is an odd sensation being so cut-off [...]

---

3 The spellings for this paragraph have not been corrected. They appear as they did in Vita's original letter.

Do thin silk clothes and sunburn make you envious? No, you wretch, you prefer your old misty Gloomsbury and your London squares. The wish to steal Virginia overcomes me, – steal her, take her away, and put her in the sun among the objects mentioned alphabetically above.

[...] I sent you a picture postcard today, just as an insult. I went down into the bowels of the earth and looked at Tut-ankh-amen. At his sarcophagus and outer mummy-case, I mean. This is merely of gilded wood. The inner one is at Cairo (I saw it) and is of solid gold. You know, the Valley of the Kings is really the most astonishing place. Tawny, austere hills with a track cut between them; no life at all, not a bird, not a lizard, only a scavenger Kite hanging miles high; and undiscovered Kings lying lapped in gold. And English spinsters in sun-helmets and black glasses. But then I got away from the spinsters and climbed where no one was, and looked down into the Valley on one side, and on to the Nile on the other, a fine contrast in barrenness and fertility; and got into a state of rapture.

You see, I have really got a very cheap mind. (You say you like to know what goes on inside, so I tell you.) If human beings are one-half as exciting to you as natural objects are to me, then indeed I see why you like living in London. I cannot explain why they should have this intoxicating quality. I can quite see why human beings should have. But why the yellow mountains, and yellower pariah dog with whom I shared my lunch? But there it is. And, – mark, – I do care so satisfactorily for the few people that matter to me. (For Virginia? Oh dear me YES, for Virginia.) Please solve this riddle for me.

I am now going to Karnak. It is full moon, and it quite frightens me to think what it will be like. Damn *that you're not here.*

Letter from Virginia

52 Tavistock Square

17 February

You are a crafty fox to write an alphabet letter, and so think you have solved the problem of dumbness [...]

I've been awfully worried by elderly relations. Three old gentlemen, round about 60, have discovered that Vanessa is living in sin with Duncan Grant, and that I have written *Mrs Dalloway* – which equals living in sin. Their method of showing their loathing is to come to call, to ask Vanessa if she ever sells a picture, me if I've been in a lunatic asylum lately. Then they intimate how they live in Berkeley Sqre or the Athenaeum and dine with – I don't know whom: and so take themselves off. Would this make you angry?

[…] Do you know it was four weeks yesterday that you went? Yes, I often think of you, instead of my novel; I want to take you over the water meadows in the summer on foot, I have thought of many million things to tell you. Devil that you are, to vanish to Persia and leave me here! […] And, dearest Vita, we are having *two* water-closets made, one paid for by *Mrs Dalloway*, the other by *The Common Reader*: both dedicated to you.

Letter from Vita

In the Red Sea
4 February
I feel as though I should like to write you a long letter. An endless letter. Pages and pages. But there is too much to say. Too many emotions, and too much Egypt, and too much excitement. And really it all reduces itself to the perfectly simple thing that I wish you were here.

You see it is so easy for you sitting in Tavistock Square to look inward; but I find it very difficult to look inward when I am also looking at the coast of Sinai; and very difficult to look at the coast of Sinai when I am also looking inward and finding the image of Virginia everywhere.

So this combination makes my letter more dumb than usual.

You manage things better. You have a more tidily sorted mind. You have a little compartment for the Press, and another compartment for Mary

Hutchinson,[4] and another for Vita, and another for Dog Grizzle, and another for the Downs, and another for London fogs, and another for the Prince of Wales, and another for the Lighthouse — no I'm wrong, the Lighthouse is allowed to play its beam over the whole lot, — and their only Common Denominator is your own excitability over whichever compartment you choose to look into at the moment. But with me they all run together into a sort of soup.

Letter from Vita

In the Red Sea
6 February

I have no brain left. It has melted. I am sticky from head to foot. I have made friends with a Parsee who specialises in Persian, and has determined that I should become proficient in the language before I reach Bombay. So I'm having a wretched time, — kept at work as hard as a schoolboy, and no brain to do it with. I like the night-sky though, with the stars getting bigger and bigger, and odder and odder, and the phosphorus in the water.

The rest of the time I read Proust. As no one of board has ever heard of Proust, but has enough French to translate the title, I am looked at rather askance for the numerous volumes of Sodome et Gomorrhe which litter the decks.

But why did he take ten pages to say what could be said in ten words?

[...] Oh my dear Virginia. Is there really a London? And are you in it? Or am I thinking of, and writing to, a wraith? Don't get ill. Be severe with les importuns. How is the novel? Blown by this hot gale, I can't write a word. But I hope my little granary is filling up, under the Southern Cross. If I don't get a letter from you at Bombay, I shall die of disappointment —

My love to Leonard.

---

4 Mary Hutchinson, the writer and model, was having an affair with Clive Bell.

Letter from Virginia

52 Tavistock Square
1 March

Yes, dearest Towzer, it is all very well about Bloomsbury being a rotten biscuit, and me a weevil, and Persia being a rose and you an Emperor moth – I quite agree: but you are missing the loveliest spring there has ever been in England. We were motored all through Oxfordshire two days ago [...] The people who took us were Leonard's brother and his wife. I promptly fell in love, not with him or her, but with being stock brokers, with never having read a book (except Robert Hitchens) [...] Oh this is the life, I kept saying to myself; and what is Bloomsbury, or Long Barn either, but a contortion, a temporary knot; and why do I pity and deride the human race, when its lot is profoundly peaceful and happy?

A lovely dumb letter came from you on Saturday, written on board ship. I extract by degrees a great deal from your letters. They might be longer; they might be more loving. But I see your point – life is too exciting.

Letter from Vita

In the Indian Ocean
8 February

The Indian Ocean is grey, not blue; a thick, opaque grey. Cigarettes are almost too damp to light. At night the deck is lit by arc-lights, and people dance; it must look very strange seen from another ship out at sea, – all these people twirling in an unreal glare, and the music inaudible. One's bath, of sea-water, is full of phosphorus: blue sparks that one can catch in one's hand. The water pours from the tap in a sheet of blue flame [...]

But by the time I come home I shall have written a book, which I hope will purge me of my travel-congestion, even if it serves no other purpose.[5] The moment it is released, it will pour from me as the ocean from the bath-tap — but will the blue sparks come with it, or only the blanket-grey of the daytime sea? (By the way, I have discovered since beginning this letter that one can draw pictures on one-self with the phosphorus; it's like having a bath in glow-worms; one draws pictures with one's fingers in trails of blue fire, slowly fading.)

For the rest, it is a perpetual evading of one's fellow-beings. Really what odd things grown-up, civilised human beings are, with their dancing and their fancy-dress [...]

We have crept onward a few hundred miles since I began this letter, and the sun has come tropically out, and the clergymen have put on their sun-helmets. Tomorrow I shall be bouncing across India in a dusty train.

Have you quite forgotten this poor pilgrim? I haven't forgotten that I am to tell you I think of you, but I think that will be a nice occupation for the Persian Gulf. In the meantime I think of you a terrible great deal. You make a wonderful cynical kindly smiling background to the turbulence of my brain. Shall I find a letter from you at Bombay I wonder?

Letter from Vita

Delhi
14 February

Well, I had India to myself for a couple of hours, while the stars paled and the dawn spread over it; and then the usual row began, and I met the Parsee in the customs house looking very foolish with a garland of white waxen flowers round his neck, over his petit complet gris-perle, like a sacrificial heifer. And I went for my letters, but there was none from you, which blackened India

---

5 Vita's travel book, *Passenger to Teheran*, was published by the Hogarth Press in November 1926.

until I remembered that I had told you to write to Rocky Hill Flats — We drove there for breakfast, and although the rooms were cool and creamy, with the windows open on the sea, and punkahs stirring the air, and great jars of oleander everywhere, still there were no letters.

As I had been counting on that letter for at least three weeks, the delicious fruits that I was given for breakfast might have been handfuls of dust for all I cared. But then suddenly a Black servant entered with armfuls of correspondence. And of course there was quite a simple explanation, that your letter had travelled with me on the [SS] Rajputana [...]

You will agree that it was a pretty setting for your letter to be read in, that had been written in the dark north — and frightened out of its life in a mail-bag down in the hold of a ship? Poor little thing, if I had known that it lay cowering there, I would have rescued it. But no; the seals of the GPO are inviolable (like Virginia) [...]

I was terribly pleased when I read that you had been excited, writing. Also terribly envious. And yet, I feel, you know, that if I could get really embarked on something I should become excited about it too. But of course there is nothing like a novel for that peculiar thing: as good as conducting an orchestra, or modelling in clay. A sense of really giving shape [...]

The tree-rats are very sweet. Like tiny green squirrels. I tried to catch one, and it bit me. Not like Virginia, who has inquisitive habits, but is a dear creature, and for whom I have a terrible and chronic homesickness. It is a persistent complaint, — sortes virginiana.

Letter from Vita

At sea in the Persian Gulf
20 February

I meant to have written such a lot, but somehow I haven't; there is always a whale or a murder to look at (a tortoise or a theorbo!), so I have written a few letters, — precious few, — and read a lot of Proust and that's all. But I shall begin now to try and collect myself, and write some articles. I don't know whether to be dejected or encouraged when I read the works of Virginia Woolf. Dejected because I shall never be able to write like that, or encouraged because somebody else can?

Letter from Vita

Baluchistan
23 February

In how fastidious and amused a grin (like Grizzle's) would your lips curl if you could see me at the present moment. Somewhere off the coast of Baluchistan, lame, and newly risen from three days of fever, I have literally pushed the other passengers (five in number) into each other's arms to dance to my gramophone. They were really too dreary for words; something had to be done about it; so I hauled the gramophone out from under my bunk, and now they are all as merry as crickets [...] You see, I am so pleased to find that I am not, after all, going to die and be buried at sea, swathed in a Union Jack and decently weighted, that I am full of the milk of human kindness towards my fellows. If anyone had told me, quite simply, that newcomers were liable to fever in these parts, I should not have lain envisaging (1) diphtheria (2) dysentery (3) plague (4) scarlet fever alone in my cabin for three days, but according to my all-too insular ideas one does not suddenly shoot up to 103 without good reason. Here, however, apparently one does. I said to myself, 'Perhaps Virginia will be a little sorry.' I wrote to you, in fact, I think, just when it was beginning. I composed telegrams so moving that when I realised I should not have to send them, I was quite disappointed [...] I wondered whether it would make my books sell any better. I feared not.

And now I am quite spry again, and have even written six pages of my new book. It is a rambling, discursive sort of affair. And I think of your lovely books, and despair [...]

The funny thing is, that you are the only person I have ever known properly who was aloof from the more vulgarly jolly sides of life. And I wonder whether you lose or gain? I fancy that you gain, – you, Virginia, – because you are so constituted and have a sufficient fund of excitement within yourself, though I don't fancy it would be to the advantage of anybody else [...] (You'll think that I'm perpetually trying to pull you down from your pedestal, but really I like you best up there. Only it would be fun to transplant you, pedestal and all, just once ...)

No, I don't really mean that. What I should really like to do would be to take you to some absurdly romantic place, – vain dream, alas! What with Leonard and the Press – Besides, by romantic I mean Persia or China, not Tintagel or Kergarnec. Oh what fun it would be, and Virginia's eyes would grow rounder and rounder, and presently it would all flow like water from a Sparklets siphon, turned into beautiful bubbles.

But I am writing nonsense, and anyway this letter cannot be posted till Baghdad. So that you will get two together, and that will be a bore.

Goodnight, darling and remote Virginia.

Letter from Virginia

52 Tavistock Square
16 March

I have been meaning every day to write something – such millions of things strike me to write to you about – and never did, and now have only scraps and splinters of time, damn it all – We are rather rushed – But, dearest Vita, why not take quinine, and sleep under mosquito nets? I could have told you about fever: do tell me if you are all right again (a vain question: time has spun a whole circle since you had fever off the Coast of Baluchistan). Much to my relief, Lady Sackville wrote and told me you had arrived: also she asks me to go and see her, to talk about you, I suppose. 'I know you are very fond of Vita'; but I haven't the courage, without you.

Last Saturday night I found a letter from you in the box: then another: What luck! I thought; then a third; incredible! I thought; then a fourth: But Vita is having a joke, I thought, profoundly distrusting you – Yet they were all genuine letters. I have spelt them out every word, four times, I daresay. They do yield more on suction; they are very curious in that way. Is it that I am, as Ly Sackville says, very fond of you: are you, like a good writer, a very careful picker of words? (Oh look here: your book of travels. May we have it? Please say yes, for the autumn.) I like your letters I was saying, when overcome by the usual Hogarth Press spasm. And I would write a draft if I could, of my letters; and so tidy them and compact them; and ten years ago I did write drafts, when I was in my letter writing days, but now, never. Indeed, these are the first letters I have written since I was married.

As for the *mot juste*, you are quite wrong. Style is a very simple matter, it is all rhythm. Once you get that, you can't use the wrong words. But on the other hand here am I sitting after half the morning, crammed with ideas, and visions, and so on, and can't dislodge them, for lack of the right rhythm. Now this is very profound, what rhythm is, and goes far deeper than words. A sight, an emotion, creates this wave in the mind, long before it makes words to fit it; and in writing (such is my present belief) one has to recapture this, and set this working (which has nothing apparently to do with words) and then, as it breaks and tumbles in the mind, it makes words to fit it: but no doubt I shall think differently next year.

Devil, you have never sent me your photograph. Angel, you wish to know about Grizzle: she has eczema, and a cough. Sometimes we peer into her throat and Leonard moves a bone.

Yes, dearest Vita: I do miss you; I think of you: I have a million things, not so much to say, as to sink into you.

Letter from Vita

Baghdad
28 February

Ah, let me see, what have I seen, done, or felt since I last wrote? I was very miserable in the Gulf with incessant fever; then I landed at Basrah, and was carried off by the Consul, and plunged for twenty-four hours into his family life. Kind people, Scotch, living in a big shadowy house; of Mrs Berry it is related that once when the tribes rebelled and the consulate was stormed by wild Arabs bent on murder, her only concern was that she had not had time to bring in the washing. That sums up her whole attitude towards life. Then I learnt all the local gossip, and what I now don't know about the goings-on of Molly Brown and Mirabelle Kernander isn't worth knowing. But one isn't a pilgrim for nothing, and next day I had to leave this kind new home, with its dogs and all [...] and start off again across Iraq.

[...] My heart goes out to you over the hat, and the mattresses, and the impossibility of privacy; I live permanently in that state; but beware: it becomes a mania. It has poisoned my life. I have quarrelled with at least three people because of it. I feel very strongly about it. I go down into precisely those troughs of desperation which you describe. Not so much through shops, which I like, as through the privacy problem. It cuts one's life up into little dice like lumps of sugar, — no, not even that, for they haven't the dignity of a cube; it's just slices, snippets, — and then one is expected to write. One is told that one has had two days undisturbed, when one is feeling like a rag-bag, a waste-paper basket, a dust-heap.

It exhausts the nerves so much the less to travel from London to Teheran, than from London to Sevenoaks [...]

I am ordering The Common Reader *for my hostess — She already has* Jacob's Room. *Its yellow face greeted me friendlily at breakfast.*

I've bought a dog. The garden here has been filled with dogs that were potentially mine, — all come from the desert, led on leash by Arabs. This one is a marvel of elegance, — long tapering paws, and a neck no thicker than your wrist. So off we set together tonight, the [Saluki] puppy and I, to face the snows in the high passes.

Like a little warm coal in my heart burns your saying that you miss me. I miss you oh so much. How much, you'll never believe or know. At every moment of the day. It is painful but also rather pleasant, if you know what I mean. I mean, that it is good to have so keen and persistent a feeling about somebody. It is a sign of vitality. (No pun intended.)

Letter from Vita

Teheran, Persia

9 March

You can't think how much I enjoy writing the above address. I have discovered my true function in life: I am a snob. A geographical snob. Every morning when I wake up, with the sun flooding into my white conventual room, I lie bewildered for a minute; then very slowly, like a child rolling toffee round in its mouth, I tell myself, 'You are in Central Asia.'

[...] Now I shall not tell you about Persia, and nothing of the space, colour and beauty, which you must take for granted — but please do take it for granted, because it has become a part of me, — grafted on to me, leaving me permanently enriched. You smile? Well, I have been stuck in a river, crawled between ramparts of snow, been attacked by a bandit, been baked and frozen alternatively, travelled alone with ten men (all strangers), slept in odd places, eaten wayside meals, crossed high passes, seen Kurds and Medes and caravans, and running streams, and black lambs skipping under blossom, seen hills of porphyry stained with copper sulphate, snow-mountains in a great circle, endless

plains, with flocks on the slopes. Dead camels pecked by vultures, a dying donkey, a dying man. Came to mud towns at nightfall, stayed with odd gruff Scotchmen, drunk Persian wine. Worn a silk dress one day, and a sheepskin and fur cap the next. Met Harold, with letters in his pocket, — two letters from Virginia, which I read first. Been taken to a party, and introduced to about 500 English people, 500 foreign diplomats, and 1,000 Persians. Dined with the Prime Minister, who has a black beard. Began to stammer in Persian. And today's my birthday.

But all this, as you say, gives no idea at all. How is it that one can never communicate? Only imaginary things can be communicated, like ideas, or the world of a novel; but not real experience [...] I should like to see you faced with the task of communicating Persia. How I wish I could bring you here; couldn't you and Leonard come next spring? No, of course you won't: what, leave the Press? I don't believe Isfahan and Persepolis are any temptation to you. I wish life was three times as long, and every day of it 48 hours instead of 24.

I wish I had a photograph of you. (Has mine ever turned up?) It is a torment not being able to visualise when one wants to. I can visualise you as a matter of fact surprisingly well, — but always as you stood on your door-step that last evening, when the lamps were lit and the trees misty, and I drove away.

There will be a vast gap between the letters I sent from Baghdad and this one, and you will think I have forgotten; but I haven't. The post-bag goes only once a fortnight from here. That in itself makes life different. One had come to take the ordinary conveniences of civilisation so much as a matter of course; but here one hears otherwise ordinary people talking in the mediaeval way of 'So-and-so was three weeks on the road', or 'Snow has fallen and So-and-so won't get through', or 'So-and-so is going down to Baghdad and can take letters' [...]

This is how you must imagine your letters arriving, and me carrying them off to read in peace, and saying 'oh darling Virginia', and smiling to myself, and reading them all over again. Whereas mine just come with the postman.

Letter from Vita

Teheran

15 March

You see from this that the muddy car has come in, and that I have had a letter from you (with a picture enclosed, which was an insult, – an insult to you, I mean). You had fallen in love with being a stock-broker. Well [...] And I had galvanised you into asking Leonard to come to the South Seas; but darling Virginia, that wasn't the point at all. The point was that you should come to Persia with me; that I should waft you to these brown plains; not that you should matrimonially disappear for a year out of my ken. Or were you teasing me? As for the South Seas, I am sure they are over-rather; vulgar to a degree; and you wouldn't like hibiscus. Whereas this ancient country [...] This is the place for you. Indeed, if you won't come by kindness, I shall have to make you come by force.

25 March

Do you know what nice little job I have on hand now? Arranging the palace for the coronation.[6] I go down there and put on an apron, and mix paints in pots in a vast hall, and wonder what the Persian is for 'stipple' [...] Why do grammars only teach one such phrases as 'Simply through the courage of the champion's sword', when what one wants to say is 'Bring another lamp'?

[...] Your letters are always a shock to me, for you typewrite the envelope, and they look like a bill, and then I see your writing. A system I rather like, for the various stabs it affords me.

Letter from Vita

Teheran

8 April

Persia has turned magenta and purple: avenues of judas-trees, groves of lilac, torrents of wisteria, acres of peach-blossom. The plane-trees and the poplars

---

6 The Shah was to be crowned on 25 April.

have burst into green [...] I have finished my poem though, and it goes off by this bag. There are large patches of Asia in it now. Will you approve, I wonder?

[...] How pleased I shall be to sit on your floor again.

I have got to go and see the Crown jewels, which is unexpectedly cutting my letter short, and I daren't risk the bag not being closed when I get back [...]

PS Just back from the palace, with ½ an hour before the bag shuts.

I am blind. Blinded by diamonds.

I have been in Aladdin's cave.

Sacks of emeralds were emptied out before our eyes. Sacks of pearls. Literally. We came away shaking the pearls out of our shoes. Ropes of uncut emeralds. Scabbards encrusted with precious stones. Great hieratic crowns.

All this in a squalid room, with grubby Persians drinking little cups of tea.

I can't write it now. It was simply the Arabian Nights, with décor by the Sitwells. Pure fantasy. Oh, why weren't you there?

Letter from Virginia

52 Tavistock Square
29 March

Now you must pretend to be interested in your friend's fortunes: but it will all seem so remote and silly to you: you have forgotten a paper called *The Nation*; Leonard was literary editor once: and since Wednesday he is no longer. We have resigned. Thank God. What a mercy – no more going to the office and reading proofs and racking one's brains to think who to get to write. We shall have to make £500 a year [...] but this is the first step to being free, and foreign travel and dawdling about England in a motor car; and we feel 10 years younger, utterly irresponsible, and please, dearest Vita, do make Harold do the same thing [...]

I cannot think what it will interest you to be told of, now you are embedded in Persia [...]

[There was] a ghastly party at Rose Macaulay's, where in the whirl of meaningless words I thought Mr O'Donovan said Holy Ghost, whereas he said 'The Whole Coast' and I asking 'where is the Holy Ghost?' got the reply 'Where ever the sea is'. 'Am I mad, I thought, or is this wit?' 'The Holy Ghost?' I repeated. 'The Whole Coast,' he shouted, and so we went on, in an atmosphere so repellent that it became, like the smell of bad cheese, repulsively fascinating [...] until Leonard shook all over, picked up what he took to be Mrs Gould's napkin, discovered it to be her sanitary towel and the foundations of this tenth rate literary respectability (all gentlemen in white waistcoats, ladies shingled, unsuccessfully) shook to its foundations. I kept saying, 'Vita would love this.' Now would you?

Letter from Vita

Teheran
17 April

What have I been doing? I went to a Persian tea-party. Ravishing *women; almond eyes, red lips, babbling like little birds, pulling their veils about them whenever they heard a noise. Completely silly, but oh so lovely! Much better than your stockbrokers. And one old monster of a mother-in-law, hanging over them, like a hawk over a flock of doves.*

[...] A curious fact: nearly all letters seem to contain at least one *irritating phrase, but yours never. They leave one feeling more intelligent, charming, and desirable than one really is.*

I wish you would do your 150 pages which shall sum up the whole of literature. It would tidy up the rubbish-heap of many people's minds, not least my own. And please don't give up the Press.

My mind is such a rubbish-heap; it distresses me.

This is a silly letter, but I shall arrive a week after it. In the meantime I am (as we say here) your sacrifice.

Letter from Virginia

52 Tavistock Square
13 April

How odd it is – the effect geography has on the mind! I write to you differently now you're coming back. The pathos is melting. I felt it pathetic when you were going away; as if you were sinking below the verge. Now that you are rising, I'm jolly again.

Letter from Virginia

52 Tavistock Square
19 May

Everybody is longing to see you. Grizzle in paroxysms. Lunch *here* at 1. Friday. Better still come to the basement at 12.30 and have a preliminary talk […] with me in my studio – then 6 or 7 hours upstairs. (Unless you'll dine with me on *Thursday*, when I happen to be alone.)

Virginia's Diary

20 May

Vita comes to lunch tomorrow, which will be a great amusement and pleasure. I am amused at my relations with her: left so ardent in January – and now what? Also I like her presence and her beauty. Am I in love with her? But what is love? Her being 'in love' with me, excites and flatters; and interests. What is this 'love'? Oh and then she gratifies my eternal curiosity: who's she seen, what's she done – for I have no enormous opinion of her poetry. I should have been reading her poem tonight.

Virginia's Diary

25 May

So Vita came: and I register the shock of meeting after absence; how shy one is; how disillusioned by the actual body; and she was shabbier, come straight off in her travelling clothes; and not so beautiful, as sometimes perhaps; and so we sat talking on the sofa by the window, she rather silent, I chattering, partly to divert her attention from me; and to prevent her thinking 'Well, is this all?' as she was bound to think, having declared herself so openly in writing. So that we each registered some disillusionment; and perhaps also acquired some grains of additional solidity – This may well be more lasting than the first rhapsody. But I cannot write. Suddenly the word instinct leaves me.

Letter from Virginia

52 Tavistock Square
7 June

Not much news. Rather cross – Would like a letter. Would like a garden. Would like Vita. Would like 15 puppies with their tails chopped off, 3 doves, and a little conversation.

Letter from Vita to Harold

Long Barn
12 June

The Woolfs are not coming today after all, because Virginia has started one of her attacks of headache again, but I am going to Rodmell tomorrow for two nights; Leonard will be away and she doesn't want to be alone. Your cabbage doesn't want to go much, thank you, and would rather stay here. I have come to the conclusion that I should like to be very eccentric and distinguished, and never see anybody except devout pilgrims who rang the front door bell (which doesn't ring), and remained for an hour talking about poetry, and then went away again. But the eccentricity is easier to acquire than the distinction. The eccentricity, indeed, is native. I am quite alarmed at the rapidity of its growth; that I don't want to see even Virginia as a dreadful symptom, for not only am I very fond of her, but she is the best company in the world, and the most stimulating.

Letter from Vita to Harold

Monk's House
13 June

I am, as you see, staying with Virginia. She is sitting opposite, embroidering a rose, a black lace fan, a box of matches, and four playing cards, on a mauve canvas background, from a design by her sister, and from time to time she says, 'You have written enough, let us now talk about copulation,' so if this letter is disjointed it is her fault and not mine [...] I can't write this letter properly, because V. who is an outrageous woman keeps on getting up and reading it over my shoulder. She says you are to give up diplomacy and find a job from £600 a year onwards.

Letter from Vita to Harold

Monk's House
16 June

I dined with Virginia and Leonard in one of their Bloomsbury pot-houses; and then went on alone with her to the ballet. She had got on a new dress. It was very odd indeed, orange and black, with a hat to match — a sort of top-hat made of straw with two orange feathers like Mercury's wings — but although odd it was curiously becoming, and pleased Virginia because there could be absolutely no doubt as to which was the front and which the back. We had press tickets, and sat in the dress circle. Virginia made up stories about everyone in the audience.

Letter from Vita

Long Barn

17 June

Dear Mrs Woolf

    I must tell you how much I enjoyed my weekend with you [...]

    I wish I were back at Rodmell. I wish you were coming here. Is it any good suggesting (you see that I am in a despondent mood) that you should do so? It is very nice here, you know; but I expect you are busy. Only, it would be a nice refuge if you wanted to escape from London, and I would fetch you in the motor. In any case I shall see you on Friday? A damned long way off, too. Is this a dumb letter? You did spoil me so at Rodmell. I was terribly happy. Tell me how you are.

Letter from Vita

Long Barn

17 June

Ha, ha! Look what I've found. Only send it back, please, because it's too precious to lose. I like my name, — I mean, Harold's name — spelt wrong.[7]

    I shall have, however, to give up reading your works at dinner, for they are too disturbing. I can't explain, I'll have to explain verbally some day. Unless you can guess. How well you write, though, confound you. When I read you, I feel no one has ever written English prose before, — knocked it about, put it in its place, made it into a servant. I wonder perpetually how you do it; like one might see a conjuror do a trick over and over again, and be none the wiser. Only one knows that it will always come off. There is an odd effect peculiar to a few writers, I don't know if you will know what I mean, and if you don't it is

---

7 Vita had rediscovered one of Virginia's early letters to Vita, which began 'Dear Mrs Nicholson'.

hopeless to make you understand: they exercise some mysterious power over print, to make certain words, — perhaps quite ordinary words, — start up out of the page like partridges out of a turnip field, getting a new value, a new surprise.

Letter from Virginia

52 Tavistock Square

18 June

Yes, I do write damned well sometimes, but not these last days, when I've been slogging through a cursed article, and see my novel[8] glowing like the Island of the Blessed far far away over dismal wastes, and can't reach land.

Letter from Vita

Long Barn

20 June

My first glimpse of Clive was somehow suitable: I ran into him as he emerged from the rear,[9] doing up his buttons. But he was prim about it, ignored my grin of welcome, my outstretched hand — nay, my opened arms, — scurried back, attended to his toilet, reappeared, not pleased to see me a bit: I was damped, crushed. During the course of the 24 hours he has recovered himself, and become friendly again; so friendly indeed that we walked round the moat after dinner, on a warm misty evening, and talked, and he made some bad breaches in my little fort of discretion. You see he was skilful enough to pique me with remarks about your general indifference, lack of response etc., and I rose like a trout to the bait. Still, I don't think I've very seriously compromised you, and Clive, at any rate, was entertained.

---

8 *To the Lighthouse.*

9 A lavatory.

Letter from Vita to Harold

Long Barn
20 June

Clive follows me all over the place. Have I been to bed with Virginia yet? If not, am I likely to do so in the near future? If not, will I please give it my attention? As it is high time Virginia fell in love.

Letter from Virginia

52 Tavistock Square
22 June

I think I won't come on Thursday for this reason; I must get on with writing; you would seduce me completely [...]

Also will you come on after your play on Thursday and see me alone? I've put off Sibyl[10] in case you can. Come early on Friday ... Of course, if you want to meet Sibyl and you've only to say so. Will you dine with me off radishes alone in the kitchen?

Letter from Vita to Harold

Long Barn
28 June

No, I am in no muddles[11] [...] Virginia — not a muddle exactly; she is a busy and sensible woman. But she does love me, and I did sleep with her at Rodmell. That does not constitute a muddle though.

Virginia's Diary

30 June

This is the last day of June and finds me in black despair because Clive laughed at my new hat, Vita pities me, and I sank into the

---

10 Lady Sibyl Colefax, the interior designer and socialite.
11 Vita and Harold's term for love affairs.

depths of gloom. This happened at Clive's last night after going to the Sitwells with Vita. Oh dear I was wearing the hat without thinking whether it was good or bad; and it was all very flashing and easy; and [I] sat by Vita and laughed and clubbed. When we got out it was only 10.30 – a soft starry night: it was still too early for her to go. So she said, 'Shall we go to Clive's and pick him up?' and I was then so light-hearted, driving through the Park, and finally came to Gordon Square and there was Nessa tripping along in the dark, in her quiet black hat. Then Duncan came, carrying an egg. Come on all of us to Clive's, I said; and they agreed. Well, it was after they had come and we were all sitting round talking that Clive suddenly said, or bawled rather, what an astonishing hat you're wearing! Then he asked where I got it. I pretended a mystery, tried to change the talk, was not allowed, and they pulled me down between them, like a hare; it was very forced and queer and humiliating. So I talked and laughed too much. Duncan prim and acid as ever told me it was utterly impossible to do anything with a hat like that. And Leonard got silent, and I came away deeply chagrined, as unhappy as I have been these ten years; and revolved it in sleep and dreams all night; and today has been ruined.

Letter from Vita to Harold

Long Barn
1 July

Well, you see, I went to the Sitwells' show with Virginia.[12] *We dined first at the Eiffel Tower, and talked about literature. So absorbing a subject was it, that we were very late for the Sitwell party. We had one complimentary ticket, and*

---

[12] A performance of Edith Sitwell's show *Façade*, where the poem was spoken from behind a screen through megaphones.

one promise from Edith (Sitwell) that we would be admitted on mention of our names. We mentioned our names, and were ushered to a back seat where even the megaphone failed to reach us. We began pushing. There were some empty seats, and to these in the interval we elbowed our way. Virginia made me go first, much as the German troops pushed the Belgian civilians before them during the war. So I bore the brunt and got all the blame [...]

I saw everyone I had ever known. I was quite impressed by the number of people I knew. Then when I had dragged Virginia away — but she gets drunk on crowds as you and I do on champagne — we went back to Bloomsbury. On the way, through one of those dark squares, we overtook Mrs Bell.[13] We stopped. Virginia hailed, 'Nessa! Nessa!' She loomed up vaguely, and said, 'Duncan [Grant] is in the public house.' We drove on. Presently we overtook Duncan, hatless, and very carefully carrying one hard-boiled egg. We drove on to Clive's. There were Leonard and [Maynard] Keynes. Presently came in Mrs Bell and Duncan. Clive produced vermouth and more eggs. The conversation became personal and squalid. I was amused.

Letter from Vita

Long Barn
16 July

Last night Pippin[14] returned home from hunting and proceeded to have convulsions. With my usual efficiency I diagnosed strychnine, and rushed her into Sevenoaks at 2 a.m. to the vet. We gave her a morphia injection, and she was immediately and magnificently sick, — really impressive it was, — and so her life is saved. But it was a dramatic dash [...]

Oh dear I do so want to see you.

---

13 Vanessa Bell, Virginia's sister. Married to Clive Bell.
14 Vita's dog.

Letter from Vita to Harold

Long Barn
27 July

Virginia was very charming and amusing [...] I took her over to Rodmell,
which was nice of me, and Clive and Leonard arrived from London with one of
Clive's shaggy sons [Quentin Bell], and there was a thunderstorm [...] I talked
to V. till dreadfully late last night [...] I told V. how much we loved each other
[...] Oh darling, she is so funny, she does make me laugh! And so sane, when
not mad. And so how[15] about going mad again. What a nightmare it must be.

Letter from Vita

Sherfield Court
4 August

If I have not written to you, it is because I have been writing for you, – tyrant,
slave-driver, how am I to write 20,000 words in 10 days, tell me? I turn a
deaf ear to all pleadings; will I play tennis? Will I come out in the punt? Will
I come and bathe? No, no, no, I say, you remember Mrs Woolf? Well, I have got
to finish a book for her to publish, so run away darlings, and don't worry; and
then back I go to Isfahan; and meanwhile Virginia sits in the water-meadows
and thinks about the Hebrides. (What, exactly, is a hebride? See Raymond
Mortimer on a 'Defence of Homosexuality'.[16] Raymond Mortimer was here for
the weekend; had rather a bad time in the shape of a good many home-truths;
but happy on the whole.)

Now that's all, because I have two chapters still to write, and several to
finish, and am getting frantic about it. Dottie[17] says I am a bore. I tell her
that it is your fault. I am a bore, I know, and nobody is allowed near the

---

15 Meaning 'pathetic'.

16 A pamphlet written for the Hogarth Press, which they were advised by their lawyers
not to publish.

17 Dorothy Wellesley, Duchess of Wellington, a poet and socialite, and Vita's lover.

writing-table except for me. As for the children, their passion for Mrs Woolf is rapidly on the decline.

Mine, alas, is not.

Letter from Virginia

52 Tavistock Square
8 August

Yes, it does seem hard, that we should make you spend all the fine weather with your nose to the pen. But think of your glory; and our profit, which is becoming a necessary matter, now that your puppy has destroyed, by eating holes, my skirt, ate L.'s proofs, and done such damage as could be done to the carpet – But she is an angel of light. Leonard says seriously she makes him believe in God [...] and this after she has wetted his floor 8 times in one day.

Letter from Vita to Harold

Long Barn
17 August

Darling, there is no muddle anywhere! I keep on telling you so [...] You mention Virginia: it is simply laughable. I love Virginia, as who wouldn't? But really, my sweet, one's love for Virginia is a very different thing: a mental thing; a spiritual thing, if you like, an intellectual thing, and she inspires a feeling of tenderness, which is, I suppose, owing to her funny mixture of hardness and softness – the hardness of her mind, and her terror of going mad again. She makes me feel protective. Also she loves me, which flatters and pleases me. Also – since I have embarked on telling you about Virginia, but this is absolutely padlock private[18] – I am scared to death

---

18 'Padlock' was Vita and Harold's code word for a secret that they must promise to keep.

of arousing physical feelings in her, because of the madness. I don't know what effect it would have, you see: it is a fire with which I have no wish to play. I have too much real affection and respect for her. Also she has never lived with anyone except Leonard, which was a terrible failure, and was abandoned quite soon. So all that remains is an unknown quantity; and I have got too many dogs not to let them lie when they are asleep [...] I don't want to get landed in an affair which might get beyond my control before I knew where I was.

[...] But, darling, Virginia is not the sort of person one thinks of in that way. There is something incongruous and almost indecent in the idea. I have gone to bed with her (twice), but that's all. Now you know all about it, and I hope I haven't shocked you [...]

Please make a comment of all this, and say you understand. But don't say you understand unless you really do. My darling, you are the one and only person for me in the world; do take that in once and for all, you little dunderhead. Really it makes me cross, when I am eating out my heart for you; and it makes me cry.

Letter from Virginia

52 Tavistock Square

19 August

Will you come on Wednesday? To lunch at 1? Leonard will be in London for the day. Would you like me to ask Clive? If so, let me know. Sleep tight.

You'll be even more uncomfortable than usual.

I say, please bring 2 bottles wine (not cider) which I want to BUY. Can't get any.

Letter from Vita

> Long Barn
> 20 August

I am going to Normandy for a week, with the boys, on the 28th, but am going to Brighton on Wednesday – could I see you? How could I see you? Sleep Wednesday night? Or lunch Thursday? We ought to decide about these photographs, and other details. I am calling it Passenger to Teheran, *which I think covers everything, 1) not too dull, 2) not too romantic, 3) explicit. Anyhow I can't think of anything better [...] It is very bad. I feel ashamed; but perhaps it will sell.*

Letter from Virginia

> 52 Tavistock Square
> 22 August

Yes – that will be perfect. I think I shall be alone on Wednesday – couldn't you come early and enjoy a scrambly lunch?

The title seems very good – far the best. I'm longing, in spite of having read 3 mss, to read yours – a great testimony to you: I'm compunctious that you should have worked so hard. Seven hours a day. My God.

Virginia's Diary

> 3 September

For the rest, Charleston, Tilton, *To The Lighthouse*, Vita, expeditions: the summer dominated by a feeling of washing in boundless warm fresh air – such an August not come my way for years.

Letter from Virginia

> Monk's House
> 15 September

They've only just sent the second batch of proofs which I have swallowed at a gulp. Yes – I think it's awfully good. I kept saying 'How I should like to know this woman' and then thinking 'But I do', and then 'No, I don't – not altogether the woman who writes this.' I don't know the extent of your subtleties [...] The whole book is full of nooks and corners which I enjoy exploring. Sometimes one wants a candle in one's hand though – That's my only criticism – you've left (I daresay in haste) one or two dangling dim places.

Letter from Vita

> *Long Barn*
> *17 September*

So happy tonight because I had your letter [...] I am glad you like the book. I did write it in a hurry, you know, so no wonder there are dim dangling places. I'm glad too that you would like to know me: we must get some common friend to arrange a meeting, dear Mrs Woolf, when I am next in London. At present I am oppressed by the thought of having to give a lecture there in October – and can think of nothing else, and the horror of it [...] I am in a bit of a turmoil, 1) The Land coming out,[19] 2) got to give a lecture, 3) Virginia likes my book. These three things trot round and round in my head, making a tune like the wheels of the railway train.

Letter from Virginia

> 52 Tavistock Square
> 12 October

Mr Barrington Gates (*The Nation* reviewer) says may he take a whole column for *The Land*, as in his opinion it is 'so outstanding' that it should not be lumped in with the others [...] So there. He's going to have a column.

---

19 Vita's poem *The Land* was published on 30 September 1926.

Letter from Vita to Harold

Long Barn
7 November

It is such a lovely day, so warm that we (Leonard, Virginia, and I) have been sitting in the sun by the big-room door all morning [...] Leonard is a funny grim solitary creature. Virginia an angel of wit and intelligence. Leonard goes back to London this evening and she stays on with me till tomorrow, which I enjoy more than anything, as she then never stops talking, and I feel as though the edge of my mind were being held against a grindstone. Hadji[20] not worry, though. It is all right.

Letter from Vita to Harold

Long Barn
9 November

Oh dear, Virginia [...] You see, Hadji, she is very very fond of me, and says she was so unhappy when I went to Persia that it startled and terrified her. I don't think she is accustomed to emotional storms, she lives too much in the intellect and imagination. Most human beings take emotional storms as a matter of course. Fortunately she is the sensible sort of person who pulls themselves together and says, 'This is absurd.' So I don't really worry. (Rather proud, really, of having caught such a big silver fish.) I look on my friendship with her as a treasure and a privilege. I shan't ever fall in love with her, padlock, *but I am absolutely devoted to her and if she died I should mind quite, quite dreadfully. Or went mad again.*

Letter from Virginia

52 Tavistock Square
19 November

Oh dear, Sibyl has given me a headache. What a bore. I can't write, except to you. I lie in a chair. It isn't bad: but I tell you, to get your

---

20 Vita's pet name for Harold.

sympathy: to make you protective: to implore you to devise some way by which I can cease this incessant nibbling away of life by people: Sibyl [Colefax], Sir Arthur [Colefax], Dadie [George Rylands] – one on top of another. Why do I put it on *you*? Some psychological necessity I suppose: one of those intimate things in a relationship which one does by instinct. I'm rather a coward about this pain in my back: you would be heroic [...]

But don't you see, donkey West, that you'll be tired of me one of these days (I'm so much older) and so I have to take my little precautions. That's why I put the emphasis on 'recording' rather than feeling. But donkey West knows she has broken down more ramparts than anyone. And isn't there something obscure in you? There's something that doesn't vibrate in you: It may be purposely – you don't let it: but I see it with other people, as well as with me: something reserved, muted – God knows what ... It's in your writing too, by the bye. The thing I call central transparency – sometimes fails you there too.

Letter from Vita to Harold

Long Barn
20 November

I got a Letter from Virginia, which contains one of her devilish, shrewd psychological pounces. She asks if there is something in me which does not vibrate, a 'something reserved, muted [...] The thing I call 'central transparency' sometimes fails you in your writing'. Damn the woman, she has put her finger on it. There is something muted. What is it, Hadji? Something that doesn't come alive. I brood and brood, feel I am groping in a dark tunnel. It makes everything I write a little unreal; gives the effect of having been done from the outside.

[...] There is no doubt about it, as one grows older, one thinks more. Virginia worries, you worry, I worry [...] Yet I would rather do this and become introspective and rattle about London, where people's voices become more and more devoid of meaning.

Letter from Vita

Long Barn
21 November

I think you are a witch, or a dowser in psychology. You must be. My respect for
you increases.

Look here, if you would like to go to the ballet tomorrow night (and Leonard)
will you ring me up before twelve and say so? I only suggest it because it is
the first night of l'Oiseau de feu, *and I would get tickets. I should like to go,*
but will only go if you will come.

I am longing to see you and have been in a state all yesterday and today. I
spent most of yesterday in bed which is why I said next weekend would be better
than this. I have been in a black temper (with myself, not with you), and have
travelled over a lot of country. If I were not going to see you tomorrow anyhow,
I should take steps to do so. Are you recovered from Sibyl? Furious with that
woman for giving you a headache. Altogether I am in a rage.

I'll come in by the basement at 2.30 or thereabouts. Thank Heaven for that.

Virginia's Diary

23 November

Fame grows. Chances of meeting this person, doing that thing, accu-
mulate. Life is as I've said since I was ten, awfully interesting – if anything, quicker, keener at forty-four than twenty-four – more desperate I suppose, as the river shoots to Niagara – my new vision of death.
'The one experience I shall never describe' I said to Vita yesterday. She
was sitting on the floor in her velvet jacket and red striped silk shirt,
I knotting her pearls into heaps of great lustrous eggs. She had come
up to see me – so we go on – a spirited, creditable affair, I think,
innocent (spiritually) and all gain, I think; rather a bore for Leonard,
but not enough to worry him. The truth is one has room for a good
many relationships. Then she goes back again to Persia.

I am re-doing six pages of *Lighthouse* daily. My present opinion is that it is easily the best of my books.

Letter from Vita to Harold

Long Barn
23 November

I am a little bothered about Virginia, but fortunately she is a busy and sensible person and doesn't luxuriate in vain repinings. She is an absolute angel to me, and the value of her friendship is not to be measured in gold. Oh my dear, what intelligence! It is amazing — what perception, sensitiveness in the best sense, imagination, poetry, culture, everything so utterly un-shoddy and real. I long for you two to know each other better. I hope to God she won't be too unhappy when I go away; she told me that last year she was terrified by her own unhappiness and I fear this will be worse. Darling, this all sounds very conceited, but I don't mean it like that, and it is padlock anyway. She is very much on the crest of the wave, which pleases her vanity, but so how always: 'I want you to be proud of me.' I think she's coming here for the weekend as Leonard has to go away.

Letter from Vita

66 Mount Street
27 November

My beloved Virginia, I am worried about you — I thought you were tired and depressed. What is it? Were you just merely tired? I feel a brute for having let you come here. Was it just the bloody flux? I oughtn't to have let you come. Don't you know that there is nothing I wouldn't do to save you a moment's pain, annoyance, fatigue, irritation? And then I go and let you come all this way to see me! I could kick myself — Please forgive me: my only consolation is that you had the motor. My darling, I will try to make up to you for the past weekend. I would ring you up and say all this instead of writing it, but the reason why I don't is obvious. I will dine and fetch you on Saturday. I miss you dearest. Perhaps I will see you on Monday? I'll ring up on Monday at 2.30. I can't get you out of my mind tonight; the corner of the sofa where you sat is haunted for me by your presence, the whole flat seems full of you —

Letter from Vita to Harold

Long Barn
30 November

I'm alone. It is very cold and wet. I have got Virginia coming for the weekend. Darling, I know that Virginia will die, and it will be too awful. (I don't mean here, over the weekend; but just die young.) I went to Tavistock Square yesterday, and she sat in the dusk in the light of the fire, and I sat on the floor as I always do, and she rumpled my hair as she always does, and she talked about literature and Mrs Dalloway and Sir Henry Taylor and she said that you would resent her next summer. But I said, No you wouldn't. Oh Hadji, she is such an angel. I really adore her. Not 'in love' — just love — devotion. Her friendship has enriched me so. I don't think I have ever loved anybody so much, in the way of friendship; in fact, of course, I know I haven't. She knows that you and I adore each other. I have told her so.

Letter from Vita

182 Ebury Street
30 November

It made me wretched to know you were tired yesterday, darling. Do take my scolding to heart! And don't be so social — you'll get like Sibyl Colefax, and develop a bright beady eye, looking for new guests. I hope you're none the worse today; would like to ring you up; but I don't want to bother. So I write [...]

I expect you both Thursday. You couldn't stay two nights, I suppose? No, I suppose not [...]

Well, I must start. Do be good, strong-minded, self protective. I hate it when you get tired and droop. It really hurts me. Bless you, sweet.

Letter from Virginia

52 Tavistock Square
1 December

Very nice to get a letter from you, dear Creature – No, it wasn't the people yesterday – I had the shivers, due to getting wet through at Rodmell – that was all – I went to bed, took aspirin, hot bottle, quite all right today, only incredibly sleepy. Still I agree – people are the devil [...]

Moreover, you can't talk – lunch at Woking, tea Virginia, Cocktail Raymond, dine Mary, supper Kitchin – There I was warm in bed, and glad to hear it was a ghastly failure. And now you're off to Brighton, heaven help you! I wish you hadn't that before you, but could drop in and talk – Here I am sitting or rather lying in front of the gas fire in perfect quiet.

Letter from Vita

Long Barn
1 December

Last night I went to bed very early and read Mrs Dalloway. *It was a very curious sensation: I thought you were in the room – But there was only Pippin, trying to burrow under my quilt, and the night noises outside, which are so familiar in one's own room; and the house was all quiet. I was very unhappy because I had had a row with my mother and very happy because of you; so it was like being two different people at the same time, and then to complicate it there was a) the conviction that you were in the room, and b) the contact with all the many people that you had created. (What a queer thing fiction is.) I felt quite light, as though I were falling through my bed, like when one has a fever. Today I am quite solid again, and my boots are muddy; they weight me down. Yet I am not as solid as usual, – not quite such an oaf, – because there is at the back of my mind all the time (slightly lifting the top off my head) a glow, a sort of nebula, which only when I examine it hardens into a shape; as soon as I think of something else it dissolves again, remaining there like the sun through a fog, and I have to reach out to it again, take it in my hands and feel its contours: then it hardens, 'Virginia is coming on Saturday.' I am going to dinner at Knole tonight, and I shall meet an oil magnate and his wife; but it will be there all the time, a will o' the wisp that lets itself be caught, 'Virginia is coming on Saturday.'*

But she won't, she won't! Something will happen. Of course something will happen. Something always does, when one wants a thing too passionately. You will have chicken pox, or I shall have mumps, or the house will fall down on Saturday morning. In the meantime there are three cows staring over the stile; they are waiting for cake. There is a nebula in their minds too, 'At four o'clock we shall have cake.' And for them, lucky brutes, nothing will happen. But for me there is the whole range of human possibility.

If ever you tried not to have chicken pox, try now. If ever you tried not to be given a headache by Sibyl Colefax, try now. (I remember, ominously, that you said you were going to tea with her on Friday.) Please try with all your might not to let anything happen. I will be responsible for you after you have arrived, – only, please arrive. (I will let you know the trains tomorrow.) Bring your work, I won't interrupt. I so want you to be happy here. I wish, in a way, that we could put the clock back a year. I should like to startle you again, – even though I didn't know then that you were startled.

Letter from Virginia

52 Tavistock Square
3 December

No – I can't come. I have caught eczema from Grizzle. My hair comes out in tufts. I scratch incessantly. It wouldn't be safe for you, or, what matters more, the puppies. I shall think of you: let that console us.

That joke being done with – yes, I'll come reaching Sevenoaks at 5.22.

It's true I'm incredibly dirty; have washed my head – hair is down – skirt spotted, shoes in holes – Pity poor Virginia dragged off this afternoon by Sibyl to meet Arnold Bennett who abused me for a column in last night's *Standard*.

Oh I'm sick of teaing, dining, reading, writing and everything, except seeing – well it *is* you, I admit. Yes it will be nice – yes it will: And shall you be very kind to me?

Letter from Vita

52 *Tavistock Square*
8 *December*

Pinker and I try to console one another. She sleeps on my bed, and clings to me as the one comparatively familiar thing in a strange and probably hostile world. She was pleased to see me when I came back from London, but ran about sniffing and looking for Mrs Woolf. I had to explain that Mrs Woolf lived in London, a separate life, a fact which was as unpleasant to me as it could be to any spaniel puppy, so she has adopted me as a substitute. I explained that everybody always betrayed one sooner or later, and usually gave one away to somebody else, and that the only thing to do was to make the best of it. I have introduced her to the insect, but he is rather frightened of her because she puts her paw down on him, so he creeps away to his legitimate abode.

So altogether it is rather a desolate party at Long Barn.

Oh, but it was a treat having you here. Such a treat, I haven't yet got over it. I wish I could think that you had been one half as happy as I was. Not but what I don't think that I am very nice, and very good for you, so you see there is no false modesty on my part. Now I think about Knole, a question over which I am prepared to make myself really disagreeable, simply because I don't think I have ever wanted anything so much, and it will be my last treat before going away. For ever so long. You will come, won't you?

Darling, you will come?

Letter from Virginia

52 Tavistock Square
8 December

Dearest Vita,

(Now why did I say that?) Yes, Monday, undern[21] 2.30. Please come, and bathe me in serenity again. Yes, I was wholly and entirely happy […]

But why, darling Mrs N., honourable Mrs N., insist upon Knole? To see me ridiculous, the powder falling, the hairpins dropping, and not a word said in private between us?

Letter from Vita

Long Barn
11 December

Disaster last night: Pinker, in sportive mood, sprang on to my writing table, upsetting the ink stand, which poured two floods of ink (one red and the other blue) down over the back of the sofa. Pippin was drenched in the blue ink, puppy in the red. Today Pippin looks like a bruise, puppy like an accident. You would have enjoyed the scene. I hope she will have regained her normal colour by January 1st when you have her back.

Oh, and you rang me up. I liked that. But surely you would like to feed stags out of a bucket? I can promise you some good moments at Knole, – and as for no private conversation, why, silly, we should be alone all day practically. We'll stick the powder on with [illegible – paper damaged] and padlock the hairpins.

Letter from Vita to Harold

66 Mount Street
21 December

My own, nothing is wrong. PADLOCK. What 'reservations' or 'half truths' have you detected in my letters? There have been none, I have told you everything day

---

21 Early afternoon.

by day exactly as it has happened. I swear to tell you at the first sign of 'muddle
with Virginia'. My dearest, how can you speak of reservations and half truths
when I have told you all about that business? Even that I did sleep with her,
which I need never have told you — but that I wanted you to know everything
that happened to me while you were away. (If you had been at home I might
not have told you.) There is nothing I will not tell you, that you want to know.
I am absolutely devoted to her, but not in love. So there.

Letter from Vita

Knole

25 December

I am spending my Christmas in bed with influenza. It is very pleasant. I am
warm, — everybody comes in looking blue with cold; an atmosphere of seasonable
jocularity prevails, I am sure, in the dining-room, — and I am exempt from
it. Kind people bring me grapes. I have a photograph of Virginia — not a very
good photograph, — but better than nothing. I lie in bed, and watch the fire
on the ceiling, and hear a clock strike, and think how delicious it will be when
you come to stay here [...]

I miss you very much, and am glad I can look forward to your coming here
as otherwise I should be really too depressed — As it is, I lie making lovely plans,
all firelit and radiant — my bed's at least nine foot wide, and I feel like the
Princess and the Pea, — only there is no Pea. It is a four-poster, all of which I
like. Come and see for yourself.

Letter from Virginia

52 Tavistock Square

29 December

One thing is I don't think Knole is possible; for this reason: I tore all
my clothes on the gorse, and can't get any more, and I couldn't ask
your butler to wait on me, nor is it for the dignity of letters that I

should eat behind a screen, so I don't see how I can come to Knole, all in holes, without a pin to my hair or a stocking to my foot. You'd be ashamed; you'd say things you would regret.

But read carefully what's coming. It's this

I am going to America.

Now that's exciting isn't it?

30 December

The *Tribune*'s[22] offered my free passages, hotel bills, and £120 to go to New York for a month in the spring and write 4 articles. I've said I will if I can arrange times, and not too much work [...]

I was partly teasing. I don't mind being dowdy, dirty, shabby, red nosed middle classed and all the rest – it's only a question of when and how – I do want to see you, I do – I do.

---

22 *New York Herald Tribune.*

1927

Letter from Vita

Long Barn
2 January

So you're going to Rodmell on Tuesday. Very well: that involves the natural consequence that I'll come up tomorrow (Monday), and come to the basement. Now never say that I don't love you. I want dreadfully to see you. That is all there is to it [...]

It's time I either lived with Virginia or went back to Asia, and as I can't do the former I must do the latter. I'm feeling, you see, like a person who has eaten too many sweets [...]

Till tomorrow then, my dear — and very nice too. You'll be nice to me, won't you? And I'll be nice to you. And we'll arrange about Knole. I shall pin you down.

Letter from Vita

Long Barn
15 January

You've no idea of the intrigues that have been going on here to ensure your getting the room I wanted you to have, — how I have lied shamelessly, tucked

Olive [Rubens] away in a room she never has, bundled her clothes out, bribed the housekeeper, suborned the housemaids. You have a curious effect of making me quite unscrupulous, of turning me into a sort of Juggernaut riding over obstacles [...]

I've got a lovely full moon (or nearly) for you — I've just been out looking at the court; it's now midnight; I like the battlements in the moonlight and the frost. You will stay over Tuesday night, won't you? And I'll motor you up to London on Wednesday morning. Do remember what a dreadfully long time it will be before I see you again [...]

I suppose I can manage to exist until Monday but I'm not sure.

Virginia's Diary

23 January

At Knole, Vita took me over the four acres of building, which she loves; too little conscious beauty for my taste: smallish rooms looking on to buildings; no views; yet one or two things remain: Vita stalking in her Turkish dress, attended by small boys, down the gallery, wafting them on like some tall sailing ship — a sort of covey of noble English life: dogs walloping, children crowding, all very free and stately; and a cart bringing wood in to be sawn by the great circular saw. They had brought wood in from the Park to replenish the great fires like this for centuries; and her ancestresses had walked so on the snow with their great dogs bounding by them. All the centuries seemed lit up, the past expressive, articulate; not dumb and forgotten [...] After tea, looking for letters of Dryden's to show me, she tumbled out a love letter of Lord Dorset's (Seventeenth Century) with a lock of his soft gold tinted hair which I held in my hand a moment. One had a sense of links fished up into the light which are usually submerged.

Letter from Vita

182 Ebury Street
28 January

Beloved Virginia, one last goodbye before I go. I feel torn in a thousand pieces – *it is* bloody – I can't tell you *how I hate leaving you.* I don't know how I shall get on without you – in fact I don't feel I can – you have become so essential to me. Bless you for all the happiness you give me. I'll write in the train. Bless you, my darling, my lovely Virginia.

Your Vita

Such ages before I can hear from you too! Please write by post soon – in fact at once – I can't bear to wait long for a word from you. Please, please.

[In pencil] Put 'honey' when you write –

Letter from Vita

London–Dover
28 January

My darling, it's so shaky I can hardly write, we are tearing through my Weald – (*see* Passenger to Teheran, *Chap. 2. passim*). So odd to have all the same emotions repeated after a year's interval – but oh worse where you are concerned. I really curse and damn at the pain of it – and yet I wouldn't be without it for anything – I shall remember you standing in your blue apron and waving. Oh damn it, Virginia, I wish I didn't love you so much. No I don't though; that's not true. I am glad I do. I don't know what to say to you except that it tore the heart out of my body saying goodbye to you – I am thankful to have had yesterday, a real gift from the Gods – Oh my darling you have made me so happy, and I do bless you for it – and I oughtn't to grumble now – ought I? But I really do feel wretched – You won't be able to read this letter – I sent you a telegram from Victoria –

Letter from Vita

Near Hanover
29 January

My darling

I hoped I should wake up less depressed this morning, but l didn't [...] The awful dreariness of Westphalia makes it worse: factory towns, mounds of slag, flat country, and some patches of dirty snow [...]

Why aren't you with me? Oh, why? I do want you so frightfully.

The only thing which gives me any pleasure is Leigh's[1] get-up. He has bought a short sheepskin coat, in which he evidently thinks he looks like a Hungarian shepherd, but horn-rimmed glasses and a rather loud pair of plus-fours destroy this effect. Dottie on the other hand has appeared in a very long fur-coat, down to the ankles, so thick as to make her quite round; she looks like a Russian grand-duke. We are all rather cross, and have rows about luggage. I want more than ever to travel with you; it seems to me now the height of my desire, and I get into despair wondering how it can ever be realised. Can it, do you think? Oh my lovely Virginia, it is dreadful how I miss you, and everything that everybody says seems flat and stupid.

I do hope more and more that you won't go to America, I am sure it would be too tiring for you, and anyway I am sure you wouldn't like it. Come to Beirut instead??

So we bundle along over Germany, and very dull it is – Surely I haven't lost my zest for travel? No, it is not that; it is simply that I want to be with you and not with anybody else – But you will get bored if I go on saying this, only it comes back and back till it drips off my pen – Do you realise that I shall have to wait for over a fortnight before I can hear from you? Poor me. I hadn't thought of that before leaving, but now it bulks very large and horrible. What may not happen to you in the course of a fortnight? You may get ill, fall in love, Heaven knows what.

---

1 Leigh Ashton, British art historian.

I shall work so hard, partly to please you, partly to please myself, partly to make the time go and have something to show for it. I treasure your sudden discourse on literature yesterday morning, — a send-off to me, rather like Polonius to Laertes. It is quite true that you have had infinitely more influence on me intellectually than anyone, and for this alone I love you [...]

Yes, my very dear Virginia, I was at a crossways just about the time I first met you, like this:

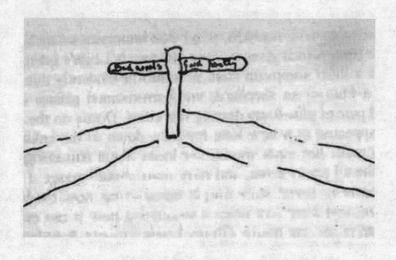

[The signpost reads 'Bad novels' on the left and 'Good poetry' on the right]

You do like me to write well, don't you? And I do hate writing badly — and having written so badly in the past. But now, like Queen Victoria, I will be good.

Hell! I wish you were here — The team of ponies prances with temper. Send me anything you write in papers, and send 'On reading'. Please. I hope you will get my letters quick and often. Tell me if I write too often. I love you.

Letter from Vita

Moscow

31 January

I tried to write to you in the train, but it was so shaky I gave it up in despair. Oh, my head is in a whirl: little patches of snow in Germany, more snow in Poland, all snow in Russia. Dark fir-woods weighted down with snow; peasants in sheepskins; sleighs; green, glaucous rivers immobilised into ice. All very beautiful, and endlessly melancholy. Fancy living in this country, feeling yourself to be only a little black dot in the middle of a flat whiteness stretching away to China. Then Moscow, with gold, green, red, blue roofs above the snow; and the scarlet Soviet flag, lit up from below at night just like the columns of Selfridges, floating over the Kremlin; and all the traffic passing to and fro over the frozen river as though it were a road; and sleighs everywhere, and coachmen stuffed out with straw. I went to see Lenin tonight. He lies embalmed in a scarlet tomb just below the red flag, and the crowd walks round his glass case two by two. A woman had hysterics just behind me; screamed like an animal; sobbed; screamed again; nobody took any notice — And oh my God, there's a dinner party of twenty-two people tonight — and I collided with Denys Trefusis in the hall[2] — and is he coming to the dinner? And shall I be put next to him? And then there's to be a concert — when the only thing I want is bed and sleep. I so nearly sent you a telegram, but thought you would think that silly; I had written it out, and then tore it up. Would you have thought it silly? Or been pleased? And do you know where I am, I wonder, or have you lost count? It's seven o'clock here, but only five in London — so you're having Sibyl to tea at this moment, instead of me, and she won't sit on the floor or say my lovely Virginia, and you won't rumple her hair — and it won't be nearly so nice. I hope you miss me, though I could scarcely (even in the cause of vanity) wish you to miss me as much as

---

2 Denys Trefusis, husband of Violet Trefusis (with whom Vita had eloped to France in 1920).

I miss you, for that hurts too much, but what I do hope is that I've left some sort of a little blank which won't be filled till I come back. I bear you a grudge for spoiling me for everybody else's companionship, it is too bad —

Oh heavens, I must dress for this thrice bloody dinner party, when I want to go on writing to you. And how angry it makes me that you shouldn't be here, and I do ache for you so all the time — damn it — it gets no better with time or distance — and I foresee that it won't — Nor shall I have a word from you for ever so long — oh damn, damn, damn — You would be pleased if you knew how much I minded —

Letter from Virginia

52 Tavistock Square
31 January

My dear Honey,

It was nice to get your telegram and letters — write as many as you can. It gives one a fillip. The only good thing that's happened to me is that the moment you left I became involved in a series of telephones, notes, scenes with Clive and Mary,[3] all very emotional which left me so angered, so sordidified, so exacerbated that I could only think of you as being very distant and beautiful and calm. A lighthouse in clean water. [...] Clive giving champagne suppers to Mary. I was amused to think how angry certain charges made against me by Mary would have made you — God, if you'd been here, what fun we should have had.

But the main good was that I've been kept on the hop the whole time: so I've been restless and scattered; it's like taking sleeping draughts: I try my best to put off thinking about you [...]

---

3 Clive Bell and Mary Hutchinson.

D'you know it's a great thing being a eunuch as I am: that is not knowing what's the right side of a skirt: women confide in one. One pulls a shade over the fury of sex; and then all the veins and marbling, which, between women, are so fascinating, show out. Here in my cave I see lots of things you blazing beauties make invisible by the light of your own glory.

No: I'm not going to America. They write that they are entertaining me at dinners, but not, apparently paying my hotel bills. So the cost would swallow up all my earnings, and l think we can cry off and go to Greece […]

I've *not* got a cold in my head, but it's like having a cold in the head, sitting here writing to you and everything at sixes and sevens. I feel dissipated and aimless for some reason […] Then it's you being away – I am at the mercy of people, of moods, feel lonely, like something pitiable which can't make its wants known. How you have demoralised me. I was once a stalwart upstanding woman. Then it's not writing novels: this journalism is such a thin draggled straining business, and I keep opening the lid and looking into my mind to see whether some slow fish isn't rising there – some new book. No: nothing at the moment.

Letter from Virginia

52 Tavistock Square
5 February

Dearest Honey,

No letter since you were careering through the snow in Westphalia – that is nothing since Monday. I hope this doesn't mean you have been eaten by brigands, wrecked, torn to pieces. It makes me rather dismal. It gets worse steadily – your being away. All the sleeping draughts and irritants have worn off, and I'm settling down to wanting you, doggedly, dismally, faithfully – I hope that pleases you. It's damned unpleasant for me. I can assure you. I had a sort of idea that I'd cheat the devil, and put my head under my wing, and think of nothing. But it won't work – not at all. I want you this Saturday more than last and so it'll go on.

I sit over the gas in my sordid room. Why can't I write except in sordid rooms? I don't think I could write a word in your room at Long Barn. Furniture that people can sit in implies people, and I want complete solitude – that's at the back of my mind, and so I get sordider and sordider. *The Voyage Out* was written in comparative splendour – a maid, carpets, fires; *To the Lighthouse* was written – as you know. So the next book will necessitate a shed. This fits in with my mood at the moment. I have banged my door on parties, dug myself into a dank dismal burrow, where I do nothing but read and write. This is my hibernating season.

Letter from Virginia

52 Tavistock Square
8 February

Yes yes yes I do like you. I am afraid to write the stronger word.

Your Virginia

Letter from Vita

Teheran
9 February

The moment we had arrived we began talking about how to get back. For one moment our mountain expedition seemed in danger, but now it is re-established; for another moment it seemed that we should return by Constantinople and Athens, by ship, in which case I conceived the dizzy idea of meeting you there; but now that is abandoned. Would you have fallen in with that plan (always assuming that you go to Greece and not to America), would you have come on board at the Piraeus and found me waiting for you at the head of the gangway?

Then we would have returned together through the Greek seas, which would I think completely have unhinged my reason. Greece, with you — in May.

God, the people here! They're still talking about the same things as when I left, only now they have got me as a new victim, 'Alors, chère amie, vous avez fait bon voyage?' 'Etes-vous contente, chère madame, de vous retrouver a Teheran?' And I must behave so pretty, and answer it all as though it were the most important thing in the world [...] But, darling beloved Virginia, I can't believe that I was intended for the diplomatic career. Harold unfortunately seems to think that he was. This is a theory which I count upon you to dispel.

But what is really odd is that I should be sitting again at the same table, with the sun pouring in through the plane-trees, writing to you as I used to do last year, and feeling again that helpless sense of impotence, travel being, as you know, the most private of pleasures. And your studio seems so much more real, and you waving on the doorstep. Oh, how I wish you would explain life to me, so that I might see it steadfastly and see it whole, or whatever the quotation is. I find it more and more puzzling as I grow older [...]

How glad I am that you exist.

Virginia's Diary

12 February

But I am forgetting, after three days, the most important event of my life since marriage — so Clive described it. Mr Cizec has bingled me. I am short haired for life. Having no longer, I think, any claims to beauty, the convenience of this alone makes it desirable. Every morning I go to take up brush and twist that old coil round my finger and fix it with hairpins and then with a start of joy, no I needn't. This robs dining out of half its terrors.

For the rest — it's been a gay tropical kind of autumn, with so much Vita and Knole and staying away: we have launched ourselves a little more freely perhaps from work and the Press. But now with Nessa

away, Clive away, Duncan away, Vita away, the strenuous time sets in:
I'm writing at a great pace; mean to make all the money we want for
Greece and a motor car.

Letter from Virginia

52 Tavistock Square
16 February

Do you realise how devoted I am to you, all the same? There's nothing
I wouldn't do for you, dearest Honey. It's true, the other night, I did
take a glass too much. It's your fault though – that Spanish wine. I
got a little tipsy. And then Bobo Mayor[4] is a great seducer in her way.
She has gipsy blood in her: she's rather violent and highly coloured,
sinuous too, with a boneless body, and thin hands; all the things I like.
So, being a little tipsy about twelve o'clock at night, I let her do it.

She cut my hair off. I'm shingled. That being so – and it'll look all
right in a month or two, the hairdresser says – bound to be a little
patchy at first – let's get on to other things. It's off; it's in the kitchen
bucket: my hairpins have been offered up like crutches in St Andrew,
Holborn, at the high altar.

[…] You shall ruffle my hair in May, Honey: it's as short as a
partridge's rump.

Letter from Virginia

52 Tavistock Square
18 February

Sweet Honey,

Yes I want you more and more. You'll like to think of me unhappy
I know. Well, you can […]

---

4 Beatrice Mayor (née Meinertzhagen), poet, novelist and dramatist.

We're still talking, you'll be surprised to hear, about love and sodomy [...]

Then Morgan [E. M. Forster] says he's worked it out and one spends 3 hours on food, 6 on sleep, 4 on work, 2 on love. Lytton [Strachey] says 10 on love. I say the whole day on love. I say it's seeing things through a purple shade. But you've never been in love they say.

Letter from Vita

Teheran

19 February

Virginia, listen. We are coming back by Greece. ('We' means Harold and I, i.e. Dottie is going home earlier.) We arrive at the Piraeus on Thursday 28th April, and leave again the same day for Trieste by Lloyd Triestino. Now, if you go to Greece, I imagine that you would be returning about the same time? Why not make it exactly the same time? Why not make it, in fact, the same boat?

I write of it in this practical and business-like way, leaving it to your imagination to reconstruct what it would mean to me if I saw you coming up that gangway; I hope, also, that it would mean something to you – though with a cold fish it is difficult to know for certain. Harold says he would like nothing better, so let's have no silliness about that *– and do not, oh I beseech you, do not let us miss such a chance through any muddle or mismanagement on your part. It's a good rendez-vous, you'll agree: meet me in Athens on April 28th at dawn.*

Letter from Virginia

52 Tavistock Square

21 February

It gets worse you'll be glad to hear, steadily worse. Today's the day when I should be trotting out to buy you your loaf, and watching for your white legs – not widow Cartwright's – coming down the basement steps. Instead you're on the heights of Persia, riding an Arab mare I daresay to some deserted garden and picking yellow tulips.

My solace is what? Dining with Ethel Sands [...] and laboriously correcting two sets of proofs. My goodness how you'll dislike that book![5] Honestly you will – Oh but you shan't read it. It's a ghost between us. Whether it's good or bad, I know not: I'm dazed, I'm bored, I'm sick to death: I go on crossing out commas and putting in semi-colons in a state of marmoreal despair. I suppose there may be half a paragraph somewhere worth reading: but I doubt it.

Letter from Vita

Teheran
23 February

Yesterday the Russian post came in; at least half of it did, for the Persians are incapable of delivering the whole of the post at one go, and think us most unreasonable for expecting them to do so, so that it arrives in driblets, spread sometimes over three days; but it was the right half that came yesterday, for it contained a letter (a nice, long, missing-me letter) from you [...][6]

I dreamt at great length, having read your letter, about what it would have been like to bring you here. Would you have got very tired on the journey? Do you like travelling? Are you the sort of traveller who constantly says, 'Oh look!'? Or do you take everything for granted? What would you like best here? Are you so much amused by people, – just as human beings, – that you have no surplus energy left for places? What would it be like to have you sitting in the room now? People become so different once they are taken away from their own surroundings – however well one knows them one discovers that one doesn't know them to the extent of being able to predict how they will

---

5 *To the Lighthouse.*
6 Virginia's letter from 5 February 1927.

react [...] I never allowed myself to indulge in these speculations about you last year, – it was too painful and made me long for you too much, – and why pray do I indulge this year? Why, for two reasons, 1) there is the chance of meeting you at Athens, and 2) there is that scheme of yours about Italy in October [...]

I have not yet found a coat for you, though I have searched. I think Isfahan will be the better place, and it's more fun to have one from there. Or Shiraz [...]

Yes, I am glad you miss me, even if it is 'damned unpleasant'. I thought from your first letter that you didn't miss me at all, and was sad about it. Now I am all pleased again. Selfish, isn't one? But I go through it too, you know, – this missing you, and wanting you, – so that I know exactly how damned unpleasant it is, and probably even better than you do.

Letter from Vita

Teheran
4 March

I have a game which I play all by myself. It consists in finding, and piecing together, the scattered fragments of Virginia's world. You see, this world was once whole and complete, and then one day some inner cataclysm burst into pieces, like the planet which burst into what is now the asteroids. (There is one little asteroid, called Ceres I think, one four miles across, the same size as the principality of Monaco, on which I have often thought I should like to live, revolving in lonely state round the sun. It would be even better than my island in the South Seas. Did you know I had got an island in the South Seas? It has a banana tree on it. But I must tell you more about Virginia's world, and never mind the South Seas.)

Well, Virginia's word was, then, whole and complete, so that it is quite easy to recognise the bits when one comes across them. One bit got itself precipitated into the caves at Cheddar, as you know, and another bit shot into the Shah's palace at Teheran. This bit was made entirely of looking-glass. Some of it flew up and flattened itself against the ceiling of a large room; some of it disposed itself round the walls in the shape of a dado. The ceiling part, of course, reflected everything upside down; not only the room, the carpet and the furniture, but also the dignitaries who were walking about on the floor or sitting on the chairs; even to the King of Kings himself; all were faithfully reflected, upside down, foreshortened, stumpy, absurd. The dado part also had great fun. It reflected people's legs up to the middle of their calves as they walked past, — big feet, little feet, flat feet, arched feet, thin legs, fat legs. But it wasn't going to be content with doing merely that, — not it. It came, remember, from Virginia's world, and consequently was mischievous, rude, irreverent, poking fun at Grand Viziers and European ladies alike. So it arranged itself in such a way as to reflect the floor going either uphill or downhill, or simply at a tilt, so that the feet climbed a cliff or descended a precipice of carpet or clung sideways like a fly, all down the length of the great room, right up to the Peacock Throne which stands at the end, and round the corner to the Bed of the Wife of Fath' Ali Shah, which is encrusted with jewels, and which has at its head a clock-like device, with jewelled hands, and the loudest tick you ever heard, — a real joke of a tick, — designed to keep the occupants from going to sleep at inopportune moments. An excellent device I thought, and one which might advantageously be adopted by Messrs Heal.

Then there were some other looking-glass bits of Virginia's broken world, which had arranged themselves in a facetted pattern in an alcove, so that they reflected only a portion of face at a time, — a nose, an eye, a chin, — endlessly repeated as one looked upward.

Great fun it all was, and I enjoyed myself very much that afternoon.

There is indeed a good deal to keep one amused. There is, for instance, the story of the clergyman who was recently stripped of all he possessed by robbers on the road, but for one garment, which they allowed him to keep on his plea that it would not be fitting for a man of God to enter Shiraz (whither he was travelling) stark naked. This one garment, however, happened to be a cut-away *tail coat. The clergyman, after some perplexity, solved the difficulty by putting it on back to front, and made his entry into Shiraz in that guise.*

Yes, there is plenty to keep one amused in a small way, but I pine for Virginia, and, to make matters worse (1) the Russian post has run amok now for two weeks, and (2) our bag, which ought to have come in yesterday, has missed the aeroplane and will not be here for a solid fortnight. This means that I get no letters. That I shan't know for ages whether you are definitely going to Greece. That I shan't even know whether you have forgotten me or not. That I shan't know if you are well. All this is damnable [...]

How nice it would be, wouldn't it, to get out of the rut of one's own thoughts for a bit; to alter the whole shape of the mind; to walk suddenly into a mental landscape as different as the landscape of Central Asia is from that of Kent.

In the meantime I should be happy if I could get another letter from you, but I can't hope to do that for at least a week. Damn these incompetent posts. It is maddening to think that our mail-bags are lying somewhere in a heap, being of no use to anybody, when we want them so badly. Or, at least, I do.

Letter from Vita

Teheran

11 March

The posts are all awry and amok; a stray Daily Mail *trickles in, then a detective story for Harold, then a letter for me posted on Jan. 30th, but no nice big lumps of post come as they ought to do. As for our missing Foreign Office bag, it hasn't turned up yet. And I haven't heard from my mother for four weeks! So Heaven knows when this letter will reach you.*

But at least, among the trickles of the Russian post, is a letter from you, of February 16th. I gather from internal evidence that one is missing, — it'll come in the bag next week, I expect.[7]

---

7 Virginia's letters from 16, 18 and 21 February would arrive at this time.

But are you really shingled? Is it true? Oh darling, do I like that? I think I preferred the dropping hairpins, that cheerful little cascade that used to tinkle onto your plate. But Mary [Hutchinson] says you look nice shingled, does she? And Mary ought to know. It makes you go all wrong in my mind, and the photograph of you at Knole no longer tells the truth, which upsets me [...]

Do you know that my time in Teheran is drawing to an end? Every night as I walk across the compound and look up at the stars through the planes, I wonder if I shall ever see Teheran again. Everybody asks me if we are coming back. I say, 'So far as I know.' But that is just official discretion: I cannot believe that the swords and silk stockings will exercise their charm much longer. In the meantime I remain wisely silent, observing a struggle going on in Harold, and knowing that an ill-placed word often makes people turn contrary [...]

I've been buying, in large quantities, the most lovely Persian pottery: bowls and fragments, dim greens and lustrous blues, on which patterns, figures, camels, cypresses, script, disport themselves elusive and fragmentary. How I am going to get them all home God knows. For the moment they stand round my room, creating a rubbed, romantic life of forgotten centuries. It's like looking into a pool, and seeing, very far down, a dim reflection. I make all sorts of stories about them [...]

Oh God, I wish I were going to be in Greece with you, lucky lucky Leonard. Please wish that I might be there. Please miss me. You say you do. It makes me infinitely happy to think that you should, though I can't think why you should, with the exciting life that you have, – Clive's rooms, and talk about books and love, and then the Press, and the bookshop, and wild-eyed poets rushing in with manuscript, and all the rest of it.

But I am going to Shiraz, it's true. This would be heaven if I didn't so much want Virginia. However, next time I go abroad it will, it shall, it must, be with you.

PS I think it is really admirable, the way I keep my appointments. I said I would be back on the 10th May, and here I am, rolling up in London at 11.50 p.m. on the ninth, with ten minutes to spare. It's like the Jules Verne man who went round the world in eighty days, and who had forgotten to turn off the gas in his flat.

Virginia's Diary

14 March

Annoyed that I have not heard from Vita by this post nor yet last week, annoyed sentimentally, and partly from vanity.

Letter from Vita

Teheran
20 March

Post going in half an hour — great hurry — beloved Virginia — so this is just to tell you we don't now go to Athens at all — can't get the Italian boat — but are coming direct to Marseilles — arriving in London late on May 5th — a few days earlier than by the other plan [...]

Bag in — got two letters from you — but too late to answer by this post. I'll send a long letter by bag on Saturday — God, here's the man for the letters.

Letter from Virginia

52 Tavistock Square
23 March

Are you well? Did you enjoy the walk? [...] I'd give a good deal to know. But the silly thing is that I'm writing before you've even left Teheran, I suppose. What I pretend to be past is all in the future. Yet to you, reading this, it's over. All very confusing, and pray God I may never have to write to you in Persia again.

How you'd laugh to see me stretched out comatose recovering from two days' high temperature – all owing to inoculations, and my principles – I know I deserve it. I urged you so lightly into it – how little I pitied you – and now you shall laugh at me. How I wish you'd walk into the room this moment, and laugh as much as you like.

Why do I think of you so incessantly, see you so clearly the moment I'm in the least discomfort? An odd element in our friendship. Like a child, I think if you were here, I should be happy.

Letter from Vita

Persepolis
30 March

I've driven a motor over nearly a thousand miles of Persia within the last week. I am dirty, sunburnt, well. We have got up at dawn every morning and gone to bed (on the floor) at 8.30. We have slept in ruined huts; made fires of pomegranate-wood and dried camel-dung; boiled eggs; lost all sense of civilisation; returned to the primitive state in which one thinks only of food, water, and sleep. But don't imagine that we have nothing but water to drink; no, indeed; we carry a demi-john filled with Shiraz wine, and though we may discard our beds (which we did on the first day, when our Ford luggage-car broke down and we strewed the street of a Persian village with chemises and tea-pots), the demi-john we do not discard. We get up at dawn, we motor all day across plains and up gorges, tearing along, and at nightfall we arrive somewhere or other, and shake out our little diminished camp, and fall asleep. A very good life, Virginia. And now (for I have moved on since beginning this letter at Persepolis) I have seen Shiraz, an absurdly romantical place, and passed again by Sivand, and slept there, a valley full of peach blossom and black kids, and came again to Isfahan, where the post was waiting for us, and a letter from you. (But before I answer it, don't imagine, please, that this life of flying free and unencumbered across Persia is in

*any sense a romantic life; it isn't; the notion that one escapes from materialism
is a mistaken notion; on the contrary, one's preoccupation from morning to night
is: Have we cooked the eggs long enough? Have we enough Bromo left? Who
washed the plates this morning, because I didn't? Who put away the tin-opener,
because if nobody did, it's lost? Far from finding a liberation of the spirit, one
becomes the slave of the practical —*

*But anyway, my darling, I found a letter from you. There it was (I've now
unpacked the ink and refilled my pen). We topped the pass, and came down upon
Isfahan with its blue domes, and there in the Consulate was our mail-bag full of
letters. You were no longer going to Greece but to Rome. You won't like Rome,
with its squaling tramlines, but you will like the Campagna. Please go out into
the Campagna as much as possible, and let your phrases match the clouds there,
and think of me. I've just been to dinner with a young Persian, — he's in love with
me, — such a nice creature, — I knew him last year, — he chants Persian poetry so
beautifully — This letter gets interrupted all the time, but I love you, Virginia —
so there — and your letters make it worse — Are you pleased? I want to get home
to you — Please, when you are in the south, think of me, and of the fun we should
have, shall have, if you stick to your plan of going abroad with me in October, — sun
and cafés all day, and ? all night. My darling [. . .] please let this plan come off.*

I live for it [. . .]

*Such a scrawl. By candlelight. The motor leaves at 4 tomorrow morning
for Teheran. I'm in a queer excited state, — largely owing to your letter, — I
always get devastated when I hear from you. God, I do love you. You say I use
no endearments. That strikes me as funny. When I wake in the Persian dawn,
and say to myself 'Virginia . . . Virginia . . .'*

The Common Reader *was in my room at Shiraz — it gave me a shock.*

*Look here [. . .] you'll come to Long Barn, won't you? Quite soon after I
get back? If I promise to get back undamaged? I'll be sweeter to you than ever
in my life before —*

Letter from Virginia

Cassis, France
5 April

I was in a towering passion – Clive had a long letter from Harold, I none from you. For some inscrutable reason after 4 days two arrived from you and one from Dottie. This has assuaged my rage, which threatened to make our journey one black and bitter pilgrimage of despair. I was very unhappy [...]

Please darling honey come back safe. We will have a merry summer: one night perhaps at Long Barn: another at Rodmell: We will write some nice pieces of prose and poetry: we will saunter down the Haymarket. We will not dine at Argyll House. We will snore.

1. Virginia is completely spoilt by her shingle.
2. Virginia is completely made by her shingle.
3. Virginia's shingle is quite unnoticeable.

These are the three schools of thought on this important subject.

I have bought a coil of hair, which I attach by a hook. It falls into the soup, and is fished out on a fork.

Are you well?

Letter from Vita

Long Barn
5 May

It is marvellous *to be actually in England. I passed Cassis yesterday! Longed to see Clive.*

Darling, darling Virginia, it's quite incredible that I shall see you tomorrow.

Letter from Vita

Long Barn
10 May

Much as I love Clive (and I have a real affection for the roystering fellow) I prefer being alone with you. I was cross and sulky [...]

Oh darling! It is nice being back, and seeing you. Damn Clive though. Dear old Clive.

I've just acquired two goats. They remind me of Persia.

Virginia's Diary

11 May

Vita back; unchanged, though I daresay one's relation changes from day to day.

Letter from Vita

Long Barn
12 May

The clock seems to have been put back a year, for I sit alone after dinner. Harold is in London, but so strong is the habit upon me that I think he is in Persia. But everything is blurred to a haze by your book of which I have just read the last words, and that is the only thing which seems real. I can only say that I am dazzled and bewitched. How did you do it? How did you walk along that razor-edge without falling? Why did you say anything so silly as that I 'shouldn't like it'? You can never have meant that though.

Darling, it makes me afraid of you. Afraid of your penetration and loveliness and genius.

The dinner is the part I like best perhaps. Then the deserted house, and the passage of time, which must have been so difficult to manage and in which you've succeeded so completely. And odd bits, like the shawl over the skull, and a phrase about the unity of things on page 101 — oh, and hundreds of phrases, scattered about, which are so like you (the flesh-and-blood Virginia, warming grey milk by the gas) that it looks odd to see them in print. And of course the relationship of Mr and Mrs Ramsay. And her shadow in the window. But I could go on for ever like that.

My darling, what a lovely book! I love you more for it. But I still can't think how you did it. It really bewilders me, even coming from you. It's as though you juggled with the coloured stars of a rocket, and kept them all alight, all flying.

Of course it is perfectly ridiculous to call it a novel.

I wonder if you know how like Mrs Ramsay you are yourself? But perhaps that's because she is your mother.

I do really love you more than before, for it. You always said I was a snob, and perhaps that is a form of snobbishness. But I do. Only if I had read it without knowing you, I should be frightened of you. As it is, it makes you more precious, more of an enchanter.

I don't feel that this is a very illuminating letter, but I leave that to your clever friends! It is simply written under a spell – I can't shake myself free.

I tore up to Hertfordshire today; tore back again; and read after dinner. I was greatly moved, when in came Louise carrying a huge dead fish on a platter. They had stuffed the hole with grass, where it had been gaffed. It looked at me with a dead cold eye. But it couldn't bring me back to my senses.

Now I must go to bed, but there will I think be more dreams than sleep. All your fault. Bless you, my lovely Virginia.

Letter from Virginia

52 Tavistock Square
13 May

What a generous woman you are! Your letter has just come, and I must answer it, though in a chaos [...] I was honest though in thinking you wouldn't care for *The Lighthouse*: too psychological; too many personal relationships, I think [...] The dinner party the best thing I ever wrote: the one thing that I think justifies my faults as a writer: This damned 'method'. Because I don't think one could have reached those particular emotions in any other way. I was doubtful about Time Passes. It was written in the gloom of the Strike: then I re-wrote it: then I thought it impossible as prose – I thought you could have written it as poetry. I don't know if I'm like Mrs Ramsay: as my mother died when I was 13 probably it is a child's view of her: but I have some sentimental delight in thinking that you like her. She has haunted me: but then so did that old wretch my father: Do you think it sentimental? Do you think it irreverent about him? I should like to know. I was more like him than her, I think; and therefore more critical: but he was an adorable man, and somehow, tremendous.

[…] I'm rather bothered about my paper; it mayn't suit; it may be dull. Ask Harold whether one can say that God does not exist to Oxford undergraduates? […]

So dearest, train, Wednesday, to arrive for dinner. I rushed into a whore's shop in Leicester Sqre and bought a coat.

Letter from Vita

Long Barn
14 May

Harold says be as rude about God as you would be at Cambridge.

Letter from Virginia

52 Tavistock Square
15 May

All right, dearest donkey. I will be outside the place where one buys tickets at Paddington at 4.35 on Wednesday, carrying a neat bag, otherwise slightly shabby, but distinguished.

Letter from Vita

Long Barn
20 May

My darling, I'm still under the spell of being with you.

This is to tell you that I am going to lunch with that old Lesbian[8] on Tuesday, but I have told her I must be back in London by a ¼ to 5. So don't put off Logan [Pearsall Smith] and the rest. It doesn't matter if I come in when they are there, does it? Only don't leave the bell unanswered!

I wish you could see my garden. It is really pretty, and will be over if you don't come till the week after next.

Letter from Virginia

Monk's House
22 May

Yes, honey, do come on Tuesday. Only stay longer than they do, whatever happens. I don't like seeing you between the legs and over the heads of Logans and Hendersons. I think it would be a tactful thing on your part if you asked L. to come to Long Barn in person. He probably thinks you don't want him etc.: being a modest man.

Letter from Vita

Long Barn
26 May

Oh dear, are you really better? I know you were feeling ill, but thought it was too many people [...]

Do stay two nights. You know how much I want you to.

---

8 Ethel Smyth.

Letter from Virginia

52 Tavistock Square
29 May

You're the only person I want to see when I have a headache — that's a compliment — But it's going off fast.

Write, dear honey, a nice letter to me.

Letter from Vita

Long Barn
30 May

My poor darling — I do hate these damned headaches that you get. I wish you were ROBUST. I wish also that you spared yourself a little more. I hate to think of you ill, or in pain [...]

I am terribly excited about your coming here. I hope it won't rain. I don't believe you have ever seen Long Barn in the summer, since the first time you came — and Leonard certainly never has.

Darling, do, do get well.

Letter from Vita

Long Barn
31 May

My darling, I needn't tell you that it makes me wretched to know that you are ill. I feared the worst the moment I saw Leonard's writing on the envelope. Oh Virginia, I'd do anything to make you well. I wish to God that if you had got to be ill, it had happened here, and then you'd have been obliged to stay, and I could have looked after you. But that's selfish really, because I suppose you'd be miserable away from your own house.

Leonard says will I come and see you towards the end of the week, so you can't be so very bad. Of course I'll come any time you like. I shall be here all the week, so you have only to get Leonard to send me a postcard — or ring up.

I send you a few flowers. I fear they won't look as fresh when they reach you as when they leave me. Put ten grains of aspirin, powdered, in the water to revive them.

Are you in bed? Yes, I suppose so. With an aching head. Able to read? Allowed to have letters? I am asking Leonard to let me know how you are. I do worry so about you, and above all can't bear the idea that you should be in pain.

Letter from Vita

Long Barn
1 June

I thought you'd like the following compliments to cheer you in your seclusion, even though they are only from my poor despised friend Hugh.[9]

'*I'm in the middle of* The Lighthouse, *ekeing it out so that it will last. Why doesn't she publish a book every day? And what fun to be in at the birth of books quite as important as Jane Austen. She is a genius and I would carry a thousand hair-shedding dogs to the gates of Hell for her did she wish it! You're lucky having her for a friend.*' (Am I?)

Darling, I know you are slipping off your pillows, and failing to reach the telephone, having genius perhaps as Hugh says for writing books, but less talent than anybody I ever knew for making yourself comfortable. I hope you may have letters, especially those that need no answer. Such as mine. I worry about you dreadfully, and Mother has sent you a box of chocolates (for you and Leonard) thinking you were coming here tomorrow. So I shall keep them till you do come. I will try not to eat them myself but won't promise.

I wrote two poems this morning (both bad) and a bit of my book; so the sap is stirring, if to little purpose.

Oh my dear, I do hope you are getting better.

---

9 Hugh Walpole, the English novelist.

Letter from Virginia

52 Tavistock Square

5 June

It's odd how being ill even like this splits one up into several different people. Here's my brain now quite bright, but purely critical. It can read; it can understand; but if I ask it to write a book it merely gasps. How does one write a book? I can't conceive. It's infinitely modest therefore, – my brain at this moment. There's Vita, it says, able to write books: Then my body – that's another person [...]

The Seafarers Educational Society has bought 2 copies of *The Lighthouse*. It's an awful thought that the merchant service will be taught navigation by me: or the proper use of foghorns and cylinders.

Letter from Vita

Long Barn

6 June

It's a very good joke about the Seamen's Union and The Lighthouse. *I shall send a presentation copy to the Lifeboat fund [...]*

Look here: I insist on your having a sofa. If you won't buy one for yourself, I shall have to buy it for you, and that will make you furious. So if one doesn't appear quickly in your room, I shall deliver an ultimatum. Now do be sensible and pay attention. It is ridiculous for someone who periodically collapses on two chairs under a golden cloak, not to have a sofa.

How you will like being at Rodmell! Dear me, what a lucky man Leonard is. I wish you were coming here instead, though.

Letter from Vita

Long Barn

8 June

What counts is that you shouldn't lavish yourself on people; and this I urge, even when I myself am the people. So do you think I'd better come on Friday?

Or will you promise to shoo me away like a chicken from your doorstep if you feel in the least tired when I drive up at about 4 on Friday? If you want to stop me, a postcard to me at White Lodge will do it. A disappointment, but no offence. I am afraid you have been worse than you admit. No, indeed I don't think you a molly coddle, — would to God that you were more of one. But I fancy I can solve the problem of getting the sofa up your stairs.

Can we go for a little walk in the water-meadows? With Pinker?

Perhaps I can come round to you with Raymond after dining with him, — but no: you mustn't see people, or be excited. Especially as you dine with Clive next day. Dear Clive, he wrote me such a nice letter; and what an angel to ask me to dinner the same night as you. I like that, because that was where and how I first saw you. Though no doubt his intention is mischievous, still I am grateful to him, and it provides a look-forward.

Letter from Vita

Sherfield Court
11 June

Do you know what I should do, if you were not a person to be rather strict with? I should steal my own motor out of the garage at 10 p.m. tomorrow night, be at Rodmell by 11.5 (yes, darling: I did a record on Friday, getting from Lewes to Long Barn in an hour and 7 minutes,) throw gravel at your window, then you'd come down and let me in; I'd stay with you till 5 and be home by half past 6. But, you being you, I can't; more's the pity.

Have you read my book? Challenge, I mean?[10] Perhaps I sowed all my wild oats then. Yet I don't feel the impulse has left me; no, by God; and for a different Virginia I'd fly to Sussex in the night. Only; with age, soberness, and the increase of considerateness, I refrain. But the temptation is great.

---

10 Vita's novel, *Challenge*, was published only in the United States in 1923, and told the thinly disguised story of her affair with Violet Trefusis: the character based on Violet is called Eve.

Letter from Virginia

52 Tavistock Square

14 June

You see I was reading *Challenge* and I thought your letter was a challenge 'if only you weren't so elderly and valetudinarian' was what you said in effect 'we would be spending the day together' whereupon I wired 'come then' to which naturally there was no answer and a good thing too I daresay as I am elderly and valetudinarian, – it's no good disguising the fact. Not even reading *Challenge* will alter that. She is very desirable I agree: very. (Eve.)

Letter from Vita

Long Barn

14 June

'Chance missed,' – DAMN. We stayed playing tennis at Sherfield and didn't get home till evening [...]

I've got nothing to say, except I wish you were here. I could so easily have fetched you this morning [...] but I expect you would have talked more than was good for you.

Virginia's Diary

18 June

This is a terribly thin diary for some reason: half the year has been spent and left only these few sheets. Perhaps I have been writing too hard in the morning to write here also. Three weeks wiped out by headache. We had a week at Rodmell, of which I remember various sights, and the immense comfort of lying there lapped in peace [...]

We saw Vita given the Hawthornden [Prize]. A horrid show up, I thought: not of the gentry on the platform – Squire, Drinkwater, Binyon only: of us all: all of us chattering writers. My word! How insignificant we all looked! How can we pretend that we are interesting, that our works matter? The whole business of writing became infinitely distasteful. But there may be a stream of ink in them that matters more than the look of them – so tightly clothed, mild, and decorous – showed. I felt there was no one full grown mind among us. In truth, it was the thick dull middle class of letters that met; not the aristocracy.

Virginia's Diary

22 June

Harold Nicolson and Duncan dined with us, and Nessa came in afterwards, very silent, inscrutable and, perhaps, critical. As a family we distrust anyone outside our set, I think. We too definitely decide that so and so has not the necessary virtues. I daresay Harold has not got them; at the same time, there is a good deal in him I like: he is quick and rash and impulsive; not in our sense very clever; uneasy; seeming young; on the turn from diplomat to intellectual; not Vita's match; but honest and cordial. L. says he's too commonplace. I liked my little duet with him. He wears a green, or blue, shirt and tie; is sunburnt; chubby; pert; vivacious. Talked of politics, but was flimsy compared with Leonard – I thought. Said it was with L. and me that he felt completely at his ease. Told stories which sound rather empty in the bare Bloomsbury rooms.

Letter from Vita

Long Barn
23 June

Darling Virginia, I am so sorry about today. I wanted to ask you and Leonard to come for your postponed visit and was going to suggest the weekend after the eclipse, or any day in the week following that. Will you let me know some time if you can and will?

Harold loved his evening with you. I am glad you thought him nice. He is nice. He does so much want you both to come here. You can rest as much as you like, — stay in bed all day if you like!

Virginia's Diary

23 June

Never have I spent so quiet a London summer. I have set my standard as an invalid, and no one bothers me. No one asks me to do anything. Quiet brings me cool clear quick mornings, in which I dispose of a good deal of work, and toss my brain into the air when I take a walk.

Vita's book [*The Land*] verberates and reverberates in the press. A prize poem — that's my fling at it — for with some relics of jealousy, or it may be of critical sense, I can't quite take the talk of poetry and even great poetry seriously.

Virginia's Diary

4 July

Back from Long Barn. Such opulence and freedom, flowers all out, butler, silver, dogs, biscuits, wine, hot water, log fires, Italian cabinets, Persian rugs, books — this was the impression it made: as of stepping into a rolling gay sea, with nicely crested waves. Yet I like this room better perhaps: more effort and life in it, to my mind. Vita very opulent, in her brown velvet coat, pearl necklace, and slightly furred cheeks (they are like Saviour's Flannel). I liked Harold too. He is a spontaneous childlike man; has a mind that bounces when he drops it; an air of immaturity. I should judge him very generous and kind hearted. Vita very free and easy, always giving me great pleasure to watch, and recalling some image of a ship breasting a sea, nobly, magnificently, with all sails spread, and the gold sunlight on them.

Letter from Vita

Long Barn
4 July

See how prompt I am in writing to you now.[11] The truth is, I have missed you horribly this evening. It suddenly turned to summer; we dined on the terrace for the first time this year; there were warm pockets of air; I wished ardently that tonight might be the last night; I sat alone on the steps watching a sickle of moon creep out from behind the poplars; everything was still and scented and soft and romantic; a moth dashed across my eyes. It is all very well, you know, but these snatches of happiness are extremely exasperating. – And why have you such an art of keeping so much of yourself up your sleeve? As to make me suspect that after twenty years there would still be something to be unfolded, – some last layer not uncoiled.

I like making you jealous; my darling (and shall continue to do so), but it's ridiculous that you should be.[12]

Letter from Virginia

52 Tavistock Square
4 July

Yes you are an agile animal – no doubt about it […] You only be a careful dolphin in your gambolling, or you'll find Virginia's soft crevices lined with hooks […]

---

11 After Vita, Harold, Virginia, Leonard, Edward Sackville-West and Quentin Bell travelled to watch the eclipse on 29 June, the entire party returned to London, except Vita, who was joined by Dorothy Wellesley. Together, these two went on to Haworth and did not return until 1 July. Virginia had confessed to feeling jealous about this side-excursion.

12 Pasted on to the verso is an illustration of a dolphin, one of Virginia's fantasy animals for Vita, with the accompanying text: 'Dolphin (Delphinus delphis) is an agile animal executing amusing gambols.'

Honey, could you remember to bring my waterproof (rose pink) and my gloves (scarlet)? I flung them down in the hall I think.

Letter from Vita

Long Barn
6 July

Slightly light-headed, — my mother kept me up till 6 a.m. this morning, — an all-night sitting. Slightly tipsy, — Harold, dismayed by my appearance, filled me up with port, — sensible man. Slightly exhausted altogether, — a combination of the bloody flux and the all-night sitting. Really my mother is a tragic character. — But there was a letter from you waiting for me; which made up for much. Am I forgiven? And are you discreet?

I sent your mackintosh (rose pink) and your gloves (scarlet) today.

Letter from Virginia

52 Tavistock Square
8 July

Yes, do come as early as ever you can on Tuesday. I'm now told that I engaged myself to go with Nessa [Bell], Duncan [Grant] and Clive [Bell] to Hampton Court on Tuesday. If so, you'll have to come — we'll dine; we'll haunt the terrace. For my part, I should prefer solitude. For yours, you'd prefer oysters. Bad Vita, bad wicked Vita. What's become of your fine gesture about promiscuity?

I've just written, or re-written, a little story about Sapphism, for the Americans.

Letter from Vita

Long Barn
8 July

Virginia, much as I love you, (and that's more than I like for your peace of mind,) I couldn't possibly go to Hampton Court with you with that party. For one thing, not being Eddy,[13] I don't relish the idea of butting in where I'm not wanted, and then — oh, lots of other things [...] I'm coming to London on Tuesday only, to see Virginia and to see her by herself [...]

Darling, write me a little note and say you won't take me to Hampton Court. I shouldn't endure it — I shall go off at full gallop if you do.

Letter from Virginia

52 Tavistock Square

18 July

My dear Mrs Nicolson,

I can't tell you how much I enjoyed myself on Sunday. It was so good of you and your husband to let me come. And what a lovely garden! I can't think how you can ever bear to leave it. But then *everything* was so delightful. London seemed more commonplace than ever after your delightful Long Barn. And I still have some of your lovely flowers to remind me of the happy time I had with you, and your husband, to whom please give my best thanks and remembrances, and with much love to you both, I am.

There, you ramshackle old Corkscrew, is that the kind of thing you like? I suppose so.

What I think will be so nice next time is the porpoise in my bath — steel blue, ice cold, and loving hearted. Some prefer dolphins — I don't. I've known one dolphin, the Mediterranean kind, ravage a whole bedfull of oysters. A lewd sort of brute that [...]

Honey dearest, don't go to Egypt please. Stay in England. Love Virginia. Take her in your arms.

---

13 Edward Sackville-West, Vita's cousin.

Virginia's Diary

23 July

It has been, on the whole, a fresh well ordered summer. I am not so parched with talk as usual. My illness in May was a good thing in some ways; for l got control of society at an early stage, and circumvented my headache, without a complete smash. I enjoyed the Eclipse; I enjoyed Long Barn (where I went twice); I enjoyed sitting with Vita at Kew for three or four hours under a cloudy sky, and dining with her: she refreshes me, and solaces me.

Letter from Virginia

52 Tavistock Square
24 July

Dearest Creature,

(By the way, why is it that you always come into my presence in letters simply and solely – not even My dear Virginia, whereas I always invent some lovely lovely phrase?) How nice it is of me to be writing to you, when you're not writing to me […]

But listen: now what am I to do about powder? Ethel[14] will take it ill if I don't powder my nose. Once you gave me some which didn't smell. Tell me quickly what to get and where. I will rise to powder. But not to rouge […]

You'll be glad to hear I've sold 4000 of the *L.*[15] in America in a month: so they think I shall sell 8000 before the end of the year. And I shall make £800 (that is with luck).

---

14 Ethel Sands, the American painter, whom Virginia was to visit at her house in Normandy.

15 *To the Lighthouse*.

Letter from Vita

Long Barn
25 July

I never begin my letters, don't I, belovèd Virginia? But as Clive (who is an authority or thinks he is on such matters) will tell you, that's the most compromising way of beginning of all.

Well, I sent you a box of powder, same as I gave you before. You must do me credit with Ethel, and without powder or with the wrong sort you certainly wouldn't do me credit. So I telephoned to the chemist and said it must be sent at once. I nearly told him to put in a box of rouge, a bottle of liquid white, a cake of eyelash blacking, and a scarlet lip-stick. I say, may I make you up one day? I should enjoy that.

God, I do wish I were going with you, instead of meeting a horde of boys[16] at Paddington and trying to get too much luggage on to the motor [...]

I went to Canterbury yesterday, and to Wye because I wanted to see where the incomparable Astrea was born.[17] I have killed her off today, which means I have done ¾ of my book. It won't be as popular as the Lighthouse, with 4 or possibly 8 thousand copies in America. What pearls before swine! I resent their reading it. You don't, but then you are a purely mercenary writer, like Michael Arlen,[18] and think of nothing but your returns.

There.

I shall write to you at Ethel's, just to keep myself fresh and green in your mind.

---

16 Her sons Ben and Nigel were returning from school.
17 Vita was writing a short book about the writer Aphra Behn (1640–89).
18 Best known for his 1924 novel *The Green Hat*.

Letter from Vita

Long Barn

27 July

Today as I was driving down Oxford Street I saw a woman on a refuge, carrying the Lighthouse. *She was an unknown woman, – up from the country, I should think, and just been to Mudie's or the Times, – and as the policeman held me up with his white glove I saw your name staring at me, Virginia Woolf, against the moving red buses, in Vanessa's paraph of lettering. Then as I stayed there (with my foot pressing down the clutch and my hand on the brake, as you will appreciate), I got an intense dizzying vision of you: you in your basement, writing; you in your shed at Rodmell, writing; writing those words which that woman was carrying home to read. How had she got the book? Had she stalked in, purposeful, and said 'I want* To the Lighthouse' *or had she strayed idly up to the counter and said 'I want a novel please, to read in the train, – a new novel, – anything'll do'? Anyhow there it was, one of the eight thousand, in the hands of the Public.*

You are in the arms of Ethel (metaphorically, I hope) by now, being motored about Normandy [...] You will be given iced grapefruit when you are called. But there won't be angel fish in your bathroom, nor many of the other delights you find at Long Barn. Please find out for me exactly what it is that one likes about Ethel. Is it the sense of civilisation and silver tea-things? Ethel, in analogy, is certainly a tea-table. But there is a scratch too.

I have got the boys, and the house from being an abode of peace has become noisy. How can one write? The door bursts open all the time – 'Where is my hammock?' 'May we play tennis?' 'What can we do now?' Nigel, however, who always likes having situations neatly defined, remarks at breakfast, 'How nice it is to have a family assembled.' I who detest families deplore this domestic sentiment in my younger son.

Darling, I like solitude, that's what I like – now do you think my poem on the subject will suffer or improve from my being thus forcibly deprived of it? I don't know when I shall ever write the poor thing. It turns over sleepily in my brain and occasionally lays a little egg in the shape of a line. Besides, most people are so gregarious that it will find no echo in any heart nearer than that of a hermit in Thibet.

My darling, come back soon, I don't like to feel you are out of England. (This comes well from me, dashing off to Persia.) I'll come over to Rodmell when you're alone there. Not on the 6th because that's Ben's birthday. But soon, please.

Letter from Vita

Long Barn
1 August

My darling, I am so upset by your saying you had no letter from me. I wrote you a long letter and posted it myself early on Thursday last. Has it ever reached you?

[…] When shall I see you?

Letter from Virginia

Monk's House
3 August

Yes, darling creature, your letter was handed me just as we left Auppegard, and caused me, I suppose, to forget my box, so that the exquisite butler had to motor into Dieppe after us. Yes, darling, it was a nice letter. Sauqueville ain't a very grand place, all the same. I looked for traces of you […]

I shall be alone Thursday night. Could you stay two nights? I don't want to seem as if I had you in secret, though it's infinitely more to my taste, exploring about in the recesses secretly […]

My God, how you would have laughed yesterday! Off for your first drive in the Singer: the bloody thing wouldn't start. The accelerator died like a duck – starter jammed. All the village came to watch – Leonard almost sobbed with rage. At last we had to bicycle in and fetch a man from Lewes. He said it was the magnetos – would you have known that?

Letter from Vita

Long Barn
4 August

NOT FOR PUBLICATION

Roshan-i-chasm-i-man,[19]

(You won't know what that means, but you say I never begin my letters, so I try to oblige.)

[…] It would in any case be difficult for me to stay two nights, though if you were alone I would certainly do so.

Are you all right? Dispirited? Over-fed? Not fond of me any longer? Something wrong, I feel, by your letter; but still am confident that by this time (i.e. midnight) next week it'll be all right. I'll come after luncheon, about 5, shall I? You can't think how I long to see you. The gaps of time are interminable.

I really would stay the 2 nights if I could, if only to make it not seem deliberate, – for your sake if not for my own.

Letter from Virginia

52 Tavistock Square
7 August

Musha-i-djabah-dal-imam

Which being interpreted means, Darling-West-what-a-donkey-you-are, all my letters in future are going to be addressed to Pippin, since it is clear you can't read them. 'Something wrong I feel by your letter.' – What do you mean? It was the nicest, lovingest, tenderest letter in the world: a little rasped at not seeing you perhaps, but after all that's

---

19 A Persian love-greeting.

your taste, isn't it? Or did you, with the marvellous intuition of the poet, discover what I have tried to keep concealed from you? That I am loved, by a man; a man with an aquiline nose, a nice property, a wife of title and furniture to suit.[20] The proposal was made the day before I left, and I have a letter now confirming it. What do you wish me to do? I was so overcome I blushed like a girl of 15.

Letter from Vita

Long Barn
8 August

I was going into Sevenoaks to pick up the boys, when I saw the postman's scarlet bicycle leaning against the village letter-box. That meant that the afternoon post had arrived. I stopped; went in; and said, 'Are there any letters for Long Barn?' There were. Among them was a typewritten envelope which contained a letter from you. I felt myself flush with rage, as I read it, – I don't exaggerate. I didn't know I was so jealous of you. Who is your damned man with the aquiline nose? Look here, I really mind. But if it comes to that, I have on my table a letter of the same sort, – which I haven't answered. What sort of answer I send depends on you. I really am not joking. If you are not careful, you will involve me in an affair which will bore me horribly. If you are nice, on the other hand, I'll send my correspondent packing. But I won't be trifled with. I really mean this.

For the rest:

1. *I'll bring my camera, only my charge is £1 per snapshot, not 2/6.*
2. *I won't bring Pippin, I think, because she might be sick in the motor.*
3. *I'll come at 4 Thursday.*
4. *I'll stay till Friday.*

---

20 The man was Philip Morrell, Ottoline's husband, who had renewed his unwelcome advances to her.

5. *I'd like to lunch at Charleston if you will* promise *to leave directly after lunch so that I may have you alone again.*

6. *I will certainly lay myself out to please you.*

I do get so angry about you.

Letter from Vita

Long Barn
16 August

I have finished with Mrs Behn — and have now only to pack her off. This, in the midst of thousands of people who arrived at Long Barn at all hours of the day and night [...] The boys splashing about in the swimming bath, Harold writing the history of biography for you, and much tennis. Such is my life — and arguments about feminism, and men and women, and lots of Alella[21] — which sharpens the wits even if it undermines the constitution — and Raymond saying 'and then Virginia of course who is unquestionably the finest living writer of English prose'.

But in the meantime no sign of life from you, — isn't it odd, these sudden, spasmodic, and violent junctions between us, and then these days of complete silence which succeed?

Letter from Vita

Long Barn
20 August

Raymond says I write bad English. I let him read my Aphra Behn, and he pulverised me. I expect you will agree. It will be out in October, — too late for you to review for America, I think. It will be an easy and grateful book to review, — very historical — picturesque [...]

Having actually put Aphra in the post, I feel as free as a lark. Free to read, free to garden, free to think, free to be nice to my children. A delirious sensation,

---

21 Spanish wine.

— but already new energies stir in me, 24 hours after Aphra is finished. God damn this energy; but thank God for it, — such are my alternative emotions. I can't be happily idle, I sometimes wish I could ...

I send you a supplementary photograph,[22] which I had in Persia, and which lived stuck into my looking glass there, and one which I took here the other day. May I have the Persian one back please? It is precious, and I don't know where the negative is. The others do not matter as I have the negatives.

Write to me?

Letter from Vita

Long Barn
30 August

It wasn't very nice, no, it wasn't, leaving you standing in the gateway on Saturday with Tray[23] and Leonard. Lucky Tray. Lucky Leonard [...]

Dear me, I do wish I had you always in the house. Have you read Oroonoko?[24] Do you like it? Do you like me? Would you miss me if I disappeared? Have you been depressed? Do you still think you are a bad writer? Did you like Harold the other day?

Sheep are bleating on the road outside. The sound whisks me straight back to the Bakhtiari road. How hot it must be there now, and how deserted. I wish I were there in camp, with you.

Letter from Vita

Long Barn
16 September

Don't go right away from me. I depend on you more than you know.

---

22 Of Virginia.
23 Raymond Mortimer.
24 Novel by Aphra Benn, which Virginia had asked Vita to lend her.

Letter from Virginia

52 Tavistock Square
21 September

Very hurried, so I can't write. And rather melancholy. This I'll explain when we meet, if you are kind.

Letter from Vita

Long Barn
22 September

My darling, why melancholy? I thought you were not quite yourself the other day, and wondered if it was all my imagination [...] I wish I were with you today, damn it all; I want to know what is the matter.

Letter from Virginia

52 Tavistock Square
25 September

Look here, I want to be told,

1. *How you are*, truthfully.
2. Any news from the Foreign Office?

But I own I'd like to see you. Then I'd tell you about my melancholy and a thousand other things.

Virginia's Diary

5 October

If my pen allowed, I should now try to make out a work table, having done my last article for the *Tribune*, and now being free again. And instantly the usual exciting devices enter my mind: a biography beginning the year 1500 and continuing to the present day, called

Orlando: Vita; only with a change about from one sex to another. I think, for a treat, I shall let myself dash this in for a week.

Letter from Virginia

52 Tavistock Square
9 October

Look, dearest, what a lovely page this is, and think how, were it not for the screen and the Campbell,[25] it might be filled to the brim with love-making unbelievable: indiscretions incredible: instead of which, nothing shall be said but what a Campbell behind the screen might hear [...]

Here occurs a terrific gulf. Millions of things I want to say can't be said. You know why. You know for what a price – walking the lanes with Campbell, you sold my love letters. Very well. So we will skip all that [...]

Yesterday morning I was in despair [...] I couldn't screw a word from me; and at last dropped my head in my hands: dipped my pen in the ink, and wrote these words, as if automatically, on a clean sheet: Orlando: A Biography. No sooner had I done this than my body was flooded with rapture and my brain with ideas. I wrote rapidly till 12 [...] But listen; suppose Orlando turns out to be Vita; and it's all about you and the lusts or your flesh and the lure of your mind (heart you have none, who go gallivanting down the lanes with Campbell) – suppose there's the kind of shimmer of reality which sometimes attaches to my people, as the lustre of an oyster shell [...] suppose, I say, that Sibyl next October says 'There's Virginia gone and written a book about Vita' [...]

Shall you mind? Say yes, or No: Your excellence as a subject arises largely from your noble birth. (But what's 400 years of nobility, all the

---

25 Vita was having an ongoing affair with Mary Campbell, which she attempted to conceal from Virginia.

same?) and the opportunity thus given for florid descriptive passages in great abundance. Also, I admit, I should like to untwine and twist again some very odd, incongruous strands in you: going at length into the question of Campbell; and also, as I told you, it sprung upon me how I could revolutionise biography in a night: and so if agreeable to you I would like to toss this up in the air and see what happens. Yet, of course, I may not write another line.

Letter from Vita

Long Barn
11 October

My God, Virginia, if ever I was thrilled and terrified it is at the prospect of being projected into the shape of Orlando. What fun for you; what fun for me. You see, any vengeance that you ever want to take will lie ready to your hand. Yes, go ahead, toss up your pancake, brown it nicely on both sides, pour brandy over it, and serve hot. You have my full permission. Only I think that having drawn and quartered me, unwound and retwisted me, or whatever it is that you intend to do, you ought to dedicate it to your victim.

And what a lovely letter you wrote me, Campbell or no Campbell. (How flattered she'd be if she knew. But she doesn't and shan't.) How right I was, – not that it needed much perspicacity, – when I realised at Clive's that here was the most [...] what shall I say? You want duty and devotion, but if I wrote what I really think you would only say that Vita was laying it on a bit too thick. So I better not expose myself to your jeers. But how right I was, all the same; and to force myself on you at Richmond,[26] and so lay the train for the explosion which happened on the sofa in my room here when you behaved so disgracefully and acquired me for ever. Acquired me, that's what you did, like

---

26 In January 1923.

buying a puppy in a shop and leading it away on a string. Still trotting after you, and still on a string. For all the world like Pinker.

Last night was the most beautiful misty moonlight night I ever saw in my life. No, I did not go down the lanes. I hung out of my window and listened to the dead leaves twirling down in the stillness. I thought how lovely and lonely it must be at Laughton.[27] I was sorry about Laughton, – a fairy-story place for Virginia to live in [...]

Darling, I can't come up tomorrow, and am sending you a telegram to that effect. I won't tell you why, – a squalid reason. I shall come up next week though, and probably stay a night in London. And what about you coming here one of these days? You said you would and the advantages are obvious.

Not a word from that bloody Foreign Office. I fear they are plotting something very dark. Harold approaches his correspondence more and more gingerly. Oh, by the way, he finished his book today and it has gone to be typed. So you will have it soon.

I wish you were here. The days and nights are beautiful as only autumn can be [...] My delight is purely aesthetic, and country bumpkin I am good, industrious, and loving; how long will it be, though, before I break out? I would never break out if I had you here, but you leave me unguarded. Now, none of that means anything at all, so don't imagine that it does. I am Virginia's good puppy, beating my tail on the floor, responsive to a kind pat.

Letter from Vita

Long Barn
14 October

Darling, this is a letter written in a hurry and a furious temper to say that Harold is going to Berlin next week. Shall you be free on Tuesday if I come after

---

27 Laughton Place, near Glynde, was a sixteenth-century moated house which the Woolfs were tempted to buy.

lunch for a bit? We are so cross, but it appears to be inevitable. We only heard this morning. Berlin for three years![28] Good Lord deliver us.

I shan't go there till the end of January.

Letter from Virginia

52 Tavistock Square
14 October

Never do I leave you without thinking, it's for the last time. And the truth is, we gain as much as we lose by this. Since I am always certain you'll be off and on with another next Thursday week (you say so yourself, bad creature, at the end of your last letter, which is where the viper carries its sting) since all our intercourse is tinged with this melancholy on my part and desire to be white nosed and so keep you half an instant longer, perhaps, as I say we gain in intensity what we lack in the sober comfortable virtues of a prolonged and safe and respectable and chaste and cold blooded friendship [...]

Orlando will be a little book, with pictures and a map or two. I make it up in bed at night, as I walk the streets, everywhere. I want to see you in the lamplight, in your emeralds. In fact, I have never more wanted to see you than I do now – just to sit and look at you, and get you to talk, and then rapidly and secretly, correct certain doubtful points. About your teeth now and your temper. Is it true you grind your teeth at night? [...] What and when was your moment of greatest disillusionment? [...]

Please tell me beforehand when you will come, and for how long: unless the dolphin has died meanwhile and its colours are those of death and decomposition. If you've given yourself to Campbell, I'll

---

28 As counsellor to the British Embassy.

have no more to do with you, and so it shall be written, plainly, for all the world to read in *Orlando*.

Virginia's Diary

22 October

'I shall let myself dash this in for a week' – I have done nothing, nothing else for a fortnight; and am launched somewhat furtively but with all the more passion upon *Orlando: A Biography*. It is to be a small book, and written by Christmas. I walk making up phrases; sit, contriving scenes; am in short in the thick of the greatest rapture known to me. Talk of planning a book, or waiting for an idea! This one came in a rush. But the relief of turning my mind that way about was such that I felt happier than for months; as if put in the sun, or laid on cushions; and after two days entirely gave up my time chart and abandoned myself to the pure delight of this farce. I am writing *Orlando* half in a mock style very clear and plain, so that people will understand every word. But the balance between truth and fantasy must be careful. It is based on Vita, Violet Trefusis, Lord Lascelles, Knole, &c.

Letter from Virginia

52 Tavistock Square
23 October

Dearest Creature,

I'm afraid you are feeling lonely tonight. I wish I were with you. Harold is a very nice man, and I'm glad I know him.

Would Wednesday, Thursday suit you for me to come, suppose Friday was difficult? But I'm not sure. What used you and Lord Lascelles[29] to talk about?

---

29 Lord Lascelles, who had been in love with Vita in 1912–13, is the inspiration for Archduchess Harriet in *Orlando*.

Letter from Vita

Long Barn
25 October

Darling lovely Virginia,

I can't make out from your letter, – do you mean Wednesday or Thursday? Because Wednesday I have got to dine with (don't laugh) the King of Iraq. But Thursday I shall be here. And alone. I shan't stay up in London Wednesday night but shall come down after dinner. I nearly came to see you yesterday, when I was in London, but I thought you might be busy and I didn't want to be a bore. I was so depressed. I was grateful to you for your letter, it was so welcome and badly needed.

I will try to remember what I talked to Harry Lascelles about! He was always very tongue-tied, so we didn't get very far. He had nice hands.

Darling, I have found some lovely pictures at Knole. I do want you to come. Pippin has six puppies. Tell Pinker. Bring her when you come. Oh I do want you to come. Let me know: Thursday or Friday – or Saturday or Sunday if you prefer.

Letter from Vita

Long Barn
11 November

I have been so really wretched since last night.[30] I felt suddenly that the whole of my life was a failure, in so far as I seemed incapable of creating one single perfect relationship – What shall I do about it, Virginia? Be stronger-minded, I suppose. Well, at least I won't create any further mistakes! My darling, I'm grateful to you; you were quite right to say what you did; it has given me a pull-up; I drift too easily.

---

30 Vita had told Virginia about her affair with Mary Campbell. Vita was reduced to tears.

But look here, remember and believe that you mean something absolutely vital to me. I don't exaggerate when I say that I don't know what I should do if you ceased to be fond of me, — got irritated, — got bored. You disturbed me a good deal by what you said about Clive even. Surely you can't mean anything serious? Oh no, that's too unthinkable. I shan't worry about that — There's plenty else to worry about.

Darling forgive me my faults. I hate them in myself, and I know you are right. But they are silly surface things. My love for you is absolutely true, vivid, and unalterable —

Letter from Virginia

52 Tavistock Square
11 November

Dearest Creature,

You make me feel such a brute — and I didn't mean to be. One can't regulate the tone of one's voice, I suppose; for nothing I said could in substance make you wretched for even half a second — only that you can't help attracting the flounderers [...] And I'm half, or 10th, part, jealous, when I see you with the Valeries and the Marys: so you can discount that.

And that's all there is to it as far as I'm concerned. I'm happy to think you *do* care: for often I seem old, fretful, querulous, difficult (tho' charming) and begin to doubt.

Letter from Vita

Long Barn
17 November

It is absolutely damnable: before getting your letter I promised to go to Brighton on Monday evening and now I can't get out of it though I have tried [...]

Oxford was a repetition of your *Oxford: dinner with Mr Aubrey Herbert, and then that assembly at St Hugh's. My paper, and then heckling. A bottle of hock on return to the hotel (the Mitre this time, not the Clarendon), and so to an exhausted sleep. I wondered why you hadn't been more tired? I felt like a dry sponge — but I remembered that you were as lively as a cricket [...] How I wished you were there. It all came back to me with a painful vividness. Why haven't we got more things to look back upon? The very few days that we have had together away from London stand out for me with just that difference that there is between that stereoscopic photograph I showed you, and an ordinary photograph [...]*

Is this a loving letter? Not very, you will think, and yet there's a lot behind it, if you only knew.

Are you well? Are you fond of me? Shall I see you at all on Monday or not? I get into despair when these contretemps happen [...] And most important of all, when are you coming here to stay? I feel this is not only important, but vital. Why not come next Saturday? [...] Give this your consideration, as really I do feel that it is urgent. You may not, but I do. I want you to come.

Letter from Vita

Oxford
22 November

Ethel [Sands] is a trump, isn't she?[31] I have accepted and have put off going to Berlin till the third instead of the first — all for love of Virginia.

I am not enjoying myself here very much, thank you, but the operation was what they call successful, so that's a comfort.[32] I don't know how long I shall have to stay here, but I should think until Thursday. Rather grim [...]

You were a nice Virginia yesterday — very nice — even nicer than usual. Why? I was glad I had come up.

---

31 Ethel had invited them both to a party on 2 December.
32 Vita's son, Ben, had an emergency operation for tonsillitis.

I say, I do hate being here — and I hate myself for hating it. How selfish one is. I expect it is good for the soul. Is it? I wish you were here, then I should love it.

Bless you, darling darling Virginia — you don't know how much I love you — how deeply — and how permanently.

Letter from Virginia

52 Tavistock Square

5 December

Shall I come Saturday for the night? — Seems the only chance. Let me know [...]

Should you say, if I rang you up to ask, that you were fond of me?

If I saw you would you kiss me? If I were in bed would you —

I'm rather excited about *Orlando* tonight: have been lying by the fire and making up the last chapter.

Letter from Vita

Long Barn

6 December

I am in despair: Saturday is the one and only evening I have somebody coming, Dottie to wit — I have tried to put her off but she says it is the only day she can come. Curse and damn. Could you come either Thursday, Friday or Sunday, possibly? I am going to Brighton tomorrow for the night, so answer to the Metropole please — If you can come, all your questions shall be answered in the affirmative. It is practically impossible to get in or out of the house here, as there is a gaping hole in front of every door, — one has to jump — very dangerous but rather exciting.[33] And stinking men crawling like beetles all over the floor. But no matter — only make a great effort, — come — and see how nice I'll be.

---

33 Long Barn was having central heating installed.

Letter from Vita

Knole

29 December

Will this ever reach you? Are you completely snowed up? Is it very beautiful among the Downs? Does Pinker like it? Have you perhaps gone back to London? Have you anything to eat? Shall I ever get to Sherfield tomorrow? Shall I ever see you again? Shall I ever write another book? I feel that the answer to most of these questions is in the negative [...]

Now tomorrow I shall be confronted with Ethel and her eagle eye; I must display, I feel, no enthusiasm about any of my friends; or I say, shall I drag a completely red herring across her path? That would be rather fun. I'll invent a new beauty, whom nobody has ever seen, I'll ask Ethel if I may bring her to dinner, a dinner which on one pretext or another will have to be permanently put off. What shall we call her? You think of a suitable name, something very romantic like Gloria Throckmorton, or Leshia Featherstonehaugh. She is only nineteen, has run away from her family in Merioneth, and taken a flat in London. She is more lovely than Valerie,[34] more witty than Virginia, more wanton than Mary, and a better golfer than Miss Cecilia Leitch.[35]

On Xmas day I went to Brighton, throwing up floods on either side, and in torrents of rain. I looked wistfully to the left as I passed through Lewes.

Knole is all soft and white, and the snow falls in great flumps as the men shovel it off the roof. We are quite cut off except by walking. No motors, no telephone. I wish you were here. You're coming to Long Barn, aren't you though? And in no Puritanical frame of mind?

---

34 Valerie Taylor, a young actress with whom Raymond Mortimer had been in love.
35 Winner of the British Ladies' Golf Championship in 1914 and 1920–21.

1928

> Knole
>
> 6 January

Was your telegram intended to convey a command or merely a message? I mean, should it be written 'Love Virginia!' — an imperative, — or 'Love. Virginia.'? Whichever way you read it, it was very nice and unexpected, and if a command it has been obeyed. Darling, Dada has been so ill; we thought it was influenza, and then it suddenly turned to pneumonia. We had an awful fright, and though he is rather better today the doctor still won't say he is out of danger. That is why I am still here, and I think I must stay here all next week — I can't leave him alone with servants and nurses in this big house, he'd be too melancholy. My fingers itch to suggest that you should come down for a night — or more — as I shall be alone; I mean, he'll still be in bed — but I don't know if you would like to? It would be very good for Orlando (say I tentatively), and I find that one can very soon have enough of the society of hospital nurses.

Rebecca West wrote an article about The Land *which succeeded in annoying me; I resent being told that my feeling for the country is not genuine, but only*

what I think people ought to feel about the country; this is not true.[1] *[...]*
So my literary temper is full of bile. Also I want to see you, but am tied here
— Damn it all —

Letter from Virginia

52 Tavistock Square
14 January

I'm frightfully sorry about your father. Lord! What a time you have of
it: I do hope he is better: and for God's sake don't catch it yourself.
Please, darling creature, be careful [...]

Damn Rebecca — who doesn't know a turnip from an umbrella,
nor a poem from a potato if it comes to that — what right has she to
pontificate about *The Land*? Let me see it.

Letter from Vita

Knole
20 January

Virginia darling, I promised to let you know how Dada was — he is terribly
ill, with pericarditis (inflammation round the heart) — and it is a very slender
chance that he may yet pull through. We can only hang on and wait to see what
the next two or three days bring forth. I have wired for Harold who arrives this
evening. It is a nightmare, especially as he suffers agonies of pain and they dare
give him hardly any drugs to relieve it [...] Don't bother to answer this but
I thought you would be wondering what I was up to.

Your miserable,

Vita

---

1 In a review for *T.P.'s Weekly* on 7 January, Rebecca West described *The Land* as 'a
poem unlikely to survive'.

Letter from Virginia

52 Tavistock Square

22 January

This is only by way of goodnight, and to say that should you ever want
to see me, I am your entirely devoted but helpless and useless creature.

Letter from Vita

Knole

24 January

*Darling, my father is much better, and I think I can come to London tomorrow
— in which case I'll be with you at 5. I'll telephone in the morning if I can't,
i.e. if he is not so well. It is absolutely miraculous his having pulled through
— as they had really despaired of his life last Wednesday — Telephone before
10 if you want to put me off. I long to see you, and am really coming for
that — otherwise I would send the boys [to school] with Harold — but I do
long to see you so.*

Your loving (and rather shattered)

Orlando —

ha-ha!

Letter from Vita

Knole

27 January

*Harold was to have left today, and I was going up to London with him, but
my father was so unwell yesterday that he put off going, and I am thankful
that he did so, as he is very much worse today, and I fear there is now very
little hope. His heart is failing at last after the long strain on it. We can do
nothing but sit and wait to see what happens. It is all the more cruel after his
apparent recovery the other day.*

Vita's father, Lord Sackville, died on 28 January. As well as losing a beloved parent, Vita lost Knole, too – as a daughter, Vita could not inherit. The house and title passed to her uncle, Charles.

Letter from Virginia

52 Tavistock Square
29 January

Darling honey,

This is only to send you my love – You don't know how much I care for you.

Letter from Vita

Knole
30 January

My darling, thank you for your very sweet little note. I find it difficult to say anything about it all – I will tell you some day. In the meantime nothing but the most grotesque ideas come into my mind, such as what good copy it would all be for Virginia's book. The whole thing is a mixture of the tragic, the grotesque and the magnificent.

Fortunately one scarcely has time to think. He lies in the chapel, and I wish you could see it. It is very beautiful, and quite unreal.

I am going back to Long Barn tomorrow after the funeral. I would like to come and see you soon if I may. In the meantime, please love me, as you say you do –

Letter from Vita

Long Barn
2 February

My darling, what an angel you are to me. I wish I was dining with you tonight [...] I think I shall come up to London on Monday, so shall I come and see you

then? In the evening. I promise not to be too gloomy – and if you would come down
for a night any time next week I should like nothing better. I needn't tell you that
though. Harold has gone, so I shall be alone. I'm not going to Berlin for three weeks.

I have just come back from Withyham, where the floor of the chapel is com-
pletely carpeted with flowers.

Darling, I do love you so, and you are so sweet to me. I do so want to see you.

Letter from Virginia

52 Tavistock Square
3 February

Yes, darling honey, I shall be in all Monday evening and shall expect
you any time after five […] Don't mind being as miserable as you like
with me – I have a great turn that way myself –

A thousand useless but quite genuine loves descend upon you at
this moment – which is I know very very horrid, my poor dear honey.

Letter from Vita

Long Barn
5 February

My darling, there is nothing in the world I should like better than to dine with
you alone tomorrow night – I did not dare propose it, not thinking that you
would be alone – I will come at about 7 – shall I?

Letter from Vita

Long Barn
8 February

My darling, I think you are not only the most intelligent but also the nicest
person I know. I shall never forget how sweet you have been to me. You have
only one serious rival in my affections, and that is Bosman's Potto.[2] I must

---

2 Bosman's Potto is a type of primate. Virginia adopts Potto as a nickname, and this
alter-ego takes on a life of its own in many of their subsequent letters.

say he's irresistible, and so are you, — not that I ever made much attempt to
resist, from that evening here when you behaved so scandalously, down to the
present day [...]

I have written letters all day, and have nearly come to an end, so perhaps
tomorrow I may be able to write a gloomy little poem for you, all about mor-
tality [...]

The N.Y. Tribune says The Land *is the dullest poem ever written in that*
genre [...] I suspect they're right.

Letter from Virginia

52 Tavistock Square

9 February

I shall arrive at Sevenoaks at 1.12 tomorrow [...] and stay till 6.30 so
I'm afraid you'll have to give me not only a bun for my tea but a bone
for my lunch [...] and by the way I'm now called Bosman's Potto, *not*
V.W. by arrangement — A finer name, don't you think?

Letter from Vita

24 Brücken-allee, Berlin

29 February

My darling, well, here I am, feeling rather like a jackdaw with a broken wing
again — but I have got a lovely sheet of paper, haven't I? To write to Virginia
on. Will you, by the way, note the address at the top? And write to me here, as
if you write to the Embassy I don't get it till luncheon, whereas if you write
here the whole morning is made more exciting by the thought that a post may
be brought to me at any moment. This is *a bloody place, to be sure; and my*
feelings which if I gave way to them would be all rebellion and despair, just
temper and tears, — are complicated by the feeling that I mustn't hate Berlin
because of Harold, i.e. it is an implied criticism of him, and a resentment,
and I can't bear to harbour any thought which reflects on him — besides he

can't help it, I suppose — so what with one emotion and another it is all very difficult [...]

I feel an awful fish out of water — and Harold now says he wants to be an Ambassador — but can you see poor Vita as an ambassadress? I can't — and the prospect fills me with dismay. Really fate does play queer tricks on one, when all one wants to do is to garden and write and talk to Potto — and instead of that one will go to pay calls in a motor with an ambassadorial footman on the box and a cockade in his hat.

Well, well. Poor Orlando.

Letter from Vita

Brücken Allee, Berlin
8 March

I know you are still alive, because Clive mentions you in his letters to Harold (yes, those documents continue to pile up, and are a source of great amusement to us), but I don't think you can love me anymore because I haven't heard a word from you. Yet I wrote you a long long letter. Have you forgotten me? Or are you just busy? Or is Potto jealous?

Have you ever heard of a fellow author of yours, called Phyllis Bottome? Hitherto I have always pronounced her name as the part one sits on, but I now learn that the correct pronunciation is Bo-tóme. Anyway, this lady has but one desire in life, and that is to make your acquaintance. As she thinks this is beyond her reach, she has consoled herself by writing a story in which she describes the meeting between you and herself. She describes you as she imagines you to be. Now how much would you give to read that story? Personally I would give a great deal, and am trying to obtain it. (It exists only in manuscript.) Miss Bo-tóme, who apparently is a best seller, does not live here, but in Switzerland somewhere. The friend who told me of this takes it quite seriously, and says it is not funny at all, but extremely pathetic; I have however persuaded her to write for the story [...]

Oh dear, I am so homesick.

Letter from Virginia

52 Tavistock Square
12 March

I fell in love with Noel Coward, and he's coming to tea. You can't have all the love in Chelsea — Potto must have some: Noel Coward must have some. I played a funny trick. I had no hat. Bought one for 7/11¾ at a shop in Oxford Street: green felt: the wrong coloured ribbon: all a flop like a pancake in mid air. Even I thought I looked odd. But I wanted to see what happens among real women if one of them looks like a pancake in mid air. In came the dashing vermeil-tinctured red-stopper-bottle-looking Mrs Edwin Montagu. She started. She positively deplored me. Then hid a smile. Looked again. Thought, Ah what a tragedy! Liked me even as she pitied. Overheard me flirting. Was puzzled. Finally conquered. You see, women can't hold out against this kind of flagrant disavowal of all womanliness. They open their arms as to a flayed bird in a blast: whereas, the Marys of this world, with every feather in place, are pecked, stoned, often die, every feather stained with blood — at the bottom of the cage.

Darling, are you happy or unhappy? Writing? Loving? Please send me a long letter, on big paper, because Potto likes that best.

Letter from Vita

24 Brücken-allee, Berlin
14 March

I have been coming to the not very original conclusion that Virginia is in every way the most charming person in the world — in fact I have spent the last three or four days thinking of very little else and being very happy in my absorption; it has been like living a little secret life that nobody knew anything about. And listen: I have got Bottome's story for you — and it will follow in a day or two [...] Bottome is so thrilled at the idea of your reading it that she rings up Berlin on the telephone out of Switzerland to know if it has yet been posted to

you — and she wishes you to be told that 'the idea came to her in a dream'.
You are called Avery Fleming in the story. You must return it when read [...]

I try to romanticise Berlin by thinking that Russia lies over there to the east.
But the only tangible reminder of Russia is the piercing east wind which comes
to us straight off the steppes. I could gladly do without it; but the sun does shine
[...] That's my life. Not as exciting as yours, no doubt, but I think a lot about
Virginia — which makes up for much — and really I have been loving Virginia
enormously lately — in an intense, absent way (absent in distance, I mean),
which has been a great satisfaction to me — like a tide flowing in and filling
a lot of empty spaces. Orlando, I am glad to reflect, compels you willy-nilly to
spend a certain amount of your time with me. Darling I do love you.

Letter from Virginia

52 Tavistock Square
20 March

ORLANDO IS FINISHED!!!

Did you feel a sort of tug, as if your neck was being broken on
Saturday last at 5 minutes to one? That was when he died — or rather
stopped talking, with three little dots ... Now every word will have to
be re-written, and I see no chance of finishing it by September — It is
all over the place, incoherent, intolerable, impossible — And I am sick
of it. The question now is, will my feelings for you be changed? I've
lived in you all these months — coming out, what are you really like?
Do you exist? Have I made you up?

Letter from Vita

Long Barn
3 April

Are you well? Are you in the sun? Oh, and Orlando. I forgot about him. You
absolutely terrified me by your remarks. 'Do I exist or have you made me up?'
I always foresaw that, when you had killed Orlando off. Well, I'll tell you one

thing: if you like — no, love, — me one trifle less now that Orlando is dead, you
shall never set eyes on me again, except by chance at one of Sibyl's parties. I
won't be fictitious. I won't be loved solely in an astral body, or in Virginia's world.

So write quickly and say I'm still real. I feel terribly real just now — like
cockles and mussels, all alive-oh [...]

Your adoring and perfectly solid,

Orlando

Letter from Virginia

Orange, France
31 March

Dearest Honey,

Are you back? At Long Barn? Happy? With the dogs? Comfortable?
Well?

I can't remember how one writes. Nothing but a heart of gold
would make me try to write now — perched on a hard chair in a bare
bedroom in a bad inn [...] I think of Vita at Long Barn: all fire and
legs and beautiful plunging ways like a young horse.

Letter from Vita

Long Barn
15 April

I have been wanting to write to you for such a long time, but I thought you would
be on your way home. My God, I shall be thankful when I know you are safely
back. I am coming up on Wednesday; shall Pinker and I come in the evening?

Letter from Virginia

52 Tavistock Square
17 April

Come punctually at 4 with Pinker, or Leonard will be gone [...] And
ain't it wretched you care for me no longer: I always said you were

a promiscuous brute – Is it a Mary again; or a Jenny this time or a Polly? Eh?

The truth shall be dug out of you at all costs.

Am I to be wearing my heart out for a woman who goes with any girl from an Inn!

Virginia's Diary

21 April

Life is either too empty or too full. Happily, at forty-six I still feel as experimental and on the verge of getting at the truth as ever. Oh and Vita – to take up the burden of facts – has had a stupendous row with her mother – in the course of which she was made to take the pearl necklace from her neck, cut it in two with a pocket knife, deliver over the twelve central pearls, put the relics, all running loose, in an envelope the solicitor gave her. Thief, liar, I hope you'll be killed by an omnibus – so 'my honoured Lady Sackville' addressed her, trembling with rage in the presence of a secretary and a solicitor and a chauffeur. The woman is said to be mad. Vita very gallant and wild and tossing her head.

Letter from Virginia

Monk's House
27 April

I rang you up just now, to find you were gone nutting in the woods with Mary Campbell, or Mary Carmichael, or Mary Seton[3] but not me – damn you.

---

3 'There was Marie Seaton, and Marie Beaton, / And Marie Carmichael, and me.' From 'The Ballad of the Queen's Maries'. Virginia would use these names for her fictitious novelists in *A Room of One's Own* (1929).

Letter from Virginia

52 Tavistock Square

4 May

Orlando,

I think I must tell Eddy about you. What do you say? He is so passionate about Knole and Sackvilles. I feel it awkward to spring the whole thing without warning – Would he keep it secret?

Letter from Vita

Long Barn

6 May

Yes, do tell Eddy. He'll be amused, and I hope annoyed. He's coming here today, to lunch. I think he would be discreet, if you impressed it well on him. The secret has been so well kept, it would be a pity for it to leak out now.

Do you know that I came and stood on your doorstep at 11.15 on Wednesday night? But the door was so firmly shut, and all the windows looked so dark, that I didn't dare ring the bell, but went sadly away like a poor dog, and drove myself home to Long Barn through the night. Yes, the nights are marvellous. Full moon, nightingales, and all that business. But where is Virginia? What about Virginia coming here for a night on Tuesday or Wednesday? Before the moon begins to wane. And the garden is so pretty [...]

You looked so lovely the other day.[4]

Letter from Vita

Long Barn

11 June

Are your ears still sore?[5] Have you enjoyed the sensation of twiddling the rings when they have stuck? A new, small, peculiar sensation.

Have you forgotten your poor Orlando already?

---

4 At the presentation to Virginia of the Femina Prize for *To the Lighthouse* on 2 May.
5 On 4 June Vita and Virginia both had their ears pierced.

Virginia's Diary

20 June

So sick of *Orlando* I can write nothing. I have corrected the proofs in a week; and cannot spin another phrase. I detest my own volubility. Why be always spouting words?

Letter from Vita to Harold

Long Barn
6 July

Virginia has just gone. She was absolutely enchanting. We talked a lot about poetry and she said it doesn't matter a bit about not being modern. Darling, really the Wolves are funnies. You see, they haven't got a garage, and it goes to Leonard's heart to pay garaging fees for the umbrella.[6] *So for some time past he has been saying what a good garage Virginia's studio would make, but she didn't respond very much because she didn't want her studio taken away from her. So Leonard didn't quite dare to suggest taking it away altogether, but finally he said, did she think they could poke a hole in the wall which abuts on to the mews, and get the motor in that way, if it wouldn't disturb her to work with a motor in the room? So now she and the umbrella are going to share the studio between them. A funny pair.*

Virginia's Diary

7 July

[At Long Barn yesterday …] Lay by the blackcurrant bushes lecturing Vita on her floundering habits, with the Campbells for instance.

Letter from Vita

Long Barn
10 July

Virginia, will you give your very serious consideration to the possibility of dashing to the vintage [Burgundy] with me between Sept. 26th and October? Having

---

6 Leonard and Virginia called their new Singer car 'the umbrella'.

got this idea into my head, where it has now been simmering for several years, I want to execute it more than anything [...]

I've been feeling very much chastened since you were here, but also curiously happy. I am never wholly crushed when you lecture me, because it shows that you aren't indifferent. And really I have a few good qualities. Ask Potto — to whom my love.

I say, we must make up for that abortive night soon? But all the same, it had a nice and unusual character of its own [...] You were very very charming really in spite of the lecture. And you are definite to me, — my goodness, you are. My silly Virginia. My darling, darling, precious Virginia.

Letter from Vita

Long Barn
23 July

I was about to write you in protest: on Saturday I caught a gleam of your handwriting among my letters; put it aside as a treat to read last; and then, coming to it full of expectation, discovered that it was for Eddy [...] Did you know I was going to marry Eddy? I didn't know it myself, but my mother told Ozzie so.[7] I am going to divorce Harold and marry Eddy, so as to get Knole. That is why I have stolen all her jewels to give them to Knole.

Will you come to my wedding?

Letter from Vita

Long Barn
9 August

But would you really? Come here, I mean? On Sunday? For the night? If October 11th is to see the end of our romance, it would be as well to make the most of the short time that remains to us.[8]

---

7 Oswald Dickinson, who was the brother of Virginia's friend Violet Dickinson.
8 *Orlando* was scheduled for publication on 11 October.

Letter from Vita

39 Manger-strasse II, Potsdam
21 August

Any more developments about France?

I found a very very old letter from you in a book, beginning Dear Vita [...]

The German army, or what is left of it, rumbles its artillery every morning over the cobbles, and the music of a distant military band echoes over the lake. In the intervals of Rilke I think about my novel,[9] and a sort of patch-work counterpane is beginning to form, but so far the patches are only laid side by side and I have not yet begun to stitch at them. It is better to be extremely ambitious, or rather modest? Probably the latter is safer; but I hate safety, and would rather fail gloriously than dingily succeed. Anyhow I don't care about what is 'better', for however many resolutions one makes, one's pen, like water, always finds its own level, and one can't write in any way other than one's own. At least I feel confident that the rank growth of my early years has been pretty severely pruned by now — and I hope has made nice strong woody growth instead. We shall see.

Poor Virginia, she will have to read that novel when it is finished — and what's more she'll have to say what she thinks of it — and with the utmost brutality too [...]

I do miss you so. I do hope we go to France, but I daren't think about it yet with any confidence. Will you write to me?

Letter from Virginia

Monk's House
30 August

Why need you be so timid and pride-blown, both at once, over writing your novel? What does donkey West mean about her ambition

---

9 *The Edwardians*.

and failure? Surely for the last ten years almost, you have cut back and pruned and root dug – What is it one should do to fig trees? [...] Please write your novel, and then you will enter into the unreal world, where Virginia lives – and poor woman can't now live anywhere else.

Letter from Vita

39 Manger-strasse II, Potsdam
31 August

I feel very violently about The Well of Loneliness.[10] *Not on account of what you call my proclivities; not because I think it is a good book; but really on principle. (I think of writing to Jix[11] suggesting that he should suppress* Shakespeare's Sonnets.) *Because, you see, even if the* W. of L. *had been a good book, – even if it had been a great book, a real masterpiece, – the result would have been the same. And that is intolerable. I really have no words to say how indignant I am. Is Leonard really going to get up a protest? Or is it fizzling out? [...] Don't let it fizzle out. If you got Arnold Bennett and suchlike, it would be bound to make an impression. (Avoid Shaw, though.) I nearly blew up over the various articles in the* New Statesman. *Personally, I should like to renounce my nationality, as a gesture; but I don't want to become German, even though I did go to a revue last night in which two ravishing young women sing a frankly Lesbian song.*

France [...] Well, you can get a pale reflection of the matrimonial miseries which I undergo. You hesitate to leave Leonard for six days; I leave Harold

---

10 Marguerite Radclyffe-Hall's *The Well of Loneliness* (1928), an overtly lesbian novel, had been banned as obscene. Many British writers were rallying to her defence.

11 Nickname for the Home Secretary, William Joynson-Hicks, who was responsible for banning the book.

*several times a year for several months. I see him off to Persia. He sees me off
to England. We are perpetually in a state of saying goodbye [...]*

*I will leave you to your own fluctuations, which amuse me a good deal. I
will only say, that you mustn't come it if's going to make you miserable all
the time. But you wouldn't.*

Letter from Virginia

Monk's House
8 September

Suppose we start (you and I and Potto) on Saturday 22nd. Sleep in
Paris. Get to SAULIEU on Monday [...]

I believe that the main thing in beginning a novel is to feel, not that
you can write it, but that it exists on the far side of a gulf, which words
can't cross; that it's to be pulled through only in a breathless anguish.
Now when I sit down to an article, I have a net of words which will
come down on the idea certainly in an hour or so. But a novel, as I say,
to be good should seem, before one writes it, something unwriteable:
but only visible; so that for nine months one lives in despair, and only
when one has forgotten what one meant, does the book seem tolerable.
I assure you, all my novels were first rate before they were written.

Letter from Vita

Long Barn
19 September

Monday, — yes. Could you send a postcard to say

1. *what time the boat starts*
2. *how much I owe you for tickets*
3. *the name of the hotel in Saulieu*

According to the time the boat starts, perhaps I may decide whether to come Sunday night or Monday morning? I'll come by train anyhow, and not by motor.

No clothes. A fur coat certainly. The other objects mentioned, – I hope unnecessary. Potto's basket. A bib for Potto.

I was in a bookshop in London yesterday and the bookseller said to me knowingly, 'I saw an advance copy of Orlando*.'*

I also am interested in this journey, but not wholly as an experiment.

Virginia's Diary

22 September

This is written on the verge of my alarming holiday in Burgundy. I am alarmed of seven days alone with Vita; interested; excited, but afraid – she may find me out, I her out. I'm afraid of the morning most; and three o'clock in the afternoon; and wanting something Vita does not want. And I shall spend the money that might have bought a table or a glass.

This has been the finest, and not only finest, but loveliest, summer in the world […] But the news of *Orlando* is black. We may sell a third that we sold of *The Lighthouse* before publication. They say this is inevitable. No one wants biography. I doubt therefore that we shall do more than cover expenses – a high price to pay for the fun of calling it a biography. I must write some articles this winter, if we are to have nest eggs at the Bank.

Vita's Diary

24 September

Walking home from the restaurant we missed our way, so sat down to drink coffee at the Brasserie Lutetia in rue de Sevres & V. & I wrote to Leonard and Harold respectively on the torn-out fly-leaves of our books. She told me how she & Leonard had had a small & sudden row that morning about her going abroad with me.

Letter from Vita to Harold

Saulieu, France

25 September

I am lying on the grass in a field, with Burgundy spread out before me. It is warm; it is sunny. There is a fair going on in Saulieu, where Virginia bought a green corduroy jacket for Leonard. I nearly bought one for you, but I was sure you would not wear it [...]

Darling, it is very nice: I feel amused and irresponsible. I can talk about life and literature to my heart's content — and it amuses me to be suddenly in the middle of Burgundy with Virginia. I like doing expeditions with you. But failing you, I could not wish for a better companion than Virginia.

Vita's Diary

25 September

We then went & sat in a field till it got too cold, & wrote letters. After dinner we went to the fair. There was a zoo with lion-cubs, a merry-go-round, & a Bal Tabarin which we watched for some time. A very lovely gipsy woman there. Virginia very much delighted with all these sights. People threw confetti over us.

Vita's Diary

26 September

We had breakfast in my room, and entered on a heated argument about men & women. V. is curiously feminist. She dislikes the possessiveness and love of domination in men. In fact she dislikes the quality of masculinity; says that women stimulate her imagination, by their grace & their art of life.

Letter from Vita to Harold

Saulieu, France

27 September

Virginia is very sweet, and I feel extraordinarily protective towards her. The combination of that brilliant brain and fragile body is very lovable. She has a sweet and childlike nature, from which her intellect is completely separate. I have never known anyone who was so profoundly sensitive, and who makes less of a business of that sensitiveness.

Vita's Diary

27 September

I got letters from H. [...] V. was very much upset because she heard nothing from Leonard [...] We went again to the post; still nothing from Leonard; so I made V. send a telegram. We hired a motor & drove to Vézelay which enchanted us. Went out to look at the cathedral, and view from the terrace; then lay in a field not talking much, but just listening to the crickets. V. seemed tired, & I made her go to bed at quarter to 10. In the middle of the night I was woken up by a thunderstorm. Went along to V's room thinking she might be frightened. We talked about science & religion for an hour — and the ultimate principle — and then as the storm had gone over I left her to go to sleep again.

Vita's Diary

29 September

Left Vézelay with great regret [...] Had chocolate in a tea-shop & found a good antiquaire where V. bought a looking-glass. Discussed Edith Sitwell. V. told me the history of her early loves — Madge Symons, who is Sally in Mrs Dalloway.

Letter from Vita

Long Barn
5 October

I was enjoying the melancholy pleasure of looking through your letters this evening, when it occurred to me that it was some time since I had had one from you, — not, in fact, since I was in Berlin. And now you are in London, besieged by Sibyls and Tom Eliots, not to mention packing up parcels of Orlando, *and you won't have time to write. Besides, if I have not had letters from you it is because I have been with you, which is better than ink and paper. And you were here, dear me, no later than yesterday.*

It was queer, reading some of your letters, in the light of having been with you so much lately. A fitful illumination played over them, — a sort of cross-light [...] played across them, projected half from the rather tentative illumination of the past and half from the fuller illumination of the present. I couldn't stop to wonder which illumination I preferred, because I saw at once that in their union they created a very lovely limpid light in which I was bathed and in which I felt extremely happy. However, no more of this, or you will think me sentimental (which I swear I am not), and I am still sufficiently respectful of you not to wish to be despised by you [...]

Burgundy seems a dream. 'Before, a joy proposed; behind, a dream.'[12] I was very happy. Were you? [...] I've returned home a changed being. All this summer I was as nervous as a cat, — starting, dreaming, brooding, — now I'm all vigorous and sturdy again, and ravenous for life once more. And all thanks to you, I believe. So you see this letter is a Collins.[13]

It is a ¼ to one, — nearly 2 hours after Virginia's bedtime. My dearest, I do love you. All the Sibyls and Tom Eliots in the world don't love you as much as I do. I do bless you for all you've been to me. This is not a joke, but very sober truth.

I dine with you on Tuesday 16th, don't I? If our friendship has survived?

---

[12] Shakespeare's Sonnet 129.

[13] Named after the obsequious Mr Collins in Jane Austen's *Pride and Prejudice*.

Letter from Virginia

52 Tavistock Square
7 October

Dearest Creature,

It was a very very nice letter you wrote by the light of the stars at midnight. Always write then, for your heart requires moonlight to deliquesce it. And mine is fried in gaslight, as it is only nine o'clock and I must go to bed at eleven. And so I shan't say anything: not a word of the balm to my anguish – for I am always anguished – that you were to me. How I watched you! How I felt – now what was it like? Well, somewhere I have seen a little ball kept bubbling up and down on the spray of a fountain: the fountain is you; the ball me. It is a sensation I get only from you. It is physically stimulating, restful at the same time.

Letter from Vita

Long Barn
9 October

I am sure you are full of people and busynesses, and don't want Vita – or Potto – who seems to be settling down. (Pinker was suffering from constipation – It wasn't that she missed Leonard. She has now had a pill, and is quite happy again – as indeed we all are when we have had pills.)

But you will send me Orlando? *Before 4. o'clock? I need hardly say that I can hardly exist till I get it [...]*

It is dreadful to think that this is the last friendly letter I shall ever write to you.

On the day before publication, *Orlando* arrived in a brown-paper parcel from the Hogarth Press. It was followed a few days later by Virginia, who presented the manuscript as a gift.

Letter from Vita to Harold

Long Barn
11 October

My own darling, I write to you in the middle of reading Orlando, *in such
a turmoil of excitement and confusion that I scarcely know where (or who!)
I am. It came this morning by the first post and I have been reading it ever
since, and am now halfway through. Virginia sent it to me in a lovely leather
binding — bless her. Oh Lord, how I wonder what you will think of it. It seems
to me more brilliant, more enchanting, more rich and lavish, than anything
she has done. It is like a cloak encrusted with jewels and sprinkled with rose-
petals. I admit I can't see straight about it. Parts of it make me cry, parts of it
make me laugh; the whole of it dazzles and bewilders me. It maddens me that
you should not be here, so that we could read it simultaneously. I scarcely slept
with excitement all night, and woke up feeling as though it were my birthday,
or wedding day, or something unique.*

*Well — I don't know, it seems to me a book unique in English literature,
having everything in it: romance, wit, seriousness, lightness, beauty, imagination,
style; with Sir Thomas Browne and Swift for parents. I feel infinitely honoured
at having been the peg on which it was hung; and very humble.*

Letter from Vita

Long Barn
11 October

My darling

*I am in no fit state to write to you — and as for cold and considered opinions
(as you said on the telephone), such things do not exist in such a connection. At
least, not yet. Perhaps they will come later. For the moment, I can't say anything
except that I am completely dazzled, bewitched, enchanted, under a spell. It seems
to me the loveliest, wisest, richest book that I have ever read, — excelling even
your own* Lighthouse. *Virginia, I really don't know what to say, — am I right?*

Am I wrong? Am I prejudiced? Am I in my senses or not? It seems to me that you have really shut up that 'hard and rare thing' in a book; that you have had a complete vision; and yet when you came down to the sober labour of working it out, have never lost sight of it nor faltered in the execution. Ideas come to me so fast that they trip over each other and I lose them before I can put salt on their tails; there is so much I want to say, yet I can only go back to my first cry that I am bewitched. You will get letters, very reasoned and illuminating, from many people; I cannot write you that sort of letter now, I can only tell you that I am really shaken, which may seem to you useless and silly, but which is really a greater tribute than pages of calm appreciation, — and then after all it does touch me so personally, and I don't know what to say about that either, only that I feel like one of those wax figures in a shop window, on which you have hung a robe stitched with jewels. It is like being alone in a dark room with a treasure chest full of rubies and nuggets and brocades. Darling, I don't know and scarcely even like to write, so overwhelmed am I, how you could have hung so splendid a garment on so poor a peg. Really this isn't false humility; really it isn't. I can't write about that part of it, though, much less ever tell you verbally.

By now you must be thinking me too confused and illiterate for anything, so I'll just slip in that the book (in texture) seems to me to have in it all the best of Sir Thomas Browne and Swift, — the richness of the one, and the directness of the other.

There are a dozen details I should like to go into, — Queen Elizabeth's visit, Greene's visit, phrases scattered about (particularly one on p. 160 beginning 'High battlements of thought, etc.', which is just what you did for me), Johnson on the blind, and so on and so on, — but it is too late today; I have been reading steadily all day, and it is now 5 o'clock, and I must catch the post, but I will try and write more sensibly tomorrow. It is your fault, for having moved me so and dazzled me completely, so that all my faculties have dropped from me and left me stark.

One awful thought struck me this morning: you didn't, did you, think for a second that it was out of indifference I didn't come to London yesterday? You couldn't have thought that? I had got it so firmly fixed in my head that Oct. 11th was the day I was to have it, that I was resigned (after all these months) to wait till then. But when I saw it in its lovely binding, with my initials, the idea rushed into my head and utterly appalled me. But on second thoughts I reflected that you could not possibly so have misunderstood.

Yes, I will write again tomorrow, in a calmer frame of mind I hope — now I am really writing against time — and, as I tell you, shaken quite out of my wits.

Also, you have invented a new form of Narcissism, — I confess, — I am in love with Orlando — this is a complication I had not foreseen.

Virginia, my dearest, I can only thank you for pouring out such riches.

You made me cry with your passages about Knole, you wretch.[14]

Letter from Virginia

52 Tavistock Square
12 October

What an immense relief! [...] It struck me suddenly with horror that you'd be hurt or angry, and I didn't dare open the post: Now let who will bark or bite; Angel that you are — But I'm rather rushed: and won't write, except this line. Sales much better. Enthusiasm in the Birmingham *Post*. Knole is discovered. They hint at you.

Letter from Vita

Long Barn
15 October

This is only to send you extracts from three letters I had this evening:

(1) 'As a work of beauty and genius it is magnificent — it leaves one breathless with admiration. The descriptions of Knole are too beautiful — they must surely

---

14 On receiving this letter, Virginia sent Vita a telegram: 'Your biographer is infinitely relieved and happy.'

*equal in beauty anything that has ever been written or said about Knole. I feel
you will be happy with those descriptions ...'*

*(2) 'How lovely your pseudobiography is. It is one of the most exquisite
pleasures that one could want, to read it. I must think that the form is peculiarly
adapted to her genius and that this is the greatest of her imaginative works.
The language is so lovely.'*

*(3) From Harold. 'What a wonderful book! The whole thing has a beauty
which makes one catch one's breath — like that sunset before Dilijan (the reference is to Persia). It is so far more than brilliance. I simply cannot believe
that such a book will not survive. The whole world of life has been poured into
it, flashing with molten flames.'*

*My darling. I am reading it all through again from the beginning. I'll come
at 6.45 tomorrow, or a little before perhaps.*

Letter from Vita

*Long Barn
17 October*

Darling, I love you.

V.

Clive adds a brief postscript: 'Orlando is a masterpiece.'

*Harold says: 'Lots to say about Orlando but shall keep it till Friday. It is
lovely and glittering and profound.'*

Virginia's Diary

27 October

A scandal, a scandal, to let so much time slip, and I leaning on the
bridge watching it go. Only leaning has not been my pose: running
up and down, irritably, excitedly, restlessly. And the stream viciously
eddying. Why do I write these metaphors? Because I have written
nothing for an age.

———

Orlando has been published. I went to Burgundy with Vita. We did not find each other out. It flashed by. Yet I was glad to see Leonard again. How disconnected this is! My ambition is from this very moment, eight minutes to six, on Saturday evening, to attain complete concentration again. I gave up reading and thinking on the 24th September when I went to France. I came back, and we plunged into London and publishing.

I am a little sick of *Orlando*. I think I am a little indifferent now what anyone thinks. Joy's life's in the doing — I murder, as usual, a quotation. I mean it's the writing, not the being read, that excites me. The reception, as they say, surpassed expectations. Sales beyond our record for the first week.

Letter from Vita

Long Barn
7 November

I do hope you are better. I had such a longing to see you on Monday night, and nearly cried when Nellie said you were out. But the fireworks were lovely, through the fog. Did you see them?

Your very very loving,

Letter from Vita

Long Barn
29 November

I am feeling something like (I imagine) a fisherman must feel between a gale and a gale. On a calm day he can go out and catch lots of little silver fishes. But there is this difference: in a gale, he can sit at home and smoke his pipe (unless he is also a member of the lifeboat crew), whereas a gale to me represents London, Eton, Oxford, — just a being blown out to sea, the little fishes all scattered. In other words, I managed to get myself home this morning, only to start off again tomorrow, early; and what sort of life is that, I ask you?

Anyway, there was a HUGE dinner,[15] *and I made a speech, in great alarm* *[...] Such a lot of people — at least 300 — and flashlight photographs — and a microphone — and Mr Winston Churchill with whom I would gladly elope if asked — and me rather miserable in the midst of it all — and wondering why I was there — and then suddenly a speech about Knole — and Jack Squire very drunk with a cold in his head. Dear me, I don't like public life. I like toasting buns over the gas-fire in Virginia's bedroom [...]*

Darling, you're my anchor. An anchor entangled in gold nuggets at the bottom of the sea.

Letter from Virginia

> 52 Tavistock Square
> 2 December

So you are just back I suppose, it being after dinner, and I had mine alone. What a good letter you wrote me! Do you know I think about your writing with interest? All your feet seem to be coming down on it now, not only the foreleg. Very few people interest me as writers; but I think I shall read your next poem with care [...]

Coming down with all her feet at once — that's what I like in a writer [...] Lord! What a pleasure you are to me.

Letter from Vita

> *Long Barn*
> *3 December*

How maddening. There was I sitting alone at Charing X from 7 to 8.30 last night, having missed my connection; and there were you dining alone the other side of London. I could have come so easily, and taken an even later train. Damn, damn, damn. But you were reading Chaucer [...]

---

15 Given by and for the National Trust.

Oxford was littered with Orlando. I nosed into all the bookshops. Such a time I had; and am slightly in love with an undergraduate, which is a sure sign of middle-age.

Darling, I'm no poet, I think. I am a lump of dough, so far as poetry is concerned. But I'd like to talk to you about it. I am rather sad about it; and think of going into mourning for my dead Muse. She died in youth, poor thing, before she had learned to talk. Or do you think she has merely been spending a few years in retreat, and will emerge again someday, grey haired but wise? I read The Land *for five minutes and thought it damned bad. Not a spark in it anywhere. Respectable, but stodgy [...]*

I wish it was Thursday. Yes, — what a pity you cannot work magic on time in real life as you can in books. Then we could make Thursday last for 300 years. Marvell seems to have had much the same idea.[16] *I now realise fully and for the first time exactly what he meant.*

Your Orlando

Letter from Vita

Brücken Allee
26 December

Did Boski remember to send you the amber beads? And will you wear them? And not scold me? And look on each of them as a kiss from Orlando? And I will think of you as a fox, a melon, or an emerald, or anything else you can devise?

Letter from Virginia

Monk's House
29 December

That wretched Potto is all slung with yellow beads. He rolled himself round in them, and can't be dislodged — short of cutting off his front

---

16 Vita was reading for her book on Andrew Marvell, published in 1929 by Faber & Faber. She is referring to Marvell's poem 'To His Coy Mistress'.

paws, which I know you shouldn't like. But may I say, once and for all, presents are not allowed: it's written all over the cage. It spoils their tempers – They suffer for it in the long run – This once will be forgiven: but never never again – The night you were snared, that winter, at Long Barn, you slipped out Lord Steyne's paper knife, and I had then to make the terms plain: with this knife you will gash our hearts I said and the same applies to beads.

Letter from Virginia

Monk's House
31 December

Please be an angel and let me have one line on receipt of this to say how you are […] If I don't hear, I shan't sleep; then I shall get a headache; then I shan't be able to come to Berlin: So you see, Love, love: and it's the last day of the year by the way.

1929

Letter from Virginia

Monk's House
3 January

I am light-headed at the moment; why, heaven knows. I have been walking alone down a valley to a Rat Farm, if that means anything to you: and the quiet and the cold and the loveliness – one hare, the weald washed away to vapour – the downs blue green; the stacks, like cakes cut in half – I say all this so excited me; and my own life suddenly became so impressive to me, not as usual shooting meteor like through the sky, but solitary and still that, as I say – well how is the sentence to end?: figure to yourself that sentence, like the shooting star, extinct in an abyss, a dome, of blue, the colour of night: which, if dearest Vita you can follow, is now my condition: as I sit waiting for dinner, over the logs […]

Do you really love me? Much? Passionately not reasonably?

Letter from Vita

> Brücken Allee
>
> 6 January

Potto, I say, stole a copy of Orlando *and had it bound for me in Niger leather — and not content with that, he also stole the [manuscript] of* Orlando *and had that bound too — so I thought I really might give him some yellow beads this Xmas without getting into a row — because I like giving Potto things — and am ordinarily so severely controlled that I never dare to. Am I forgiven? And is Potto forgiven? For having rolled himself in them?*

[...] Is it true — can it be true? — that you are coming to Berlin? Heavens, I wish you were coming alone. But Virginia in Berlin [...] Very odd. It almost reconciles me to Berlin, that Berlin should be going to contain Virginia. The red tongue creeps across my calendar, eating up the days: only ten days more. Don't oh don't get ill and be prevented from coming [...] Because, really, you have no idea how miserable I am here. I almost cease to exist. I shall revive when you come, like a watered flower.

I shall meet you at the station.

I'd better stop now, or I should write you too wild a letter of love and longing.

Letter from Virginia

> 52 Tavistock Square
>
> 8 January

What station it will be I will tell you later. Vita will say Hullo Virginia! Leonard will stoop and pat the dog. He will compare her with Pinker, and if you are tactful you will say, 'But Pinker's a much better colour, Leonard' and then we shall all feel happy [...]

Orlando has now sold 13,000 copies in America: that's the last time I mention him.

Letter from Vita

> *Brücken Allee, Berlin*
> *12 January*

I count the days, for you don't know the full pathos of how I devise little schemes for making January and February go; and with your advent a whole clock of time resolves itself, from the bright 17th to the black 24th [...]

We went to a sodomites' ball.[1] A lot of them were dressed as women, but I fancy I was the only genuine article in the room. A very odd sight. We also went to a bicycle race which lasts for 6 days and 6 nights, round and round a banked-up track under arc-lights. There are certainly very queer things to be seen in Berlin, and I think Potto will enjoy himself.

Now I won't say any more, except that there are 483000 seconds between now and your arrival, and that that is the moment I am living for.

Virginia, Leonard, Vanessa, Duncan Grant, Quentin Bell and Eddy Sackville-West visited Vita and Harold at the British Embassy in Berlin. The group was too large, and they got on each other's nerves. Virginia was able to spend a few hours alone with Vita, and seems to have declared her love again, to which Vita responded guardedly.

Letter from Vita

> *Brücken Allee, Berlin*
> *25 January*

My darling lovely Virginia
* It is so empty here without you [...]*

---

1 *Ball der Jugend.*

You won't get this, thanks to the English non-Sunday post, till after you have been to Long Barn, which I hope will have reminded you of me a little and perhaps revived in you something of those feelings to which you gave such startling and disturbing expression in the Funkturm?[2] I say, you don't know what a difference your week here has made to me. It just shows how little the actual duration of time really counts. Formerly, the whole of Berlin was pure loathsomeness to me; now, there are just a few places which are invested with romance. Prinz Albrecht-strasse, Potsdam, the Funkturm; even Brücken-allee holds something of your flavour. So your transporting of four people to Berlin has not been wasted [...] THEN, comes Long Barn and the spring, and the nightingales and your big bedroom, and all the rest of it. But will you be in a different frame of mind by then? Or unfaithful to me? [...] God, I'd never forgive you — No — save yourself for your own.

Letter from Virginia

52 Tavistock Square
27 January

Well, here I am in bed. I had to be hauled out of my berth at Harwich — a mixture of the somnifeine, flu, and headache — apparently. Quite drugged. But I'm better. Only of course the dr makes me stay in bed and do nothing. I wish it had happened in Berlin. I wish I could see you. Do write. I'm much better today. Berlin was worth it anyhow.

Letter from Vita

Brücken Allee, Berlin
29 January

Oh dear oh dear, what it is, to be far away, and to hear of things days after they have happened — What a wretched journey you must have had — and

---

2 The Berlin radio tower where Vita and Virginia had dined.

Harwich at six o'clock in the morning — with the flu — it just doesn't bear thinking about. I hate you to be ill; it matters more for you than for other people. I say, look here: if you'd like to escape to the country [...] You know that all the servants are at Long Barn twiddling their thumbs, and you could go there and be comfortable (the comforts of a first class hotel etc.), and nothing in this world would make me more happy than to think you were benefiting by my empty ideal little house — except to be there with you myself [...]

Think what I owe you! I got a great sheaf of white lilac suddenly, with a card: 'For Orlando.' I felt I ought to pack it all up and send it to you.

Darling I do feel so worried about you; are you all aches and miseries? Have you recovered?

Letter from Virginia

52 Tavistock Square
29 January

Here is another selfish invalid's bulletin, but I like to write to you, and you won't mind it all being about myself.

I am really better today, only still kept in bed. It is merely the usual headache which is now making me rather achy and shivery but passing off [...] It's odd how I want you when I'm ill. I think everything would be warm and happy if Vita came in.

Letter from Vita

Brücken Allee, Berlin
31 January

Your little shaky pencil letters simply wring my heart — oh, how damnable space and time are — you see, all my pictures of you are at two days' remove. I know you were in bed still when you wrote, but what I don't know is whether you're in bed now — or whether you've been promoted to the sofa.

Letter from Virginia

52 Tavistock Square
31 January

I shall now have my little treat of writing to Vita, I say to myself. I wish
I'd heard from you, but perhaps I shall. No I am not to see anybody –
not Mary [Hutchinson] even [...]

Everything is put down to Berlin. I am never to walk round a gallery
or sit up drinking again. All my adventures are to be lying down – which
will suit, in some ways. Really I am rather better, and make up a book
to be called *The Moths*[3] hour after hour.

Letter from Vita

Brücken Allee, Berlin
2 February

No parties, no romances – poor, poor Virginia. Although I am all for the kennel
(with a little write run) I don't like it to be for that reason;[4] *would rather have*
Virginia well and naughty, than Virginia ill and good. Much, much rather [...]

Oh damn, it is so tantalising to be such miles away, and not able to do
anything for you, except make suggestions which I greatly fear you will scorn.
But everything which is mine is yours, as you very well know – even to my heart.

Letter from Virginia

52 Tavistock Square
4 February

Dearest – what a time your letters take to come! One posted Thursday
comes this morning – to my great delight. You can't think what a difference it makes when they bring in a blue envelope. I'm still in bed

---

3 The Moths would become *The Waves* (1931).
4 Virginia had written 'You want Potto and Virginia kept in their kennel'.

[…] And no pain for two days and no sleeping draughts, only Bromide. I've had this sort of thing before, especially after flu, slight though that was and it always takes some time to go off […]

A woman writes that she has to stop and kiss the page when she reads O[rlando] – Your race I imagine. The percentage of Lesbians is rising in the States, all because of you.

Letter from Vita

Brücken Allee, Berlin
5 February

Having stopped at the book shop on the way and bought Orlando *in Tauchnitz I began to read, and so lost myself that the evening is already nearly gone. Do you know, I never read* Orlando *without tears pricking my eyes? You may believe this or you may not but it is true. Sometimes they even spill over. Whether it is the mere beauty of the book, or whether it is because it is you, or because it is Knole, or because it is all three, I don't know; anyhow you like facts, and there is a fact for you. There never was a book that so bewitched and moved me. All this, in spite of my being forbidden to mention O——o. Perhaps today the effect was heightened by the damnable fact of your being ill. When I am old and dying I shall cause* Orlando *to be read aloud to me.*

Letter from Vita

Brücken Allee, Berlin
6 February

I prefer to write to Virginia – not that I have anything to say except that I love her and wish she were not ill. I can't believe it's the 'racketing' of Berlin; really, you might have spent every night for a week till 5 in the morning indulging in orgies – to hear you talk – or Leonard talk, rather, and the doctor. No, no; it was the flu, but whatever it was it's very distressing. Now look how well you were when I brought you back from France; all round and rosy, and Potto's

coat a treat to see. Do you know what I believe it was, apart from flu? It was
SUPPRESSED RANDINESS. So there — You remember your admissions as the
searchlight went round and round?[5]

Letter from Virginia

52 Tavistock Square
7 February

[Leonard] is a perfect angel – only more to the point than most angels
– He sits on the edge of the bed and considers my symptoms like a
judge. He brings home huge pineapples: he moves the gramophone
into my room and plays until he thinks I'm excited. In short, I should
have shot myself long ago in one of these illnesses if it hadn't been for
him. As it is, I hope to go into the Square next week: but as I say this
sort of thing takes time.

Letter from Vita

Brücken Allee, Berlin
7 February

Oh Virginia, darling, they are good.[6] *I have stuck them up all around the room.*
I don't know which I like best. May I keep them till tomorrow? Absurd question,
since you can't say either yes or no — and by then I'll have decided. (Of course
there's nothing to prevent my ordering them all from Lenare myself if I want
to!) Do you like them yourself? Does Leonard? You will find that they are a
source of perpetual expenditure to you, as people will ask you for them. You are
an angel to have sent them — I was longing for them. Very tidy you were, that
day, and I'm glad you have no hat on.

---

5 At the Funkturm on 19 January.
6 Vita had received a parcel containing photographs of Virginia, taken by Lenare.

Letter from Vita

Rapallo, Italy
13 February

We found this tiny villa on Monday when we were out for a walk; it would be delicious in warm weather, for it is practically in the sea, and from the windows you can see right down the coast as far as Spezia. Did I tell you this? I forget. But now the sea lashes the rock on which it is built, and the oranges look simply silly. Southern countries look much sillier in wintry weather than northern ones do in summery. I don't quite know what I mean by that but I know I mean something.

My darling, are you better?

Letter from Virginia

52 Tavistock Square
12 February

I have been out. I have twice walked round the square leaning on L.'s arm – very cold and ugly it is, and a cat had chosen to die on the path. Then I undress and lie on the sofa […] L. wrapped me up warm; and I am very cheerful again. It's awfully difficult to say how long it's going to take though. I agree it was the flu; but I think I was foolish also in Berlin – you don't realise what a valetudinarian life mine is, usually, so that what's nothing to anybody else is rackety to poor Potto. Never mind. I shall be in robust health by the 4th. But can't you look in for a bite on the 2nd?

Letter from Vita

Brücken Allee, Berlin
16 February

I return the week after next, which is not so very long to wait, and you know I'd look after you like the most expensive of Scotch nannies with a new baby to powder [...] My poor darling – I mind more than you know. I mean, I keep feeling I haven't the right to be well and in the sun, when you are lying on the sofa with a headache. I would exchange with you, if only an archangel would appear and give me the chance.

Letter from Virginia

52 Tavistock Square

19 February

I am sometimes pleased to think that I read English literature when I was young; I like to think of myself tapping at my father's study door, saying very loud and clear, 'Can I have another volume, Father? I've finished this one.' Then he would be very pleased and say, 'Gracious, child, how you gobble!' [...] and get up and take down, it may have been the 6th or 7th volume of Gibbon's complete works, or Spedding's Bacon, or Cowper's Letters. 'But my dear, if it's worth reading, it's worth reading twice,' he would say. I have a great devotion for him – what a disinterested man, how high minded, how tender to me, and fierce and intolerable – But I am maundering.

Letter from Vita

Brücken Allee, Berlin

23 February

My darling Virginia I have been feeling so grim about Berlin that I have not had the heart to write any letters. If I wanted to describe what I felt about it, I should have to enlarge my vocabulary. And the cold! Thick snow, and the thermometer fallen to nothing. I feel completely atrophied. Now, as I write this, I shall probably be in England by the time you get it, and next morning I shall see you, – shan't I? – so that's a nice thought.

Letter from Vita

Long Barn
12 March

'You might write,' you said; and the days have drifted, and I haven't [...] But do
I dine with you on Friday? Clive asked me to dinner that night, and I refused.
Will you send a postcard on receipt of this to say where and when I am to come?
    It has been warm, and I have wished you were here.

Letter from Vita

Long Barn
3 April

You know, or rather, you don't know, how dilatory I am, except when writing
books for the Hogarth Press, and that's because I am frightened of Leonard.
You know, for example, that it took me 15 years to get my ears pierced, not
wholly due to cowardice; and things lie about the house for five and seven
years before anything is done about them. But when I get two photographs
of Virginia they go straight to Sevenoaks to be framed, which is where they
now are [...] Darling, I love them. I wish Potto had been sitting on your
knee, that's all.

Letter from Virginia

Monk's House
5 April

Come on Tuesday; to the basement, not a wink later than 3 [...] Do
NOT bring Dottie. This I feel strongly about. Twice lately she has utterly
ruined my serenity with you; and I won't have it. Choose between us.
Dottie if your taste inclines that way by all means; but not the two of
us in one cocktail [...]

I told Nessa the story of our passion, in the chemist's shop the other day. 'But do you really like going to bed with women?' she said, taking her change. 'And how d'you do it?' And so she bought her pills to take abroad, talking loudly as a parrot.

Letter from Vita

Long Barn
6 May

And am I ever going to see Virginia again? A despair has settled down on me about it. My own fault, no doubt [...] I say, the novel is about the Edwardians, – a fascinating subject, if only I can do it justice. It is absolutely packed with the aristocracy. Shall you like that? I feel that for snobbish reasons alone it ought to be highly popular! I hope so, because Leonard's offer was very handsome, and I should hate to ruin the Press, towards which I feel avuncular as you know.

Letter from Vita

Long Barn
15 May

This is too tantalising! I would rather you had come to tea, which would have been hopeless, but to miss you by an hour is dreadful.

Letter from Vita

Long Barn
10 June

I shall feel forlorn in London with no Virginia when I go up to broadcast on Thursday. Shan't go up till the evening in consequence. No nice expedition or anything. No bunloaf – no affection – no Potto to stroke. Damn [...] Harold and I are going – We're going to no, I shan't tell you that: you'd laugh. You'll find out for yourself fast enough.[7]

---

7 On 17 June Vita and Harold broadcast a discussion on marriage.

Letter from Vita

> Long Barn
> 4 July

Are you writing and very happy? I am very, very miserable, because Pippin has disappeared. All efforts to trace her have failed. I am left with Jane and the five little orphans, and a gnawing anxiety at my heart to know what can have happened to her. Is she lying hurt in some trap in a soaking wood? Is she poisoned? Do you think the BBC (which I look on as my pocket borough) would broadcast an SOS?[8]

Letter from Virginia

> 52 Tavistock Square
> 9 July

Darling, we are so unhappy about Pippin. We both send our best love – Leonard is very sad.

Letter from Vita

> Savoy, France
> 24 July

I am writing to you in an Alpine hut with a thunderstorm imminent outside.[9] We are at the quite respectable height of 9300 feet, surrounded by a ring of white peaks. Up here grow gentians and other lovely little creatures, which seem to become brighter and more fragile the higher one climbs. And there are butterflies and beetles which would rejoice your entomological heart.

By this time I have a good many miles of Savoy in my legs [. . .] Hilda is an admirable companion; is content to read for hours together; can make a pudding

---

8 Pippin was found dead on 7 July.
9 Vita was on a walking tour in Savoy alone with Hilda Matheson, a pioneering radio producer at the BBC and its first Director of Talks. Virginia was jealous.

out of apricot jam and snow, and a waste-paper basket out of The Times. *Also she can read maps so we do not get lost as we cross the hills.*

But how does one write a novel? I have come to the conclusion that I am a good walker but a bad novelist. One writes and writes, and at the end of the time one re-reads and decides that it might all just as well have remained unwritten [...]

This is perhaps not what you call an intimate letter? But I disagree. The book that one is writing at the moment is really the most intimate part of one, and the part about which one preserves the strictest secrecy. What is love or sex, compared with the intensity of the life one leads in one's book? A trifle; a thing to be shouted from the hill-tops. Therefore if I write to you about my book, I am writing intimately, though it may not be very interestingly QED? But you would rather I told you I missed Potto and Virginia, those silky creatures with a barb under their fur – and so I do, and wonder very much whether they will come and stay with me when I get back? Potto would like the puppies, Virginia would like her nice big bed and coffee at eleven, – and all the affection that would be shown her at hours licit and illicit [...]

I watch the beetles, – winged, black, splotched with red, – at their amours on hot slopes here, and would like to enclose one of them. But it would get squashed in the post. So I just send you my love, unsquashable.

Letter from Vita

Savoy
30 July

So now Harold becomes a journalist.[10] *Well, well! Life is very exciting to be sure. Plus the mountain air, it has all gone fairly to my head [...] I have done a lot of my novel since I have been here; it is a very honest little book, quite straightforward with no fal-lals, and I fear you will find it quite devoid of all interest save for a few details about the servants' etiquette, which is of a*

---

10 Harold had accepted the unexpected offer of a post at the *Evening Standard*.

nature to please you. What with one thing and another, I feel like a boat in a
maelstrom — only not in any unpleasant sense — and looking forward terribly
to seeing Virginia again.

Virginia's Diary

Yes it was a scattered summer; I felt as if the telephone were strung to
my arm and anybody could jerk me who liked. A sense of interruption
bothered me. And then I'm cross with Vita: she never told me she was
going abroad for a fortnight — didn't dare; till the last moment, when
she said it was a sudden plan. Lord Lord! I am half amused though;
why do I mind? What do I mind? How much do I mind?

One of the facts is that these Hildas are a chronic case; and, like the
damned intellectual snob that I am, I hate to be linked, even by an arm,
with Hilda [Matheson]. Her earnest aspiring competent wooden face
appears before me. A queer trait in Vita — her passion for the earnest
middle-class intellectual, however drab and dreary. You can choose
between us, I say, stopping writing; and I get some satisfaction from
making up caustic phrases.

Letter from Vita

Long Barn
9 August

Oh dear I posted my letter in the blotting book, where I have just found it, and
now it is all out of date, containing as it does messages about trains. So I don't
send it. I am however sending my proofs, which will you glance at? I'm very
doubtful about the poem called 'Nocturne' on p. 56 and 57; shall I cut it out?
It seems to me meaningless now, though pregnant enough when I wrote it![11]

---

11 Vita's new volume of poems, *King's Daughter*, contained several lesbian poems that
had clearly not been intended for Virginia, but for Mary Campbell.

Virginia's Diary

10 August

Well, Heaven be praised; it is all over and calm and settled [...] I'm too deliciously relieved to have seen Vita this moment and find that her story to me was precisely true. Indeed I was more worried and angry and hurt and caustic about this affair than I let on, even to the blank page; yet too afraid of exaggeration. [...] And I'm pleased – oh very pleased – about Vita.

Letter from Virginia

Monk's House
12 August

I don't think I shall be able to come this week – I've had to retire to bed with the usual old pain, not very bad and the price of the value I set on your honesty. Lord!

[...] Meanwhile will you at least send a line to say what happened about Hilda – I particularly want to know the situation with respect to Janet, as I have anyhow to write to her.[12] And please make Hilda see that it was all your donkeyism.

Letter from Vita

Long Barn
13 August

Oh dear, oh dear, oh dear. I feel so miserably responsible, you can't think. Poor, poor Virginia – and that means you can't write – can do nothing in fact except stroke Potto's ears. But I love you enormously, – more, if possible, since this incident.

---

12 Virginia's friend Janet Vaughan, from whom she had heard about Vita and Hilda's walking tour in Savoy, which had aroused Virginia's jealousy.

No harm was done by my impulsiveness. [Hilda] had the sense not to write to Janet Vaughan, so there is no need for you to make any allusion to it unless you wish to. I have told her it was mostly due to a misunderstanding on my part, and she says she will not say anything either, when she dines out with [Janet]. So although a donkey I have not been a mischievous donkey, and there is no need for you to take any action [...]

Oh you will never know what miseries I went through before seeing you. I couldn't bear to see your manuscript on its shelf or your photographs in my room. They were all like so many daggers. What should I have done [...] but my imagination revolts. All having ended well, I must admit that the incident was very illuminating. Only I cannot feel it has ended well if your headache is really due to it; if that is true, then it has ended disastrously.

Letter from Virginia

52 Tavistock Square
15 August

I took up my pen to say that I hope, if you see Hilda, you will make her understand, not merely superficially, that Janet Vaughan was as blameless as anybody could be – mere joking and affectionate at that, – I mean I shouldn't have minded to hear what she said of me; and to show how casual and lightly meant it was, she never even gave me a hint that Hilda could seriously entertain those passions. It was merely Oh how amusing it would be if Hilda could fall in love – and then nothing more, but what I took seriously – that the plan had been made many weeks or months.

Letter from Vita

Long Barn
16 August

I have been in bed for the last three days. It would be incorrect to say I was better, but I am getting more ingenious: i.e. I have learnt what positions are to be avoided, and I have got a rope slung round a beam, by the aid of which I can raise myself at least two inches [...]

Geoffrey [Scott] has died of pneumonia in New York, which has upset me a good deal.[13] How horrible to die alone in a foreign hospital away from one's friends — Poor Geoffrey — what a disastrous life [...]

Letter from Virginia

52 Tavistock Square

18 August

[William] Plomer is a nice young man, rather prim and tight outwardly, concealing a good deal I think; though I'm completely bored by speculating as to poets' merits. Nobody is better than anybody else — I like people — I don't bother my head about their works. All this measuring is a futile affair, and it doesn't matter who writes what. But this is my grey and grizzled wisdom — at his age I wanted to be myself. And then, — here is a great storm of rain. I am obsessed at nights with the idea of my own worthlessness, and if it were only to turn a light on to save my life I think I would not do it. These are the last footprints of a headache I suppose. Do you ever feel that? — like an old weed in a stream. What do you feel, lying in bed? I daresay you are visited by sublime thoughts ...

Anyhow, my dear Creature, let me know truthfully and exactly how you are. Potto kisses you and says he could rub your back and cure it by licking.

Letter from Vita

Long Barn

22 August

It is a very queer thing, being ill, when you are not used to it. I suppose in the course of time, if one became really bed ridden, one would evolve ingenious

---

13 The author Geoffrey Scott had been in love with Vita in 1923–4 and his wife divorced him because of her.

methods of dealing with the difficulties of bed-life [...] for at present everything either seems to fall on the floor or else become submerged under blankets and sheets. Also litter — what does one do about litter? My room is like Hampstead Heath after a Bank Holiday. And the worst of bed is that it is not really comfortable, except to sleep in. Trying to prop oneself up in bed is misery, isn't it —What do you do about it, you who must have spent so many months of your life in this situation? [...]

One's mind seems to extend itself into different directions when one lies awake and everybody else is asleep — not unhappy exactly, but speculative and enlightened in a calm way. One thinks about dying. I find also that one thinks (with some distress) about the falsity and difficulty of one's relations with people; how there is probably nobody in the world who knows all round one; how one show separate sections to different people, not on purpose, but willy-nilly, and the best one can hope for is that they will guess the rest. Besides one would probably not like it if anybody did see all round and all through. And what does it matter any how, which brings one back to dying again [...] The reverse is the case, when one is normal and well.

But about knowing people, I have read the two volumes of Miss Mayne's life of Byron[14] — and that's illuminating: being presented with first one letter and then another, both written the same day and flatly contradicting each other, to two different people [...] Instead of seeing just one flat section of his mind at a time, you see right through (so to speak) down into the next section, in a way that his contemporaries couldn't do. Now you write to me, and how do I know that next minute you won't snatch up your pen and write something completely different to Vanessa? And even you yourself don't know which you really mean. There is nothing to prevent me from writing to Harold in an hour's time, and swearing at the horrors of illness, whereas to you I have written of its charms. But that's a thing you would never know unless you had second sight.

Anyway I should be very glad if I could write letters like Byron's.

---

14 Ethel Colburn Mayne's Byron, 2 vols (1910).

Letter from Virginia

52 Tavistock Square
24 August

Might I come on Wednesday for the night? Could you let me know?

[...] And how are you? The best sleeping draught is audit ale at bedtime: any fellow of a college will get it, and if you don't like it, I will drink it.

A thousand different varieties of love are rained upon you, like the showers from a gigantic watering pot by Virginia.

Letter from Vita

Long Barn
13 September

I have several things of the highest importance to tell you:

1. *Harold has resigned from diplomacy.*
2. *He has engaged himself to Lord Beaverbrook from Jan 1st 1930.*
3. *We have written to my mother telling her we will be dependent upon her no longer after the end of this year.*
4. *Harold has withdrawn his objections to* King's Daughter *so that's all right.*

Now there is a fine packet of news for one letter [...] We are feeling very proud and free. I suppose there is no chance of your being in London next Thursday when I am coming up? No, I suppose not. But I have a longing to see you.

Letter from Virginia

52 Tavistock Square
15 September

A thousand congratulations from us both.

I daresay these are the happiest days of your life.

No, alas, I go to London on Friday not Thursday.

Yes, very pleased about *King's Daughter*.

Thank Goodness, no more dealing with Lady S. [...]

How business like this letter is!

And looks like a sonnet.

Letter from Vita

Long Barn
16 September

I dreamed last night that you and Leonard had never been really married, and that you decided it was high time to hold the ceremony. So you had a fashionable wedding. You were dressed in a robe of mediaeval cut, made of cloth-of-gold, and you wore a long veil, and had an escort of bridesmaids and pages. You did not invite me to the wedding. So I stood in the crowd, and saw you pass on Leonard's arm.

For some reason or reasons (not far to seek) this dream made me extremely miserable, and I woke in tears, and have not yet thrown off the effect of it.

Will you tell your bridegroom that I sent back the proofs of King's Daughter *to Mrs Cartwright last week? I am sending him a fleacomb, enclosed, which is better than Keatings [...]*[15]

Will I ever see you again? I have a great and urgent craving to. But you seem very remote [...] At any rate, all sorts of different landscapes seem to open, whichever way I look, not just the vista of a dinner table with gentlemen in gold-braided uniform and ladies in low dresses. Oh Christ, how much I always want to see you when life becomes exciting.

Your Orlando

The fact that I don't see you prevents these from being (some of) the happiest days of my life.

---

15 Flea powder for dogs.

Virginia's Diary

16 September

Another reflection – nothing is so tiring as a change of atmosphere. I am more shattered and dissipated by an hour with Leonard's mother than by six hours – no, six days, of Vita [...] The tremendous great changing that has to take place grinds one's machinery to bits.

Letter from Virginia

52 Tavistock Square
17 September

And when shall we meet? I'm a little dismal. Another of these cursed headaches. How I get them I can't imagine – Whether it's writing, reading, walking, or seeing people. Anyhow it's not been bad at all – only it makes Leonard gloomy and tightens my ropes – I mustn't walk, or do anything but sit and drink milk – you know the old story.

Letter from Virginia

52 Tavistock Square
26 September

No, I didn't mean I was ill – only an ordinary headache, and I'm perfectly all right again [...]

I'm reading an Oxford undergraduate ms novel, and his hero says, 'Do you know these lines from *The Land*, the finest poem, by far the finest of our living poets?' – but for all that, we shan't publish him.

I have only one passion in life – cooking. I have just bought a superb oil stove. I can cook anything. I am free for ever of cooks. I cooked veal cutlets and cake today. I assure you it is better than writing these more than idiotic books.

[Vita heavily scored out five lines at the end of this letter, so that they are no longer readable. They may have been about Hilda Matheson.]

Letter from Vita

> Long Barn
> 28 September

Did I, or did I not, detect a note of annoyance in your letter? A quick scratch? Anyway you are quite wrong: if I go to Barcelona at all, it will not be with Hilda Matheson but with Dottie, in her motor, and in any case I don't think the scheme will mature.

Letter from Virginia

> 52 Tavistock Square
> 30 September

No, no, no, I meant Dottie, not H. M. (about going to Barcelona) and the reference was to your late travels and it was only a joke and Potto made it and said hah hah to show it was a joke and only a Donkey's bray.

Letter from Virginia

> 52 Tavistock Square
> 13 November

Yesterday I was in mischief – in the arms of Osbert [Sitwell], and very fat they are too; on the carpet of Mrs Courtauld,[16] and that is as thick and resilient as Osbert's arms. Lord! What a party? I flirted and I flirted – with Christabel [McLaren], with Mary [Hutchinson], with Ottoline [Morrell]; but this last was a long and cadaverous embrace which almost drew me under. Figure us, entwined beneath Cezannes which she had the audacity to praise all the time we were indulging in those labyrinthine antics which is called being intimate with Ottoline; I succumb: I lie; I flatter; I accept flattery; I stretch and seek, and all

---

16 Elizabeth Courtauld was the wife of the wealthy industrialist and art collector, Samuel Courtauld. Her house at 20 Portman Square was a centre of cultural life in London.

the time she is watchful and vengeful and mendacious and unhappy and ready to break every rib in my body if it were worth her while. In truth, she's a nice woman, eaten with amorosity and vanity, an old volcano, all grey cinders and scarcely a green plant, let alone a shank left. And this is human intercourse, this is human friendship, so I kept saying to myself while I flattered and fawned [...]

I hope, oh I hope, you are now comfortable and quiet and warm and loving your

Potto and V.

1930

None of Vita's letters to Virginia survive from 1930 and 1931, although Vita kept over seventy of Virginia's. The letters were likely lost unintentionally, as the affectionate tone of her replies suggests Virginia would have considered them worth preserving.

Their diaries show that between September and the end of 1930 Vita and Virginia met at least eight times. Early in 1930, Vita and Harold purchased Sissinghurst Castle, leading Vita to become increasingly withdrawn from social life as she worked on its restoration and garden – it remains one of the most famous gardens in England. She also published a bestselling novel – *The Edwardians* – with the Hogarth Press. Virginia made a new friend, the composer Ethel Smyth, who became her most frequent visitor and correspondent, even if she never replaced Vita in her deepest affections.

Virginia's Diary

16 February

Two nights ago, Vita was here; and when she went, I began to feel the quality of the evening – how it was spring coming; a silver light; mixing with the early lamps; the cabs all rushing through the streets; I had a tremendous sense of life beginning; and all the doors opening; and this is I believe the moth shaking its wings in me; ideas rush in me. It is no use trying to write at this stage. I would like to lie down and sleep, but feel ashamed. Leonard brushed off his influenza in one day and went about his business feeling ill. But as I was saying, my mind works in idleness. To do nothing is often my most profitable way.

Letter from Virginia

52 Tavistock Square
25 April

'I don't think I can stand, even the Nicolsons, on happiness for three quarters of an hour,' I said at 8.15.

'Well, we can always shut them off,' said Leonard. At 9 I leapt to my feet and cried out, 'By God, I call that first rate!' having listened to every word.

This is (for a wonder) literally true. How on earth have you mastered the art of being subtle, profound, humorous, arch, coy, satirical, affectionate, intimate, profane, colloquial, solemn, sensible, poetical, and a dear old shabby sheepdog – on the wireless? We thought it a triumph.

Virginia's Diary

16 June

The summer is in full swing. Its elements this year are Nessa and Duncan, Ethel Smyth, Vita and re-writing *The Waves*. Ethel Smyth drops in; dropped in yesterday for instance [...] I get, generally, two letters daily. I daresay the old fires of Sapphism are blazing for the last time. In her heyday she must have been formidable – ruthless, tenacious, exacting, lightning quick, confident; with something of the directness and singleness of genius, though they say she writes music like an old dryasdust German music master.

Virginia's Diary

26 July

Just back from a night at Long Barn, and am all of a quiver with home coming to L., to two newts in the bathroom, letters (from Ethel, and flowers), books, &c. A very nice homecoming; and makes me a little amazed at my own happiness. I daresay few women are happier – not that I am consistently anything; but feel that I have had a good draught of human life, and find much champagne in it. It has not been dull – my marriage; not at all.

Virginia's Diary

25 August

Ethel came for a night on Friday, and let me pelt in a few notes of this curious unnatural friendship. I say unnatural because she is so old, and everything is incongruous. Her head is an enormous size over the temples [...] Lying in my chair in the firelight she looked eighteen; she looked a young vigorous handsome woman. Suddenly this vanishes [...] I am conscious, I suppose, of the compliment she pays me. But then she is over seventy. I had some interesting moments. About jealousy for instance. 'D'you know, Virginia, I don't like other women being fond of you.' 'Then you must be in love with me Ethel.' 'I have never loved anyone so much. Ever since I saw you I have thought of nothing else &c. I had not meant to tell you.' But what I like in her is not I think her love, for how difficult it is to make that intelligible – what

I like is the indomitable old crag; and a certain smile, very wide and benignant. But dear me I am not in love with Ethel.

Virginia's Diary

2 September

My map of the world lacks rotundity. There is Vita. Yes — she was here the other day, after her Italian tour, with two boys; a dusty car, sandshoes and Florentine candlepieces, novels and so on tumbling about on the seats. I use my friends rather as giglamps: there's another field I see; by your light. Over there's a hill. I widen my landscape.

Letter from Virginia

52 Tavistock Square
6 November

Dearest Creature,
I was so much touched by your staying up to dine with me last night — Potto and I were so happy.

Virginia's Diary

16 December

I will never dine out again. I will burn my evening dress. I have gone through this door. Nothing exists beyond. I have taken my fence; and now need never whip myself to dine with Colefax, Ethel, Mary again. These reflections were hammered in indelibly last night at Argyll House. The same party: same dresses; same food. To talk to Sir Arthur [Colefax] about Queen Victoria's letters, and the Dyestuff Bill, and — I forget — I sacrificed an evening alone with Vita, an evening alone by myself — an evening of pleasure. And so it goes on perpetually. Forced, dry, sterile, infantile conversation. And I am not even excited at going. So the fence is not only leapt, but fallen. Why jump?

1931

Though no letters from Vita to Virginia survive from this year, their diaries show that they met at least nine times in the first four months. Vita continued work on Sissinghurst Castle and published another bestselling novel, *All Passion Spent*, with the Hogarth Press. Virginia published *The Waves*.

Letter from Virginia

Monk's House
24 May

Dearest Creature

I've wasted 4 days when I wanted to write. And I've spent them partly reading Princess Daisy of Pless[1], speculating upon her real character and life and longing for a full account from you – who appear in a footnote as a distinguished author. What a chance the British aristocracy had and lost – I mean if they'd only grafted brains on to those splendid

---

1 *From My Private Diary* (1931), by Princess Daisy of Pless. She was the daughter of Colonel W. Cornwallis-West, distantly related to Vita through the De la Warrs.

bodies and wholesome minds [...] Could Bloomsbury be grafted on to Mayfair: but no: we're too ugly and they're too stupid. And so the world goes to rack and ruin.

Letter from Virginia

Monk's House
27 May

I'm quite recovered and have been sauntering over the downs alone – Lord – why go back to London? They look so lovely this evening, from my garden room, with the low barns that always make me think of Greek Temples. And we've been to a village wedding and seen the bridal party perched on kitchen chairs driven off in a great blue wagon, drawn by colossal farm horses with ribbons in their tails, and little pyramids of bells on their foreheads. What an odd mixture English country life is of squalor and magnificence!

[...] Perhaps Ethel is sleeping with you tonight?[2]

Letter from Virginia

Monk's House
8 August

As for Katherine [Mansfield], I think you've got it very nearly right. We did not ever coalesce; but I was fascinated, and she respectful, only I thought her cheap, and she thought me priggish; and yet we were both compelled to meet simply in order to talk about writing [...] I dream of her often – now that's an odd reflection – how one's relation with a person seems to be continued after death in dreams, and with some odd reality too.

---

2 Ethel Smyth was spending the night with Vita at Sissinghurst.

Virginia's Diary

14 October

A note. *The Waves* has beaten all my books: sold close on 5,000; we are reprinting. The reviews I think the warmest yet. But Vita found it desperately dull – anyhow for 100 pages. What shall I say to Virginia? I can't get through it.

Letter from Virginia

Monk's House
29 December

And how happy the sound of your voice made me, coming over the fields, and lighting up the fishmonger's window as it did this time how many years ago?

[...] But Vita, on the other hand, should write a long poem for Virginia; and before she does that she should sit down and write ever so long and intimate a letter to Virginia.

1932

Vita was now forty, Virginia fifty. In the spring, Virginia and Leonard went to Greece with Roger Fry and his sister Margery. On her return, Virginia led a far more sociable life than Vita did at Sissinghurst. Vita published another popular novel with the Hogarth Press, called *Family History*.

Letter from Virginia

Athens, Greece
24 April

Well, you haven't written to me, not one word, not one postcard, so perhaps Sissigt. is blotted out – the Tower fell, crushing the daughter of the Sackvilles to pink pulp – a very fitting end for a woman who forgets old but humble, humble, but old, friends. It's Sunday at Athens; we've been lunching, not too well, and looking for 2 hours at Byzantine relics – because it's a sultry wet day [...] Still it's a beautiful island, and I padded up to the hill top, picking wild irises and unknown yellow stars, and little purple, violet, blue, white, pearl flowers, all about as big as the stone on your ring no bigger. And we went to Daphnis, and wandered in olive woods, and to Sunium, the Temple on a cliff, which cliff is soft with flowers, all again no bigger than pearls or topazes. Margery Fry is a maniacal botanist, and squats – she's the size of a Russian bear – on the rocks digging with a penknife […] There! That's to make you feel envious. (I see you've got foot and mouth disease in Kent.)

Our drawbacks – these you'll want to know – are bitter winds, stormy grey skies, and vast helpings of soft sweet pudding. Also Roger has the piles – can't walk, also Margery suffers – like all spinsters aged 63 from unrequited loves 20 years ago for Englishmen who were killed in the war […] But I don't want Tavistock Sqre at the moment: I like the life here – you should see the donkeys, with paniers full of anemones; and the Square, all ablaze with flowers, and The Acropolis. Have I described our afternoon on The Acropolis – when a storm rushed up from the Aegean, black as arrows, and the blue was as blue as hard china, and the storm and the blue fell upon each other and 10 million German tourists rushed across the temple precisely like suppliants in their grey and purple mackintoshes – no I haven't described the Acropolis – You may thank your stars I know my place as a prose writer and leave that to someone who, about this time 4 years since, won from Jack Squire, a silver beaker[1] to drink her pop from. There! That's my revenge for your not thinking of me. Ethel thinks of me.

Letter from Vita

Sissinghurst Castle
25 April
My dear, remote, romantic Virginia – yes, indeed, I see the moon in English muddy puddles, and I wonder where you are: sliding past the Dalmatian coast

---

1 Symbolising the Hawthornden Prize, which Vita received for her poem *The Land*.

(I think at one moment), passing Corfu and Ithaca (and oh God! what associations they all have for me!), and then the Piraeus and Athens — (more associations), and then what happens to you? For I simply don't know, — the hinterland of Greece, I suppose, which is a closed country to me so far — and is likely to remain closed unless I go there with Ethel, which God forbid. Why didn't you ask me to come with you? I would have thrown everything to the winds, and would have come. But you didn't.

In the meantime I cultivate my garden and April cheats me of all its advertised joys: the wind is howling at all hours, and the rain is raining at most of them. A bloodier April England never saw. So be glad that you are in the sun (I hope) of Greece.

I am glad for your sake, but England is empty without you.

Will you come here when you come back? Shall you be dazed by all the things you have seen? You have been to Greece before, and your recollections will be strong, I know. It is rather appalling, to think what things people live through, — people one loves, — when one isn't there with them. Yes, I do wish I were with you [. . .]

You will be seeing those lavender and tawny slopes, I suppose: and all the wild spring flowers which I have never seen, — for I was in Greece in October. How I envy you. How I envy the people who are with you.

Life is too complicated, — I sometimes feel that I can't manage it at all.

Letter from Virginia

Hotel Majestic, Athens
8 May

Well I have just got your letter, and it was very nice to get your letter though I can't help feeling, being as you know a very polyp emotion, that you're somehow rather saddened, worried, bothered — why? Why is life so complicated at the moment? Money? Dottie? Writing? God knows [. . .]

Yet it was so strange coming back here again I hardly knew where I was; or when it was. There was my own ghost coming down from the Acropolis, aged 23; and how I pitied her!

Letter from Vita

Long Barn
17 May

We've had no posts here since Saturday! The consequence was that I only got your letter this morning. DAMN. I was in London yesterday and could perfectly well have come, but I never thought you'd be in London on Bank Holiday. I got a lovely lovely letter from you from Greece — two, in fact — yes, it sounds ravishing and I wish you'd taken me with you in your pocket.

When shall I see you now? I shan't be in London till the 30th, unless I come up for the flower-show. I am tempted to come up, but I ought to stick to my book. What would be really nice, would be if you and Leonard motored down here on a fine day. Telephone and say you are coming, Sissinghurst 250 — but our number is a deep dark secret, so tell it to no one. Sissinghurst really is looking nice just now, — but of course you are spoilt for our simple English beauty. Still, the bluebell wood is really a dream.

No, I'm not depressed and I certainly didn't mean to write a depressed letter. I may have been feeling rather harassed, and you always know when my coat is at all ruffled. I do long to see you.

Letter from Virginia

52 Tavistock Square
25 May

There's only one person I want to see, and she has no burning wish for anything but a rose red tower and a view of hop gardens and oasts. Who can it be? It's said she has written a poem and has a mother, a cow, and a moat. I'm so illiterate — I've seen so many people — life offers so many problems and there's a hair in my pen.

Letter from Virginia[2]

52 Tavistock Square
24 August

No more room, or I would pitch you a very melancholy story about my jealousy of all your new loves.

And when am I going to see you? Because you know you love now several people, women I mean, physical I mean, better, oftener, more carnally than me.

Letter from Virginia

Tavistock Square
12 October

I've just bought the 6,000th copy of *Family History* – 6,000 sold before publication – my God! And my fingers are red and whealed with doing up parcels for 3 dys incessantly [...] orders pouring in – we all working till 7.30 – thought we were just finished – then a batch of orders discovered hidden in a drawer another hour's work – clerks panting – telephones ringing carriers arriving – parcels just finished in time to catch the vans – Oh Lord what it is to publish a best seller.

Letter from Vita

Long Barn
16 October

Oh dear, not content with making you tie up six thousand family histories I made you tie up the common reader too.[3] An extra parcel. I won't apologise though.

---

2 This letter, along with three others (dated 8 August 1938, 11 August 1938 and 26 February 1939), were discovered after Vita's death, hidden in a drawer in her Sissinghurst office.

3 Vita's *Family History* was published on the same day, 13 October, as Virginia's *The Common Reader: Second Series*.

If you knew what pleasure it gave me, you wouldn't want me to apologise [...]
Lord, you ARE a good writer, aren't you? And a good critic. I take off my hat;
I sweep it off, so that its plume raises the dust.

I've got an extra broadcast talk to do tomorrow, and am scrapping three
books in order to put yours into it.

That is why this letter is not longer: because I've got to write my talk.

Yes, do please come to Sissinghurst soon. Remember, I'll be in America for
nearly four months (January–April 1933).

Letter from Virginia

52 Tavistock Square

18 October

Yes dearest Creature – that was very nice of you. Pinka and I sat erect,
blushing, as our praises poured forth from the trumpet.[4] I think you
gave me too much – I hope the three you supressed weren't listening
too. But anyhow, you soothed my vanity – there are people who say
I'm vain – did you know it? [...]

You would have been still nicer if you had told me you were in
London, and come here. I prefer you, bodily, to you vocally.

Oh I was in such a rage of jealousy the other night, thinking you had
been in love with Hilda that summer you went to the Alps together!
Because you said you weren't. Now were you? Did you do the act under
the Dolomites? Why I should mind this, when it's all over – that tour – I
don't know. But I do. D'you remember coming to confession, or rather jus-
tification, in my lodge? And you weren't guilty there, were you? You swore
you weren't. Anyhow my Elizabeth comes to see me, alone, tomorrow.[5] I

---

4 Vita reviewed *The Common Reader* on the radio.
5 Elizabeth Bowen, the Irish novelist whom Virginia had met through their mutual
friend Ottoline Morrell. Since 1923, Bowen had married to Alan Cameron.

rather think, as I told you, that her emotions sway a certain way. (That's an elegiac.) I'm reading her novel to find out. What's so interesting is when one uncovers an emotion that the person themselves, I should say herself, doesn't suspect. And it's a sort of duty, don't you think – revealing peoples true selves to themselves?

Letter from Virginia

52 Tavistock Square

8 November

Well, my faithless sheep dog, – yes, you'll be turned into a very old collie if you don't look out, blind of one eye, and afflicted with mange on the rump – why don't you come and see me? Poor Virginia can't come to you. She – that is, I suppose, I – had another, very slight though, fainting […]

I'm divinely happy, because I wrote all the morning – Oh how you'll hate my novel, and how it amuses me![6] – and then I go for a walk, or drive, and then I come back to tea, carrying one muffin which I eat, with honey, and then I lie on the sofa, and – who d'you think came and talked to me t'other night? Three guesses. All wrong. It was Violet Trefusis – your Violet.[7] Lord what fun! I quite see now why you were so enamoured – then: she's a little too full, now, overblown rather; but what seduction! What a voice – lisping, faltering, what warmth, suppleness, and in her way – its not mine – I'm a good deal more refined – but that's not altogether an advantage – how lovely, like a squirrel among buck hares – a red squirrel among brown nuts. We glanced and winked through the leaves; and called each other

---

6 Virginia was writing the end of *Flush* (published in 1937), when she then suddenly put it aside to begin the 'essay-novel' that would be published in 1937 as *The Years*.

7 Vita's former lover, Violet Trefusis, had come to talk to the Hogarth Press about her third novel, *Tandem*, 1933.

punctiliously Mrs Trefusis and Mrs Woolf – and she asked me to give her the *Common R.* which I did, and said smiling, 'By the way, are you an Honourable, too?' No, no, she smiled, taking my point, you, to wit. And she's written to ask me to go and stay with her in France, and says how much she enjoyed meeting me: and Leonard: and we positively must come for a whole week soon.

1933

Vita and Harold went on a lecture tour of the United States for the first four months of 1933, which would be Vita's last sustained public performance. She withdrew to Sissinghurst, published her *Collected Poems* and cultivated her garden. Virginia published her short novel *Flush* in October, and was writing *The Years*. Although they wrote that they missed each other, Vita and Virginia met only half a dozen times in the year.

Letter from Virginia

Monk's House
7 January

I was seized with gloom when you left — ask Ethel. Isn't it odd what tricks affection — to leave it at that — plays? I don't see you for six weeks sometimes; yet the moment I know you're not there to be seen, all the fishmonger's shops in the world go dark.[1] I always think of you

---

1 In December 1925, Vita had ordered fish at a shop in Sevenoaks, and Virginia often returned to this memory of her when the physical part of their relationship began.

as a pink shop with a porpoise in a tank. Now there are no porpoises. No, Sissinghurst is grey; Sevenoaks a drab coloured puce. Here I sit at Rodmell, with a whole patch of my internal globe extinct. Yes – that's a compliment for you […]

By the way, are you lecturing on me at Albertvilleapolis Pa? If so, do send me your notes. Please do. And let them say something of love, and Horne the butler [at Long Barn]. Let them slip in one word to say Vita loves Virginia better than the whole world wrapped in a nutshell. Better than all those ardent but anaemic herring grillers with whom – Lord love her soul! – she consorts. Because Virginia is so clever, so good […] Yes; you are adventurous woman, and make me envious. Please, for God's sake, don't catch the flu, or the pneumonia – both I see rampant in New York. Don't do a thing that can diminish your splendour in my eyes. Come back soon, before I start, as I intend, for the East […]

Shall you now clear a space among the spittoons and write to me? Describe everything, down to the lace on women's nightgowns. Then add a terse but compendious statement why I love Virginia next best to my husband and sons.

And take great care of yourself.

Letter from Virginia

Monk's House
24 January

Yes, dearest Creature, I did write to you but I called you Nicolson, and did not say forward; so you may not have got it. As it was the very most passionate letter I ever wrote, and the loveliest and wittiest what a pity. (This is trusting you never got it.)

You wrote to me from the high seas. How like you – to have waves 80 miles high, and to stand on the Bridge with the Captain.

Now the point of you is that everything is like you – that's very profound [...]

I daresay you're eating clams on a skyscraper at this moment – 5.30 on Tuesday evening, the time you should be with me. And we wasted our last evening. I raging against Eddy, and you very honourably upholding him. Did you ever discuss it with him? I've not seen him since; nor ever shall, I daresay, for I can't manoeuvre my friends' tempers [...]

I am writing all the morning: and I like writing; but you won't much care for it. Never mind. Oh and tonight they're dancing *Orlando* on the ice, and I shan't be there. It's a remarkable fact – the whole British peerage says they descend from the Courtiers I invented, and still have the snow boots which they wore on the frost which I invented too. It's all true, every word of it.

They charge 30/- a ticket, and I would willingly have gone and hired skates if you'd have come [...]

Oh I must boast, for I can't bear to think of all you're doing and seeing, and I not there, and I not there! Please, please, write down every scrap for me; and know how not a tassel on a table or a stain on a mat comes amiss. And how I miss you! You wouldn't believe it. I want coloured windows, red towers, moats and wans, and one old Bull walking up and down an empty stable: you, in short. But you don't want me. You are enchanting, chiefly with the glamour of your title and the glow of your pearls, all the Coons in Canada. Tell me that too: about the white soft women and their blazing eyes. I wish I couldn't see them so clearly couched on glittering frosty grass with the daughter of The Sackvilles.

Letter from Vita

En Route Through the Rockies
16 March

This writing paper appeals to me so much that I must write you a letter on it. This is a Thursday; I left New York on Monday and have been travelling ever since through unending prairies until this morning when I woke to find a semi-circle of snow mountains edging the horizon, their peaks just turning pink as the sun rose over the opposite rim of the plain. Then we got to Denver, at the foot of the Rockies, and by breakfast time we were climbing right up into the mountains and are now some 7,000 feet up. It is very beautiful, very desolate, the sun is hot, and I've seen a cowboy. So I'm very happy. It is all, quite suddenly, un-American and subtly Spanish [...]

I find I can post this right up at the top of the mountains — so you must look at the postmark, which apparently is a special one. The scenery is altogether too scenic for my taste, — terrific gorges and roaring rivers — it gives me claustrophobia [...]

The time keeps on changing, which is very disconcerting; from 'Mountain Time' we have now got to 'Pacific Time', and there is 6 hours' difference between us and you. Do you realise that California is more than twice as far from England than Persia?

Harold wants to go for a walk now.

Letter from Virginia

Monk's House

18 March

Well, do you remember me? I wrote you a very long and passionate letter the other day, but stuck it in my case, forgot it, left it, and found it so out of date — it was all about earthquakes and banks failing — that I can't send it.

I saw Sibyl the other day; and she had seen Harold, and Harold said you are a roaring raging success; which, I said, don't matter a straw with Vita. She'll shake her coat, and the grease and the oil will run down her. A great compliment to you. Shall you net anything after all — with the dollar collapsed? — There'll be the experience, as they call it — all those virgins you've ravished — teas you've eaten, shrines you've visited, fat old women you've intoxicated [...]

Please Vita darling come back soon. We shall be off in the car to
Italy if you don't – we want to try the fluid fly wheel on the Alps.[2]
Please come snuffing up my stairs soon, just the same, in your red
jersey. Please wear your pearls. Please bring Sarah.[3] And then ask me
to Sissingt. Lord, how you'll love your first night there and sun rise
seen from the pink Tower! Write to me.

Letter from Vita

Smoke Tree Ranch, South California
28 March

*I have been trying to write to you for days and days, but life has been too thickly
populated with movie stars and so forth. I am now in a three-roomed cottage
in the middle of the desert (I send you a photograph of it), with nothing but
a few cowboys and a stray coyote to interrupt. Magnificent stars overhead, and
mountains all round. The desert itself is carpeted with rosy verbena. It is exactly
like Persia, and we are as happy as larks [...]*

*Los Angeles is hell. Take Peacehaven, multiply it by 400 square miles, sprinkle
it all along the French Riviera, and then empty the Chelsea Flower Show over
it, adding a number of Spanish exhibition buildings, and you have the Los
Angeles coast. The Americans have unequalled genius for making everything
hideous. Hollywood however is fun. It is pure fantasy, – you never know what
you will come on round the corner, whether an ocean liner, or Trafalgar Square,
or the façade of Grand Hotel or a street in Stratford-on-Avon with Malayan
houris walking down it [...]*

*A young lady rushed up to me in Pasadena and said she was writing a book
about you and me. Isn't that nice for us? Would I give her an interview to tell
her our (yours and mine) views on Imagery? Fortunately I was able to say I had
only just time to catch my train [...]*

---

2 Virginia and Leonard were driving to Italy in their new car at the beginning of May.
3 One of Vita's dogs.

From here we go to Arizona and then to New Mexico, and then to Milwaukee, and then to South Carolina, and then to New York, and then to that blessed Bremen[4] which will bring us home. Battered but enriched, – not only by dollars.

Lord, but I am dying to see you.

Letter from Vita

Charleston, South Carolina
9 April

We have been amusing ourselves by reckoning up the distance we shall have travelled by the time we get home, and find that it comes to over 33,000 miles – We've been to 72 different cities, and have spent 63 nights in the train. I hope you are impressed by these statistics [...]

I don't think I wrote to you from the Grand Canyon which is the most astonishing thing in the world. We are going to come back to America in order to motor all through Texas, Arizona, California and Mexico, taking tents with us in order to camp in the desert. You can't imagine, Virginia, what the Painted Desert is like. It is every colour of the rainbow, broken by great pink cliffs the colour of the rocks in Devonshire. And the sun blazes every day, and the air makes you want to leap over the moor. Why don't you and Leonard come with us? [...] Doesn't it appeal to you? If you liked, you could give a couple of lectures which would practically pay for your expenses [...]

Lord, I must stop. But think, next week – next week, – we shall be home.

Letter from Virginia

Monk's House
19 April

I say this is exciting!

You're back – Thank the Lord my porpoise is in the fishmonger's again! But when shall I see here? We are here (Lewes 385) till Sunday

---

4 A German liner.

afternoon. Then London for 10 days: then Italy. Could you ring up –
don't tell me you've changed your voice too – and suggest any time,
which I'll keep even if it means murder [...]

Now you must attend to your world. Lord how I envy you your
pink tower after all America.

Letter from Vita

Sissinghurst Castle
24 April

Yes your porpoise is back on the marble slab. But with four months accumulation
of stuff to deal with, – a real nightmare. I don't feel I shall ever get straight.
I can hardly find 8 inches x 8 inches of space on my table to put this paper
on. And there isn't a chair to sit on, – all loaded up with books and papers
and cowboy hats. I sit on the floor mostly, and Sarah wriggles into my lap,
upsetting everything [...]

So you're going to Italy. Well, well, Damn. I shall come up to London to see
you before you go [...]

Your bewildered, happy, home-unsick,

V

P S You are the one and only person I want to see. Where is the promised
Flush?[5]

Letter from Vita

Sissinghurst Castle
17 May

Well, you have disappeared, – vanished from my ken, – lost in Italy [...] And
I daresay it is so lovely, – Italy in May, – that I won't even tell you about

---

5 Virginia finished the typescript of *Flush* in January and it was published in October
1933.

the bluebell woods here, which are better than anything in the Middle West, I promise you. Nor will I tell you about our charcoal-burner, — a new denizen of Sissinghurst, — nor about the two swans which have miraculously appeared on the lake [...] No, you have abandoned me, and I am left with nothing but Pinka for consolation — and do you know what? She won't take any notice of me. Pinka, who can sniff me even while I'm still on the doorstep in Tavistock Square, and makes a piss, you'll admit, when I come in, won't have a thing to do with me when my guest [...]

She's been having copious doses for worms, tell Leonard. Louise calls her Mrs Pinka, I don't know why.

Are you very very happy? I am sending Ben to Italy for two months — wouldn't you like to be eighteen and going off to Italy alone for two months? I would. He is very nice, is Ben. How I love the young. I should like you to see him again now. You know his admiration for you; that ought to dispose you kindlily towards him, or are you sick of admiration?

[...] Darling, it does seem a bit hard that you should have vanished like this just when I have travelled 33,000 miles in order to see you again. But of course I can't hope to rival the attraction of a fluid fly-wheel.[6] You'd better come back soon though, or I shall begin exploring London for a divertissement. I have to go there tomorrow, and just fancy, I'm lunching with Sibyl [...]

Would it surprise you to learn that I miss you very very much indeed? In order to console myself I am thinking of taking up with Marlene Dietrich. So don't linger too long at Montepulciano if you value the rather touching fidelity of your old sheep dog.

---

6 Virginia had boasted about her new car: 'silver and green, fluid fly wheel, Tickford hood – Lanchester'.

Letter from Virginia

Spotorno, Italy

20 May

This is a strictly business like (only I happen to be tipsy, having drunk more than my half bottle tonight).

Yes, I am half dazed with travelling, so many cities have I seen, and smelt: now it's the waves breaking, and the scent of stocks in the garden [...] We're so brown cheeked, red nosed and altogether dusty shaggy shabby – what a state my clothes are in – even I hesitate to wear them – for we lunch in the fields, under olives, off ham, and it's my duty to wash up, which affects my clothes.

Letter from Vita

Sissinghurst Castle

5 June

Virginia, darling, you are an angel, – an angel, I mean, to understand so unfailingly when one really minds about something as I minded my mother telling Ben about my morals and Harold's.[7] Not that I am in any way ashamed of my morals or H.'s. Only Ben might have had a horrid imprint sealed on his mind. Lucky he didn't – a tribute, I think, to our bringing up of him? (That's a boast. But you, also, even you, boast sometimes [...]) Anyway you are a darling to have realised that I minded.

I am slight and unseasonably tipsy, for I went to a party at my tenants' here, to celebrate their golden wedding, and had to drink their health at lunch.

---

7 Virginia and Leonard lunched at Sissinghurst on 28 May. Lady Sackville had recently told her grandson, Ben Nicolson, about his parents' affairs. Ben's diary recounts how his grandmother had spoken to him about 'M. [Vita] getting hold of women and D. [Harold] of men – about Violet Keppel, Virginia Woolf etc.' Ben then repeated this story to Virginia, who 'listened ... with her head bowed. Then she said: "The old woman ought to be shot."' See Nigel Nicolson's *Portrait of a Marriage*.

It was the sort of party you would have liked; the old lady, who is just on 80, had tied a yellow ribbon round her neck, with the most coquettish little bow just behind her ear, and kept assuring me how happy her husband had looked on this day fifty years ago. The whole house was draped in Union Jacks. Why is it that patriotism must play a part in the most intimate family gathering? [...] I enjoyed it more than any party I've been to for years. They were all more like characters in a novel than any character in a novel I've ever read. The old lady said to me, rather grimly, when I congratulated her, 'Well it's better than divorce, anyhow.'

Letter from Virginia

52 Tavistock Square
8 June

Would you dine with me *alone* upon my honour, on Monday next MONDAY 12th – anytime you like. It is only that I shall be alone. Otherwise, I don't think it's worth anyone's while to come to London. Could you angelically ring the telephone? [...]

Forgive the scrawl

Potto is the writer

Letter from Vita

Sissinghurst Castle
11 June

Isn't it enraging that of all people in the world your own particular Ethel [Smyth] should be the one to prevent me dining with you tomorrow? But there it is, the engagement has been arranged for weeks past, – I get letters fairly trumpeting with excitement from Ethel by every post – supplemented by postcards and telegrams – and so I felt I simply couldn't put her off – much as I longed to. Anyone else, – any herring griller, – could have gone to hell. But Ethel, I reflected, is 75 and one cannot play fast and loose with the old.

She's coming for the night [...] Says she wants to hear all about America. My God.

You haven't got another evening available, have you? I won't tell you how much I want to see you, because you wouldn't believe me — cynical woman that you are — not knowing the meaning of love.

Letter from Vita

Sissinghurst Castle
24 June

Yes it was nice to see you, but I feel rather like a starving man given one solitary crust. Oh I've got so much to say to you — but it takes hours — I mean, the sort of things I want to say to you require prolonged intimacy before they can squeeze themselves out. (That sounds horribly like Ethel.) Do you remember a night in Burgundy [...] when I came along the dark passage to your room in a thunderstorm and we lay talking about whether we were frightened of death or not? That is the sort of occasion on which the things I want to say to you, — and to you only, — get said.

Well, I go off to Italy on Monday, if you felt inclined to write and say you still had some affection for me [...]

Letter from Vita

Sissinghurst Castle
21 July

Come and lunch with me at the Café Royal on Wednesday? Or will you be too busy? Still, you must lunch somewhere.

Will you tell your husband, please, that I return his announcement herein with two suggestions — and tell him please that I shall be a terrible bore to him about this edition [of Collected Poems*], because it is the only book of mine I shall ever have minded about — I.e. I don't give a damn for my novels, but I do give ½ a damn for my poems, — which is not saying much.*

Normally I don't think I'm much of a bore as an author, vis a vis my publisher. But on this occasion I may become one.

Letter from Virginia

Monk's House
16 August

Poor Virginia has been in bed; and thought how nice it would be to see Vita! And is now up and says, How nice it would be to see Vita! And L. says (this is a terrific compliment), 'I should like to see Vita.' What about coming one day next week for the night? Could it be?

And who's Lady Roehampton in *The Edwardians*? Please tell me [...]

But can you come?

If so, I'll write a long long letter. This is only Potto's scrawl

Letter from Vita

Sissinghurst Castle
18 August

Dear Mrs Woolf

(That appears to be the suitable formula.)

I regret that you have been in bed, though not with me — (a less suitable formula.)

About next week. I am more flattered than I can say by your suggestion that I should come to Rodmell, knowing how much you dislike invasion. I am all the more flattered by Leonard's support — yes, I really do take that as a compliment. But next week is rather difficult, though not impossible. The point is, that I've got my sister-in-law staying here, and she's been ill, and I am supposed to provide the cure. Country rustication and all that [...] she is editing a book, at the moment, on advice to Parents, which I find fascinating, [8] *— I mean, I*

---

8 Gwen St Aubyn, Harold's younger sister. She was editing *The Family Book* (1934).

like seeing a really expert mind at work technically on such difficult matters.
We sit on the steps of the tower discussing why some women get their physical
satisfaction interiorally or exteriorally, and what connection there may or may
not be between the inner part of the nerve and the outer — and what connection
there may be between perversion and normality — and so on.

A very interesting question.

I might tell you more about it at 3 in the morning — but not in cold blood.
Anyhow, it's a better subject for 3 in the morning than butler's wages [...]

The Edwardians, — oh, that bloody book! I blush to think you read it.
Lady Roehampton is Lady Westmoreland, — a lovely sumptuous creature who
came to Knole when I was eight, and who first set my feet along the wrong
path, I fancy, but who died, herself relatively young, of drugs and a plethora
of lovers. (No, it wasn't Lady Westmoreland who set my feet along the wrong
path, now I come to think of it, but the Queen of Roumania who appeared in
my schoolroom one day.)

Here is the post going.

Letter from Vita

Sissinghurst Castle
1 September

Tell Leonard a rival publisher is trying to bribe me away with £1,000 — but
I won't be bribed, and have said so.

A faithful sheep dog? Nicely trained to heel?

Letter from Virginia

Monk's House
15 September

I am a wretch never to have written — not that you care. But there
has been such a rain of visitors on my head that I couldn't escape [...]

My word, what a nice woman you are! That's the véry words I said, on reading your letter to Leonard. Moreover, they confirmed my own saying. He was rather in a stew, and thought we were making demands on your honour, integrity, friendship, magnanimity and so on. I said, Oh but Vita is like that. Then your letter comes to confirm it. It was a noble act though, tossing 1,000 guineas into the duckpond, or cesspool, for to tell the truth, I don't like Hart Davies in the flesh, nor Cape in the spirit.[9]

Letter from Vita

Sissinghurst Castle
16 September

I had begun to wonder if you were X with me – though I didn't know why and had a clear conscience. 'After the 23rd' fits in beautifully, because it appears that they are producing All Passion Spent *at the Croydon Theatre on that date [...] and I suppose I'll have to go and see a rehearsal one day next week, in order to prevent them from committing too many howlers. You might tell Leonard, would you, about this, if he doesn't know? Because he would probably like to arrange with the theatre to have the book on sale there [...]*

Try to come before Oct 4th when Ben goes to Oxford, because Ben liked you. Isn't that odd?

No it wasn't Cape who offered me the 1,000 guineas. It was Cassell.[10] Cape was quite a separate bribe [...]

I say: my poems are so thin. It really appals me, re-reading them all in a bunch, and thinking, 'Is that all I've got to show for half a life's experience?' I can hardly hope that you won't even glance at them, in your capacity as ½ my

---

9 Rupert Hart Davies, a publisher for Jonathan Cape.
10 Cassell & Co publishers.

publisher, so I shall send you a copy in which I shall mark the only specimens I could bear you to read, and shall trust to your honour not to eavesdrop on the others [...]

Lord I must go and plant fritillaries.

When will you come?

Letter from Virginia

Monk's House

30 September

We dined with Mary [Hutchinson], and her Jeremy wants to meet your Ben, so I said I would hand on the message.

Mary makes love to me – yes: other people don't. I daresay at this very minute you're couched with some herring griller in the straw God damn you.

Letter from Virginia

52 Tavistock Square

1 November

'I saw Vita lunching at the Cafe Royal today,' said Jack Hutchinson last night.

Oh such a pang of rage shot through me! All through dinner, and the supper, which ended with champagne and iced cake at 12.30, I was going back and foraging in my mind for the seed in my pillow: (you know what I mean: the pea under the mattress) and that was it. And I couldn't say, 'Who was with her?' And it burnt a hole in my mind, that you should have been lunching at the Cafe Royal and not come to see me.

How pleased you'll be! You did it on purpose I daresay. But who were you with? You knew I should get wind of it – yes and it was a woman you were lunching with, and there was I, sitting alone and and and … I break off my writing, which is all dish water […]

Dearest Creature, do write and tell me who you were lunching with at the Cafe Royal – and I sitting alone over the fire!

I've had your book [*Collected Poems*] in my hands – and very stately it is, like a slab of ivory engraved with steel; but I didn't read it, because you are giving it me.

Oh the Cafe Royal! When Jack said that – not to me, but to the company, you could have seen my hand tremble; and then we all went on talking […] and the candles were lit, and I chose mine, a green one, and it was the first to die, which means they say that out of the 8 or 9 people there, I shall be the first to wear a winding sheet. But you'll be lunching at the Cafe Royal!

Letter from Vita

Sissinghurst Castle
3 November

My lunch at the Cafe Royal! Well, I was taking Gwen to a nursing-home, and took her to have some luncheon there first. We didn't then know if she had to have her head cut open or not. Thank goodness, it turns out to be not. *But they say she won't be well for a year; perhaps not for two. She's having treatment for it, – a red-hot rabbit-hutch that they put over her head twice a day, and which makes her faint. They seem to think that this will dispel the injury to her brain […]*

I can't tell you how gratified I was by your annoyance (as you predicted) on discovering me in unknown company at the Cafe Royal – but if I hadn't been on so grim a mission you may be sure I should have let you know. As it was, I was with doctors and specialists all day – and didn't dare make any other appointments because of them and their erratic movements […]

Tell me about dinner on the 13th — if you still have any affection left for
a rather shabby sheep dog that gnaws its bone at the Cafe Royal.

Letter from Virginia

52 Tavistock Square

22 November

Oh faithless — why has everybody got a book and not I?[11] Didn't I
give you *Flush* and *Orlando*? Aren't I a critic too — aren't I a woman?
Don't you care what I say? Am I nothing to you, physically, morally
or intellectually?

Letter from Vita

Sissinghurst Castle

23 November

Do you know, it was my native modesty which prevented me from sending you
my book. I couldn't believe you really wanted it. However, here it is. I wish
somebody would review it, as at present it seems to be completely still-born [...]

Such *a lot of gardening going on here — we are planning the loveliest*
shrubs — and Sissinghurst is going to be a riot.

Is it true that Berners is going to marry Violet?[12] *I suspect the rumour of*
being a joke either on his part or on hers. Lord, to think how angry I should
have been once!

Letter from Virginia

52 Tavistock Square

26 November

And the book came. And I've read one or two of the new ones. And
I liked them yes — I liked the one to Enid Bagnold; and I think I see

---

11 Vita's *Collected Poems*.

12 Indeed it was not true. Lord (Gerald) Berners was a lifelong bachelor, with no intention of marrying Violet Trefusis, nor she him.

how you may develop differently. You're an odd mixture as a poet. I like you for being 'out-moded' and not caring a damn: that's why you're free to change; free and lusty [...]

Oh dear me, I wish I could read behind some of the poems!

1934

Only three of Vita's letters to Virginia remain from the years 1934–6. Vita kept twelve replies in 1934, eleven in 1935, and nine in 1936, but she had moved away emotionally. Vita's closest friend was now her sister-in-law, Gwen St Aubyn, and Virginia's was Ethel Smyth, who continued to shower her in attention.

Letter from Vita

Castello, Portofino
6 February

I am writing to you on the terrace of a tiny old castle perched above the sea.[1] Two great stone-pines shield me from the sun, which is almost too hot. There is a rustle of lizards among the aloes. The sea sparkles three hundred foot below. In the distance are snow-mountains. A Franciscan monk with a rope round his waist and a vast grey beard has just been to call on me. A large bottle of golden wine stands at my elbow. I write and write and write — which reminds me, would you please tell Leonard that I can probably give him my book by May or June [...][2]

---

1 Vita was with Harold and Gwen, and then went to Morocco for three weeks.
2 Vita's *The Dark Island* was published by the Hogarth Press in October 1934.

You see, I couldn't resist the castle. I started in a little hotel down in the village, and every evening I used to watch the castle turning pink in the sunset. So I made enquiries; found it was empty and to let; rang up the agent in Genoa, and in five minutes had arranged with him for immediate occupation. There is only one path up to it, so half the population turned out to carry our luggage up on their backs. And we were greeted at the door by the gardener with a large bunch of irises and narcissus.

Letter from Virginia

52 Tavistock Square

18 February

Yes it certainly sounds very nice, your castle. But you will have left it by now. You will be at Marrakesh, with the Princess Royal and Lord Harewood – this piece of news stares me in the face in Sunday's paper [...]

I've been laid up on the sofa in my dressing gown almost ever since you left – what a bore! I hope I didn't infect you that day in the car: the usual little chill; then the usual damned headache.

Letter from Vita

Fez, Morocco

27 February

I see your books everywhere in Morocco, both in French and English – the latter in Tauchnitz. It's odd to meet Orlando *in Marrakesh and* La promenade au phare[3] *in Rabat. I'm sure you like this!*

[...] Well I must go and have my luncheon, but I shall toss off a large glass of Moorish wine (which is rather good) to your recovery. My darling Virginia, my poor darling Virginia, I am really deeply unhappy to think of you ill in the fogs of London.

---

3 *To the Lighthouse.*

Letter from Virginia

52 Tavistock Square

5 March

Yes, I am ever so much better. It was only the usual little temperature, which makes the headache hang about. But I am back in my room again, writing [...]

And I'm flirting with a rather charming – oh dear me, this won't make you jealous, sipping rosé at Fez.

Letter from Virginia

52 Tavistock Square

13 April

Yes, I must really write to you, because I want to know what is happening. But that said, I've nothing to say. That's because you're in love with another, damn you! Aren't I a nice nature, though, like a flight of green birds alighting now and then? I had meant, God knows, to apologise for being so d—d dull, so obtuse, drowsy and dreary that night at King's Bench.[4] I said to myself, No wonder Vita no longer loves you, because you bore her and if there's one thing love won't stand, it's boredom [...]

The week after next we go to Ireland,[5] driving all across by land, and then leaping the Channel [...] and so up to the wildest islands, where the seals bark and the old women croon over corpses of drowned men, don't they? And there I may be windswept in to the sea. But what would Vita care [...] She'd bury me under, wouldn't she, Vita? And yet how clever, how charming I am!

---

4 Harold Nicolson's London flat.
5 They visited Virginia's friend Elizabeth Bowen.

1935

Harold entered Parliament in 1935 and became involved in great issues of foreign affairs. Vita focused on her garden and her books: she wrote poetry, *The Dark Island*, and published her *Saint Joan of Arc* with Cobden-Sanderson. Virginia wrote her only drama, *Freshwater*, based on her great-aunt, Julia Margaret Cameron. The Prime Minister proposed to recommend Virginia for the King's Birthday Honours; she declined.

Letter from Virginia

52 Tavistock Square
15 February

I'm longing for an adventure, dearest Creature. But would like to stipulate for at least 48½ minutes alone with you. Not to say or do anything in particular. Mere affection – to the memory of the porpoise in the pink window.

I've been so buried under the dust and rubbish. But now here's the spring [...]

My mind is filled with dreams of romantic meetings. D'you remember once sitting at Kew in a purple storm?

[...] So let me know, and love me better and better, and put another rung on the ladder and let me climb up. Did I tell you about my new love?

Virginia's Diary

11 March

It was the bitterest Sunday for twenty-two years. We went to Sissinghurst in the bitter wind with the country all lying in its June green and blue outside the window. Now that's an odd observation I have to make. My friendship with Vita is over. Not with a quarrel, not with a bang, but as ripe fruit falls. But her voice saying 'Virginia?' outside the tower room was as enchanting as ever. Only then nothing happened. And she has grown very fat, very much the indolent county lady, run to seed, incurious now about books; has written no poetry; only kindles about dogs, flowers, and new buildings. Sissinghurst is to have a new wing; a new garden; a new wall. And there is no bitterness, and no disillusion, only a certain emptiness. In fact – if my hands weren't so cold – I could here analyse my state of mind these past four months, and account for the human emptiness by the defection of Vita; Roger's death; and no one springing up to take their place; and a certain general slackening of letters and fame, owing to my writing nothing; so that I have more time on my hands, and actually ask people to come here now and again. (But the week fills unbidden mostly.) Coming back in the snowstorm from Vita's: the snow was like long ribbons of paper; whipping, mixing, getting entangled in front of the car.

1936

Virginia finally completed *The Years,* and suffered another period of ill health. Lady Sackville, Vita's mother, died early in the year. Although Vita loved her, Lady Sackville had become increasingly erratic, and her death helped to ease some of Vita and Harold's personal and financial difficulties.

1937

Vita paid tribute to her mother in *Pepita*, a dual biography that was instantly acclaimed. In July, Virginia's twenty-nine-year-old nephew Julian Bell died in the Spanish Civil War. Virginia spent much of her time comforting her grieving sister, Vanessa. The event re-opened relations between Vita and Virginia, and their meetings and communication became full of vitality and meaning once again.

Letter from Virginia

52 Tavistock Square
21 July

Dearest Creature

I wired to you because Julian was killed yesterday in Spain. Nessa likes to have me and so I'm there most of the time. It is very terrible. You will understand.

Letter from Vita

Sissinghurst Castle
22 July

I am so terribly sorry. You know how often one says one is sorry, and one is, but there is a difference between being very sorry and sorry-to-matter. I am

sorry-to-matter about Julian. He was such a charming alive person, – do you
remember when you took me to tea with him in his rooms at Cambridge? – and
he might have done so much and enjoyed life so fully, and now! [...]

Darling Virginia – I wish I could do or even say something. You are so very
dear to me, and you are unhappy – and I can do nothing – except be your
ever very loving

Letter from Virginia

52 Tavistock Square
26 July

Dearest Creature,

I was very glad of your letter. I couldn't write, as I've been round
with Vanessa all day. It has been an incredible nightmare. We had both
been certain he would be killed, and the strain on her is now, perhaps
mercifully, making her so exhausted she can only stay in bed [...] Lord,
why do these things happen? I'm not clear enough in the head to feel
anything but varieties of dull anger and despair [...]

I should like to see you.

Letter from Vita

Sissinghurst Castle
21 September

Don't you know how I love seeing you always? And what an especial joy it
is to have you here? And what a benefit you confer on me, a lasting treasure,
by coming?

Second, thank you for the letter. I return it.[1] I agree with Leonard that it
is the effusion of a maniac [...] I hope you won't follow his advice, but still I

---

1 An American had written to Virginia asking her to write an article about Vita, adding
that Virginia's 'affair with V. Sackville-West' should make her an authority upon the subject.

have a certain secret pride in the thought that 'your affair with V. S-W.' should enable you to write with authority. Would it? There is much to be said on the subject but perhaps it would be better said by firelight on a winter evening when one had omitted to turn on the lights [...]

This is a private postscript. I had a note from Vanessa which ends thus: 'I cannot ever say how Virginia has helped me. Perhaps, some day, not now, you will be able to tell her it's true.'

Perhaps I ought not to quote this to you, but I don't see why not. In any case, please keep it to yourself.

Letter from Virginia

Monk's House
1 October

We have been so ridden with visitors that I never had a moment to write. In fact I was so touched by your letter that I couldn't. Isn't it odd? Nessa's saying that to you, I mean, meant something I can't speak of. And I can't tell anyone — but I think you guess — how terrible it is to me, watching her: if I could do anything — sometimes I feel hopeless. But that message gives me something to hold on to.

Letter from Vita

Sissinghurst Castle
13 November

My (once) Virginia

You said I was a fool not to write to you when my pen wriggled to do so. Well, it wriggles now. I write from the pink tower, which you like.

I hear echoes of you — from Eddy for instance, who says he went to tea with you. I felt envious. I felt I could have come to tea with you on far closer terms than Eddy. Why don't I? Just because I am not in London — and Eddy frequently is. Isn't it a pity that geographical distance should make such a difference?

Anyway we are going to have some jaunts of our own liking in January, aren't we? Where shall we go? To Kew? Do you ever think of me?

If you do, please imagine a Sissinghurst very muddy, with busynesses going on, such as gardening (ask Leonard, who is a gardener, and he will tell you that all gardeners have an orgy of planting and transplanting at this time of the year. You may have seen him and Percy busy at it).

Such an unpleasant party of people came here, their hands shaky from drink and drugs, I don't know which; I hated them; they made the sort of impression one doesn't forget.

Is this just a letter to be put up behind your paperweight on the mantelpiece, to be answered some day? If so, I'd rather you didn't answer it at all. Or among Ethel's letters? What an awful thought!

No, Virginia, please don't answer it. I shall know it has arrived and that you will recognise it as a thought of love from your Orlando.

The servants made such a lovely bonfire here on Guy Fawkes' day. I thought of you, as the flames shot up. They had fireworks too, and turned the whole front of Sissinghurst pink as though it blushed. They put the fireworks into a dustbin, and blew the lid up into the sky.

Behind all this nonsense, is the horror of Spain. I do mind about it so much. And all the rest of the world too — Only, Spain is in the foreground for the moment.

A rather inconsecutive letter, I fear (I've just read it over, — you know how one does, at the bottom of the page), but somehow I always turn to you when I feel like the dustbin with fireworks inside it.

Letter from Virginia

Tavistock Square
25 Nov

Why 'once' Virginia? Why mayn't I answer your letter? That of course is the way to make me sit down at once and answer it. Why are you a dustbin? And why shouldn't we go for a jaunt? Why, why, why?

Just because you choose to sit in the mud in Kent and I on the flags of London, that's no reason why love should fade, is it? Why the pearls and the porpoise should vanish.

No. I can't see your argument. In January I will take you to the place where we once had a glass of wine in a bow window overlooking the river [...]

So no more – but if your pen should again take to twisting, let it.

Because, my dear Vita, what's the use of saying '*once* Virginia' when I'm alive and here now? So's Potto if it comes to that.

Yr faithful old servants and adorers

P and V

Letter from Virginia

Monk's House
26 December

12,000 copies of *Pepita* sold. I'm thinking of buying a fur coat.

Letter from Vita

Sissinghurst Castle
28 December

Glad Pepita *is going to furnish you with a fur coat. I continue to get the oddest and nicest letters about her [...]*

I regret not being closer to Virginia whom I love. Lord, how lovely you looked the other night in your black and scarlet!

Your pink porpoise
Orlando

1938

Virginia published *Three Guineas*, a condemnation of male vanity and aggression with which Vita did not wholly agree and which led to their only quarrel. In her new poem *Solitude*, published by the Hogarth Press, Vita hinted at the contrast between her ephemeral love affairs ('Those cheap and easy loves') and what Virginia still meant to her.

Letter from Virginia

52 Tavistock Square

3 May

Oh I'm so sick of this blasted London; its perpetual drab, its drip today, its grey everyday, and all these people. The Press however is now chained to John Lehmann,[1] or will be in October; and I hope (not with great sanguinity though) to be quit of those eternal [manuscripts]. Six lie before me at this moment. And we've had such a good year and made so much money, and I can't help some pride when I think of the type in the carpet at Hogarth House; and now they say it's worth, the Press, £10,000. Much thanks to the noble daughter of all the Sackvilles.

1 John Lehmann had purchased Virginia's half-share in the Hogarth Press.

Letter from Vita

Sissinghurst Castle
30 May

I thought I must have committed some crime when I saw a typed letter from you signed 'yours faithfully Virginia Woolf,' but I quickly saw it was all right, and have sent a small donation to the library [...][2]

*What about your [*Three Guineas*]? I thought it was coming out this month but have seen no more about it.*

How very nice it was, coming to dinner with you. You know, I like your house better than any other house; its atmosphere, I mean. I always come away feeling that life is more worth while. This sounds like a phrase, but is the right truth.

Letter from Virginia

52 Tavistock Square
1 June

[*Three Guineas*] comes out tomorrow. It's only a piece of donkey-drudgery, and as it repeats in still soberer prose, the theme of that very sober piece *The Years*, which, rightly, you didn't like, I hadn't meant to send it. But I will, by way of thanks, and you need neither read it nor write and say you have. Both those books are now off my mind, thank God. Why did I feel I must write them? Lord knows.

Letter from Vita

Sissinghurst Castle
15 June

If I haven't written to thank you for your Three Guineas, *it is only because I knew you were going off to Skye, not because I didn't savour it. You are a*

---

2 Virginia was an enthusiastic patron of a feminist library in Marsham Street, and was appealing to her friends for subscriptions.

tantalising writer, because at one moment you enchant one with your lovely prose and next moment exasperate one with your misleading arguments. You see, so provocative a book can't be thanked for in a mere letter; it would need a reply as long as the book itself, and that would mean a publication by the Hogarth Press. And far be it from me to cross swords with you publicly, for I should always lose on points in fencing, though if it came to fisticuffs I might knock you down. So long as you play the gentleman's game, with the gentleman's technique, you win. — I am not explaining myself very well, indeed very badly and confusedly, so shall we leave it till we meet? In the meantime, let me say that I read you with delight, even though I wanted to exclaim 'Oh, BUT Virginia … ' on 50% of your pages.

Letter from Virginia

George Inn Challerford, Northumberland
19 June

Of course I knew you wouldn't like *3 gs* — that's why I wouldn't, unless you had sent a postcard with a question, have given it to you. All the same, I don't quite understand. You say you don't agree with 50% of it — no, of course you don't. But when you say that you are exasperated by my 'misleading arguments' — then I ask, what do you mean? If I said, I don't agree with your conception of Joan of Arc's character, that's one thing. But if I said, your arguments about her are 'misleading' shouldn't I mean, Vita has cooked the facts in a dishonest way in order to produce an effect which she knows to be untrue? If *that's* what you mean by 'misleading' then we shall have to have the matter out, whether with swords or fisticuffs. And I don't think *whichever we use,* you will, as you say, knock me down. It may be a silly book, and I don't agree that it's a well-written book; but it's certainly an honest book: and I took more pains to get up the facts and state them plainly than I ever took with a thing in my life […]

Letter from Virginia

52 Tavistock Square
22 July

Leonard says you have sent a poem, and would like to know what I
think of it. Now I would like to read it and normally would fire off an
opinion with my usual audacity. But I want to explain: constituted as I
am (not as I ought to be) I feel I can't read your poem impartially while
your charges against me, as expressed in a letter I have somewhere but
won't quote, remain unsubstantiated. I feel, I mean, that you thought
me dishonest in *3 gs*: you said something about its being 'misleading'
and suggested that if only you weren't incurably clumsy, honest and
slow witted yourself you could demolish my specious humbug. You
could knock me down with your honest old English fists and so on.
And then you sicklied me over with praise of charm and wit.

Letter from Vita

Sissinghurst Castle
23 July

*But my darling Virginia, never in my life have I ever suspected you of humbug or
dishonesty! I was absolutely appalled by your letter this morning. Obviously you
have never had a letter I wrote you while you were away, and perhaps foolishly
sent to Skye. I of course cannot now remember exactly how I expressed myself
in it, but it was to the effect that I had never for a moment questioned your
facts or their accuracy in 3 Guineas, but only disagreed in some places with
the deductions you drew from them. And this, after all, is a matter of opinion,
not of fact. By my unfortunate allusion to the elegance of your style I meant
that you almost succeeded in convincing one in spite of oneself, until I stopped
to reflect afterwards in cold blood. To take an example, I question very much
whether any Englishwoman feels that England is not her country because she
will lose her nationality if she should happen to marry a foreigner (p. 196).*

Again, on p. 194, you suggest that 'fighting is a sex characteristic which she cannot share', but is it not true that many women are extremely bellicose and urge their men to fight? What about the white feather campaign in the last war? I am entirely in agreement with you that they ought not to be like that, but the fact remains that they frequently are. The average woman admires what she considers to be the virile qualities.

However, it is boring to go on adducing examples, but I hope I have said enough to show you that your honesty, integrity, and good faith were never for an instant under suspicion. I am truly upset to think you may have been nourishing this idea for the last weeks, and I wish to God you had got the letter I wrote to Sligachan.[3] You know there are few people in the world whom I should hate to hurt more than you, and few people whose integrity I respect or trust more. That you should feel you can't read my poem because of some barrier between us shows me that I must have hurt you, though God knows I never meant to, nor was there any cause for offence in my mind, only I must have expressed myself clumsily. At any rate I know you will believe me. Your very contrite and entirely devoted

Letter from Virginia

52 Tavistock Square

23 July

What on earth can I have said in my letter to call forth your telegram? God knows. I scribbled it off in five minutes, never read it through, and can only remember that it was written in a vein of obvious humorous extravagance and in a tearing hurry [...]

But, as I say, let's leave it: and I apologise, and will never write a letter so carelessly again. And I've no grievance whatever; and you need say no more, because I'm quite sure, on re-reading your letter, you

---

3 On Skye.

didn't mean that I was dishonest: and that's the only thing I minded.
So forgive and forget

Letter from Vita to Harold

Sissinghurst Castle
3 August

*I went to Rodmell last night, and very nice it was too. We sat out in the garden
watching the late sunlight making the corn all golden over the Downs. Then
I had a long talk this morning with Virginia, who was in her most delightful
mood [. . .] Oh my dear, what an enchanting person Virginia is! How she weaves
magic into life! Whenever I see her, she raises life to a higher level. How cheap
she makes people like Teenie [Cazalet] seem. And Leonard too. I know he is
tiresome and wrong-headed, but really with his schoolboyish love for pets and
gadgets he is irresistibly young and attractive. How wrong people are about
Bloomsbury, saying that it is devitalised and devitalising. You couldn't find two
people less devitalised or devitalising than the Wolves [. . .]*

Virginia's Diary

4 August

I liked seeing Vita, so free and easy again. We sat out here and discussed
her loves; death; Ben [her son]'s tears, on being scolded by Vita; Willy
Maugham; Clive, who's writing a book, secretly, on war; Julian; Nessa;
looking so ill; so many women have lost sons and lovers; I forget how it
went. Also she brought a basket of peaches and half a bottle of Château
Yquem from her mother's cellar. And off she went in her great black
car [. . .] She was much like old times.

Virginia's Diary

7 August

Yesterday I saw six tanks with gun carriages come clambering down
the hill and assemble like black beetles at Rat Farm. Small boys playing

idiotic games for which I pay. Harold is very dismal, Vita says: predicts war, but not this week. A lull at the moment. And terrifically hot.

Letter from Virginia

Monk's House
27 October

Yes, Mrs Nicholls handed me a copy of your book: which I certainly consider my due, with an inscription. I don't believe you care a damn what I think of it. However, I'll tell you when I've read it, if you want to know [...] We plan to retire here for ever: in which case I should sink as deep in solitude as even you could wish.

Virginia's Diary

30 October

Words, words, words, so many and so many – That I think is the vocalisation of my little sensation this morning. I am tired of writing. 'Words' refers partly to Vita's new poem, *Solitude*. Does it jab on the nerve? Is it only sleek eloquence? The words I found on my lips were 'Suave and sumptuous'. I suspect there's a good deal more. But no doubt I'm at an angle. I don't want reflections on God: nor do I altogether forget her superficial view of *Three Guineas*: that she never troubled to think out what I meant. This is partly personal; partly not.

Letter from Vita

Sissinghust Castle
19 December

Virginia mine – This is to bring you my love – and to say I have ordered a paté for you for Christmas – and also to say I hope you weren't bored at luncheon[4]

---

4 On 14 December Vita invited Virginia to lunch with Freya Stark, the author and traveller.

— and how much I regretted that you weren't there when Father d'Arcy and I went to admire the lizard Freya Stark has brought back from Arabia, a magnificent animal which spends its life in England lying on a hot water bottle under an electric light globe, surrounded by relics of Ur dug up by Leonard Woolley. And was the Freudian dinner a success?

I would have liked some moments alone with you after luncheon but all I got was compliments about you from Miss Stark, who thought you very beautiful [...] So did I, if I may be allowed to say so, — very beautiful indeed in your brown fur cap and your exquisitely ethereal slenderness.

Well, well [...] I had better conclude with wishing you a happy Christmas, like any old housekeeper. And to think how the ceilings of Long Barn once swayed above us! [...] and dolphins sported on the marble slabs.

Letter from Virginia

Monk's House
25 December

Well that was a princely thought — the paté, and better than a thought, it practically saved our lives; pipes frozen; electric fires cut off; nothing to eat, or if there were, it couldn't be cooked; and then behold the parcel from Strasbourg! So we dined and then lunched and then dined off that — I can eat it for ever — I could have been content to freeze almost, if I could eat such gooses liver for ever. But what an extravagant Prince you are! How tremendously in the vein of the pink, and the pearls and the fishmonger's porpoise this pink cream with the black jewels embedded is — or was.

[...] and Mitzi[5] died in the night of Christmas Eve. It was very touching — her eyes shut and her face white like a very old woman's. Leonard had taken her to sleep in his room, and she climbed onto his foot last thing.

But enough — don't die —

---

5 Leonard's pet marmoset.

1939

Vita and Virginia were brought closer by the emotion and anxiety generated in the approach of the war. Both Vita's sons were in the Army. The women met frequently, though travel between Kent and Sussex was made more difficult by petrol rationing.

Letter from Vita

Sissinghust Castle
14 January

I have several things to say to you — First that I was deeply distressed for Leonard on hearing of the death of Mitzi. Please give him all my sympathy, and tell him he'd better acquire a lemur as soon as possible — they are the most enchanting pets, and said to be more closely allied to the human race than any other animal. I find this hard to believe, judging by their appearance, but biologists affirm that it is so [. . .]

Second, that I lost my heart to a friend of yours the other day, Margery Fry. I want to know more about her from you some day, please. What a lovely face and sense of humour.

Letter from Virginia

Monk's House
19 February

It is rumoured that a large shaggy sheepdog was lately seen in Piccadilly. On being questioned, it answered to the name of V. Sackville-West.

I don't know why it came into my head to tell you this fact; except that I think it's time V. Sackville-West answered to her name [...]

You have a ladder: on which rung am I?

Letter from Vita

Sissinghust Castle
22 February

How funny: I had just thought to myself overnight, 'It is a long time since I heard anything from Virginia, – I will write to her tomorrow,' – and then your letter came.

So our thoughts clashed and clicked –

Well, it can't be true that the shaggy sheepdog was seen recently in Piccadilly, because it hasn't gone near London since Feb. 2nd – when it suggested coming to have a meal of rabbit and dog-biscuit with you – and you replied that you would be going away to Rodmell that day – so that suggested appointment was off [...]

Anyhow, listen, Virginia mine: will you be in London on Friday, March 31st? And if so could I dine with you – or would you dine with me? I will stay up in London for the night if you will consent to do this.

Harold is flying to Egypt on April 4th – This worries me out of all proportion. I tell you this because I know you will understand. Damn, damn, damn, – I wish flying had never been invented. I shan't know a restful moment until he gets back. Nor would you, if it was Leonard.

You wish somebody would write a long poem, although you won't read any new poetry for a year. Well, I am writing a new poem[1] — a sort of companion to The Land — but I won't ask you to read it — only you might tell my publisher Mr Leonard Woolf that perhaps he may be offered a new poem sometime in 1940.

And tell him also (which he will be more interested in), that I am in the process of buying a neighbouring farm with 200 acres.

Lord, how rich life is, when one takes it the right way! Acres of farm-land, and a new poem in a big foolscap book, — what more could anyone ask from life?

Now more than ever seems it rich to die ...[2]

I would like to correct that into,

Now more than ever seems it rich to live ...

But if Harold gets killed by Imperial Airways, flying to Egypt, everything will go black.

Letter from Vita

Sissinghust Castle
23 April

This is Sissinghurst 250 — is that Museum 2621? — Is that Virginia? This is Vita speaking, — yes; Vita, — a person you once reckoned as a friend — Oh, had you forgotten? Well, dig about in your memory and perhaps you will remember a porpoise on a marble slab. — Yes, it is pronounce Veeta, not Vaita — Now you remember, do you? You remember a thunderstorm at Vézelay and the ceilings of Long Barn gently swaying round?

The purpose of this message is manifold. Its principal object is to say that I don't like being cut off from you and thus am making an attempt to get in touch. Will you and Leonard ever come here, on your way down to Rodmell?

---

1 Called *The Garden*.
2 A quote from Keats' 'Ode to a Nightingale'.

I would so like Leonard to see my garden. You, I know, are no gardener, so I confine this interest to Leonard. I do wish you would both come.

Letter from Virginia

Monk's House
19 August

Isn't it nice sometimes to write a letter one doesn't have to write? So this is one. I've been walking on the marsh and found a swan sitting in a Saxon grave. This made me think of you. Then I came back and read about Leonardo – Kenneth Clark – good I think: this made me also think of you. And in a minute I must cook some macaroni [...] Now I've enjoyed writing when I needn't; that's not to say you've enjoyed reading. And which rung are we one – my poor Potto and V.?

Letter from Vita

Sissinghust Castle
25 August

Virginia darling, you are very high up on the rungs – always –

Harold has gone off to join his boat again,[3] and I have asked him to telegraph to me when he is likely to get near to Newhaven. He wants me to fetch him from Newhaven – with the car – so if we aren't at war before then (Monday or Tuesday) I will telephone to you and ask if I may come for the night.

I find one's war-psychology very strange, – don't you? Up to 12 o'clock noonday I am the complete coward, dreading air raids, bombs, gas, etc. – then after 12 noonday I become all brave and British again – and remain brave until the next morning – when the whole thing starts up again in its terrifying cycle of fear, dread and shrinking cowardice.

---

3 A small sailing boat named *Mar*, which Harold had purchased for occasional weekend sailing trips. It was destroyed by bombs in 1940.

I think you are much braver than I am; or should I call it more philosophical? I don't know what you feel. —What strange stages of feelings one passes through, these days! I could not write about this to anyone I did not love as I love you. It is all too private and secret.

I have got Eddy coming here for the weekend. I fear he is very wretched for various reasons. I respect him enormously for volunteering to drive an ambulance or a car in London during air-raids. That seems to me really brave, for a person of his type especially – and delicate at that – He goes up in my estimation –

Letter from Virginia

Monk's House
29 August

But I don't think I'm philosophic – rather, numbed. I'm so hot and sunny on our little island – L. gardening, playing bowls, cooking our dinner: and outside such a waste of gloom. Of course I'm not in the least patriotic, which may be a help, and not afraid, I mean for my own body. But that's an old body. And all the same I should like another ten years: and I like my friends: and I like the young

[…] indeed, my dearest creature, whatever rung I'm on, the ladder is a great comfort in this kind of intolerable suspension of all reality – something real.

Letter from Vita

Sissinghust Castle
1 September

Virginia darling

Harold came back. So my Newhaven scheme fell through. I had meant to ring you up and ask if Nigel and I might come to luncheon tomorrow, but my best-laid plans have gone agley and seem likely to go agley-er and agley-er for

some years to come. So what can one say? I know you must feel all that I feel, and that millions feel. I keep thinking of Vanessa, with Quentin as a young man and Julian already gone. Perhaps she will now not feel so bitter about Julian's lost life, because he did at least sacrifice it voluntarily for a cause he believed in, which is nobler than being conscripted against his will into a general holocaust.

I do sympathise with you in the minor but still exasperating worry of removing from Tavistock to Mecklenburgh Square.

Well, – there it is, – and I must now go and arrange to darken our windows. Luckily there is a certain amount of comic relief always – and I find myself still able to laugh over ludicrous things which occur. This is called 'Keeping the brave British smile' by the Daily Sketch, *but I find myself keeping it at moments without conscious effort. I wonder how much longer we shall keep it?*

V

I do hope Potto doesn't mind the Second German War too much.

Shall you stay at Rodmell? It would be folly to go to London unnecessarily.

Letter from Virginia

Monk's House
2 September

Yes, dearest Creature, come at any moment you like and share our pot. Alone today and what a mercy!

I did like your letter. And if I'm dumb and chill, it doesn't mean I don't always keep thinking of you – one of the very few constant presences is yours, and so – well no more. Yes, I sit in a dumb rage, being fought for by these children whom one wants to see making love to each other.

So come: and I'll write to you, if to no one else, when ever I've a moment free.

Dearest creature, how I go on seeing you, tormented.

Letter from Vita

Sissinghust Castle
16 September

How much I liked getting your letter. Let us write to one another sometimes: I find that there are few people these days who give me any sense of real contact, but you certainly do; I suppose one's sorrow sifts out the rest. You ask what I feel, and I can tell YOU: on the top I mind what you call the incessant bother of small arrangements, — no physical solitude; people constantly about the place; questions, responsibilities, voices; five six seven eight people to every meal; the necessity of having my mother-in-law to stay here for God knows how long; never knowing who is coming or who is going away; the whole house upside down with people sleeping on sofas, — all this is very trying on the surface and makes one realise how profoundly selfish one has always been about one's private personal life. Perhaps it is salutary no longer to be able to indulge oneself in one's own idiosyncrasies?

Then, underneath this, on the second layer, come the anxieties, the young men one cares about whose lives are upset and who are probably going to lose them in a horrible manner, Ben with an anti-aircraft battery, learning to fire low, at 600 feet, in case of aeroplanes swooping down with machine guns; Nigel waiting, waiting, to be called up into the Guards; Piers (aged 18) already with the HAC; John, my nephew, aged 20, waiting to be called up at any moment; Harold fretting because no job has as yet been allocated to him; and when he does get a job it will mean his living in London more or less permanently — with air-raids and all that.

Then on the third layer, deepest of all, comes one's own grief and despair at the wicked folly of it all —

One is very unhappy and very tired always, don't you think? I have never felt so tired, — physically and spiritually, — in all my life. I think this is the dominant impression I get, so far, from the Second German War: complete exhaustion and weariness. Terror no doubt will come later on, within a fortnight or so, when they have finished with Poland.

I would like to see you. May I telephone in the morning and ask if I can come to lunch? Petrol is still available – or would you prefer to come here, in order to get away from your clerks?

Bring Potto.

'Où sont les neiges d'antan?'[4]

Your

V

I am glad at any rate that Quentin should be safe – I am glad of that both for Vanessa and you –[5]

Letter from Vita to Harold

Sissinghurst Castle

28 September

I very much enjoyed seeing the Wolves. It was a lovely day and the Downs looked very beautiful in the sunshine. Virginia seemed well in health, though naturally unhappy in mind. She says the only good thing which has come out of the war for her so far is that Ethel (Smyth) has fallen in love with her next-door neighbour, who, like herself, is aged 84. For years they have lived side by side avoiding each other, but the war caused them to talk over the garden fence, with the result they discovered they were twin souls [...]

I do like the Wolves so much. They always do me good. Virginia was so sweet and affectionate to me. I was touched. She told Ethel that she only really loved three people: Leonard, Vanessa, and myself, which annoyed Ethel but pleased me.

---

4 'Where are the snows of yesteryear?' François Villon (1931–63).

5 Quentin Bell had been excused military service on medical grounds, and was working on a farm.

Letter from Virginia

Monk's House

3 December

That was nice of you – to send me your book [*Country Notes*]. It really touched me. I've not read it (and I don't suppose you'd care a damn to know what I thought, if I thought about it considered as a work of art – or would you?) – but I dipped in and read about Saulieu and the fair and the green glass bottle [...] I shall keep it by my bed, and when I wake in the night – so shan't use it as a soporific, but as a sedative: a dose of sanity and sheep dog in this scratching, clawing, and colding universe.

1940

The Woolfs' London houses were made uninhabitable by German bombing, and they retreated permanently to Monk's House in Sussex. Vita visited Virginia here three times, thinking each time might be the last. A German invasion of Britain was expected throughout the summer, with Kent and Sussex on the front line. Vita sent Virginia presents from her farm to supplement her food ration.

Virginia's Diary

31 January

Vita is offered £1,850 for a 25,000 word story. My righteous backbone stiffens. I wouldn't for any money write 25,000 words.

Letter from Virginia

Monk's House
12 March

Oh what a pleasure to get your letter! And how odd! – I was saying to L. I felt that you felt we were out of touch: as for myself, I *never* feel out of touch with Vita. That's odd but true [...]

Here I am in the week of influenza – can't get normal, but hope to be up by the end of the week. A d——d sore throat.

And this is the only scrap of paper I can find.

But my dear how nice to get your letter! How it's heartened me! And how I long to hear from your own lips what's been worrying you – for you'll never shake me off – no, not for a moment do I feel ever less attached. Ain't it odd? And so I didn't write but waited – Yes, do, do come. What fun, what joy that'll be.

Letter from Virginia

Monk's House
19 March

Dearest,

I have a horrid little fear, as you've not written, that I said something idiotic in my letter t'other day. I dashed it off, I was so glad to get yours, with a rising temperature, and perhaps said something that hurt you. God knows *what*. Do send one line because you know how one worries in bed, and I can't remember what I wrote.

Forgive what is probably the effect of flu […] This is to show why I'm being, as I expect, foolish and exacting. It also shows how much I depend on you, and should mind any word that annoyed or hurt you. One line on a card – that's all I ask.

Letter from Virginia

Monk's House
22 March

Potto here licks the page in love of you.

Letter from Vita

Sissinghust Castle
24 April

Thank you for letting me come to stay with you and for being so permanently loving towards me —

Your friendship means so much to me. In fact it is one of the major things in my life —

Would you please tell Leonard that I inadvertently told him wrong about the plant I brought him: it should be Lewisia HECKNERI, *not* TWEEDII *—*

[…] I am so grateful to you: you sent me home feeling that I really ought to go on with my novel — Before I came to you, I was in the dumps about it.[1]

Then I told you something about it, which I would never have said to anybody else, and you said just the right thing.

So instead of despairing about it, I fished it out again this evening instead of trying to avoid it.

Did I leave a little golden box on your breakfast table? Don't send it, but keep it for me against the day we meet at Penshurst.[2] I apologise. There is nothing more tiresome than a guest who leaves something behind […]

Don't forget about Penshurst, and our picnic.

Your Orlando

Letter from Virginia

Monk's House
28 April

Oh Potto was so glad to huddle upon the Rung again. Yes, it was a great treat having you. In fact, isn't it a duty, in this frozen time, to meet as often as possible? So that even in the cold night watches, when all the skeletons clank, we may keep each other warm?

---

1 *Grand Canyon*, set in Arizona. Leonard rejected it for publication by the Hogarth Press.
2 Penshurst Place, Kent. Virginia, Vita and Leonard visited the house on 14 June.

Please dearest Vita, come soon again. You've got a hoard in your tank.[3]

Letter from Virginia

Monk's House

[early May]

What a dream I had of you! A cow flew over us & crushed your nose – it went black. I had tapioca pudding handy, & applied it. The nose gradually blew out like a toy pig. What's the interpretation? Horror & guilt both strongly present.

Virginia's Diary

14 June

Paris is in the hands of the Germans. Battle continues. We spent the day seeing Penshurst with Vita – picnicked in the park. Very fine and hot [...] Odd to have seen this Elizabethan great house the first day that invasion becomes serious. But I like Monk's House better.

Letter from Vita

Sissinghurst Castle

1 August

Virginia darling, you were an angel to send me your book which has just arrived.[4] And I am forwarding a parcel to Ben, which I take to be a copy for himself. This is really lavish of you and I needn't tell you how delighted he will be [...]

Everything has seemed so uncertain (I refer to the invasion) that I hesitated to write and suggest a night for my visit.[5] But if things continue to drag on as they are now doing, may I come one day this month?

---

3 I.e. of petrol, which was rationed.
4 *Roger Fry: A Biography* was published on 25 July.
5 There were rumours of a German invasion in southern England.

I didn't want to get caught and be unable to get back home! Think if you had been landed with me for the duration of the war.

Would you ever come here if I gave you enough petrol coupons? You know you like a jaunt, and your book is off your mind now. So consider it.

Letter from Virginia

Monk's House
6 August

I've been in such a pelt that I couldn't write before. So now merely suggest, emphatically, *Friday 16th* [...] stay the night and it's understood that means all Saturday – no evasions about lunch, or someone waiting at Sissinghurst. Great lorries are carrying sandbags down to the river: guns are being emplaced on the Banks. So do come before it's all ablaze.

Letter from Vita

Sissinghust Castle
9 August

Look, I can't come on the 16th because I have promised to go to a demonstration of thatching (Women's Land Army) on the 17th, but may I come on the 26th? Which seems to be my first clear run. I am short of petrol now, as they have unexpectedly emptied my reserve tank, but will save up coupons for the pleasure of seeing you. Isn't that polite? But more genuinely meant than most polite remarks [...]

I will now repeat my urgent invitation that you should come here – only damn it, I am no longer in a position to fill your tank with petrol. I was so petrol-proud last week, and now all my lovely gallons have gone [...] Anyhow I think I could still produce a gallon for you – if only you'd come.

[...] Did I ever tell you that I sent my jewels and my Will away to a safer place some time ago, and that the only other treasure I sent was the manuscript of Orlando*?*

Letter from Virginia

Monk's House
30 August

I've just stopped talking to you. It seems so strange. It's perfectly peaceful here – they're playing bowls – I'd just put flowers in your room. And there you sit with the bombs falling round you.

What can one say – except that I love you and I've got to live through this strange quiet evening thinking of you sitting there alone.

Dearest – let me have a line […]

You have given me such happiness.

Virginia's Diary

31 August

Now we are in the war. England is being attacked. I got this feeling for the first time completely yesterday. The feeling of pressure, danger, horror. Vita rang up at 6 to say she couldn't come. She was sitting at Sissinghurst, the bombs were falling round the house. I'm too jaded to give the feeling – of talking to someone who might be killed at any moment. 'Can you hear that?' she said. No, I couldn't. 'That's another. That's another.' She repeated the same thing – about staying in order to drive the ambulance – time after time, like a person who can't think. It was very difficult talking. She broke off – Oh how I do mind this, and put the telephone down. I went and played bowls. A perfect quiet hot evening. Later the planes began zooming. Explosions. Planes very close. A great raid on London last night. Today quiet here. When I rang up Sissinghurst after dinner, someone cut in with 'Restricted Service. Things very bad there just now.' Of course this may be the beginning of invasion. A sense of pressure. Endless local stories. No – it's no good trying to capture the feeling of England being in a battle.

Letter from Vita

Sissinghust Castle
1 September

Oh dear, how your letter touched me this morning. I nearly dropped a tear into my poached egg. Your rare expressions of affection have always had the power to move me greatly, and as I suppose one is a bit strung-up (mostly sub-consciously) they now come ping against my heart like a bullet dropping on the roof. I love you too; you know that.

I didn't like to go away last Friday because they had no other ambulance-driver for the village ambulance but me — and fights were going on all day and distant sinister thuds — not so very distant. But I have now secured the services of a lady who could drive the ambulance in my place if necessary. She has a most romantic life-history which you would enjoy — It includes a vine-yard in Corsica which she ran for 5 years until brigands made her life impossible. But that is nothing to her matrimonial tragedies.

Anyhow, it means that I can now get away. So may I telephone one morning and ask if it would be convenient for me to come? [...]

Your loving, very and permanently loving
V

Letter from Virginia

Monk's House
4 October

'Oh I'm glad' — those were the very words Leonard spoke when I said Vita says she'll come. If you could hear what the Wolves usually say when people say they're coming —

So do. *Wednesday* we suggest: and the compact is you stay for Thursday luncheon [...]

Air raids pretty constant. Two bombs as I ordered dinner, a mile away in the marsh [...]

Virginia's Diary

10 October

Rather flush of ideas, because I have had an idle day, a non-writing day – what a relief once in a way – a Vita talking day. About what? Oh the war; bombs; which house hit, which not; then our books – all very ample easy and satisfying. She has a hold on life, knows plants and their minds and bodies; large and tolerant and modest, with her hands loosely upon so many reins: sons; Harold; garden; farm. Humorous too, and deeply, I mean awkwardly, dumbly affectionate. I'm glad that our love has weathered so well.

Letter from Vita

Sissinghust Castle
10 October

How nice it was to be with you – how much I enjoyed my visit. I like being with you more than I can say. You know I love you, and you know I like Leonard. There is a difference between love and like. So you are my love and Leonard is my like. I do like Leonard extremely [...]

Darling – thank you for my happy hours with you. You mean more to me than you will ever know.

Letter from Virginia

Monk's House
29 November

I wish I were Queen Victoria: then I could thank you – From the depths of my *Broken* WIDOWED heart. *Never* NEVER NEVER have we had such a *rapturous* ASTOUNDING GLORIOUS – no, I can't get the hang of the style. All I can say is that when we discovered the butter in the envelope box we had in the household – Louie that is[6] – to look.

---

6 Louis Everest, the Woolfs' live-out 'daily'.

That's a whole pound of butter, I said. Saying which I broke off a lump and ate it pure. Then in the glory of my heart I gave all our week's ration – which is about the size of my thumb nail – to Louie – earned undying gratitude; then sat down and ate bread and butter. It would have been desecration to add jam [...]

Bombs fell near me: trifles; a plane shot down in the marsh: trifles: floods damned – no, nothing seems to make a wreath on the pedestal fitting your butter.

Letter from Virginia

Monk's House

26 December

If my admiration for you could be increased, it would be by the fact that your divine butter arrived on Christmas morning. Anybody else, I that is, would have sent it any other day. As it was, Leonard and I, economising with a duck this year, had such an orgy of butter eating it was worth ten turkeys. Oh what a gift!

Oh Vita what a Cornucopia of Bounty you are!

[...] Two pounds of fresh butter.

And I never give you a thing – I wonder why that is. Then I have to add about £2,000 from your books, let alone the meaning of 'em.

1941

At Monk's House on 17 February, Vita and Virginia met for the last time. They wrote their last letters to each other in March.

Letter from Vita

Sissinghust Castle
14 January

(Dear me, I never realised your dislike of poor Hilda was so vigorous – I thought it was just a negative feeling –) [...]

I don't feel that any of the foregoing remarks are useful for keeping friendship in repair – if indeed it needs repair – does it? Personally I had quite lost the drifting feeling. All the same, what can I tell you that will evoke a sense of intimacy? So little has happened to me since the snow came and incarcerated me completely among my ruins. Harold has been away touring England and Scotland, and as I've been without a car since Christmas day (Ben having taken it away and left it out all night so that it got frozen and isn't back yet) the outside world has quite ceased to exist. But before that happened my past arose and looked me in the face in the person of Violet (Trefusis) whom I hadn't seen for about 10 years.[1] *We had a queer a la recherché du temps perdu luncheon together on the neutral ground of a country inn. She had lost everything in France, and now the MSS of her book has been burnt in Paternoster Row. Much to my relief she has taken herself off to Somerset, after threatening to take a house near me, but we correspond. She is rather pathetic really, − so forlorn − with her house and all her possessions gone −*

Oh how I look forward to the 3rd Tuesday in February

Your

V

Violet asked me what's known as a leading question about you and me.

Letter from Virginia

Monk's House
19 January

I must buy some shaded inks − lavenders, pinks, violets − to shade my meaning. I see I gave you many wrong meanings, using only black ink. It was a joke − our drifting apart. It was serious, wishing you'd write. It was not true that I disliked Hilda. I only felt − What? Something opaque, pulverising: my fault, as much as hers. And one pang of wild jealousy seized me, inopportunely, dining at Sibyl's. No, no, I must buy my coloured inks [...]

What did you say when Violet T. asked you a leading question? I still remember her, like a fox cub, all scent and seduction [...] Now why did you love her? And did you love Hilda? We must go into all this. I rather think I've a new lover, a doctor, a Wilberforce, a cousin − ah! Does that make you twitch? Am I still on the 3rd rung from the top?

---

1 Violet had fled France after the German invasion, and visited Sissinghurst several times during the war, but there was no renewal of her passionate intimacy with Vita.

Letter from Vita

Sissinghust Castle
27 February

Shame on me, I have never written you a Collins[2] nor sent you the promised firelighter. But here they are, arriving together. The firelighter is known in America as the Little Wonder, and indeed deserves the name [...]

I was interrupted here by an officer wanting to climb to the top of my tower. I asked why, being cautious. His reply was truly Elizabethan: 'Because we are coming to guard from dawn to dusk. You will have the Home Guard from dusk to dawn.'

Letter from Virginia

Monk's House
4 March

Oh dearest Creature – now you've topped the whole hill of your benefactions with a firelighter. Po: butter: wool: books: firelighter on top. There you must stop. You can't add anything to fire. You see the poetic fitness of ending there. What a magnificent conception of life you have – O damn the law. Leonard says we can't use your petrol. Another gift [...]

I suppose you haven't any Hay to sell? Octavia Wilberforce's cows at Henfield, which give us butter, are starving. So I said I'd ask.

Silence means no.

Letter from Vita

Sissinghust Castle
6 March

HAY! Good God, hay! Have I not been scrounging all over the Weald of Kent for hay? No hay; scarce milk: and that's why you haven't had any more butter

---

2 A thank-you note for her visit to Rodmell on 17–18 February.

— and that's why all the lawns of Sissinghurst are not going to be mown this year but allowed to grow. Hay! My holy aunt!

Leonard was mistaken for once about the petrol coupon. I wouldn't do anything illegal any more than he would. However, if you can really bear to come by bus I can easily meet you at Hawkhurst. I'd take you to Ellen Terry in the afternoon, and restore you to Hawkhurst later. All you have to do is to let me know. Any day except March 19th and 20th. On the 19th I have a committee and on the 20th — guess what? A local Women's Institute.

Virginia's Diary

8 March

No: I intend no introspection. I mark Henry James's sentence: Observe perpetually. Observe the oncome of age. Observe greed. Observe my own despondency. By that means it becomes serviceable. Or so I hope. I insist upon spending this time to the best advantage. I will go down with my colours flying. This I see verges on introspection; but doesn't quite fall in. Occupation is essential. And now with some pleasure I find that it's seven; and must cook dinner. Haddock and sausage meat. I think it is true that one gains a certain hold on sausage and haddock by writing them down.

Oh dear yes, I shall conquer this mood. It's a question of letting things come one after another. Now to cook the haddock.

Letter from Virginia

Monk's House
22 March

No, I don't keep budgerigars.

Louie's survive: and she feeds them on scraps — I suppose they're lower class, humble, birds. If we come over [to Sissinghurst] may I bring her a pair if any survive? Do they die all in an instant? When shall we come? Lord knows —

Virginia's Diary

24 March

A curious seaside feeling in the air today. It reminds me of lodgings on a parade at Easter. Everyone leaning against the wind, nipped and silenced. All pulp removed.

This windy corner. And Nessa is at Brighton, and I am imagining how it would be if we could infuse souls.

Octavia's story. Could I englobe it somehow? English youth in 1900. L. is doing the rhododendrons.

On 28 March 1941, Virginia left her last letter on the writing block in her garden lodge. It was a note to Leonard which thanked him for giving her 'complete happiness [...] from the very first day till now'. She then walked the half-mile to the River Ouse, filled her pockets with stones, and threw herself into the water.

Letter from Vita to Harold

Sissinghust Castle
31 March

I've just had the most awful shock: Virginia has killed herself. It is not in the papers, but I got letters from Leonard and also from Vanessa telling me. It was last Friday. Leonard came home to find a note saying that she was going to commit suicide, and they think she had drowned herself as they found her stick floating on the river. He says she had not been well for the last few weeks and was terrified of going mad again. He says, 'It was, I suppose, the strain of the war and finishing her book, and she could not rest or eat.'

I simply can't take it in. That lovely mind, that lovely spirit. And she seemed so well when I last saw her, and I had a jokey letter from her only a couple of weeks ago.

Virginia's body was discovered on 18 April. She was cremated at Brighton on 21 April, with only Leonard present. Her ashes were buried under an elm tree at Monk's House, with the penultimate words of *The Waves* as her epitaph: 'Against you I will fling myself, unvanquished and unyielding, O Death!'

As soon as Harold heard the news, he came down to Sissinghurst to be with Vita. Many years later she wrote, 'I still think that I might have saved her if only I had been there and had known the state of mind she was getting into.'

Vita died from cancer on 2 June 1962. Her writing desk at Sissinghurst remains as she left it, decorated with two photos: one is of her husband, and the other is of Virginia.

FURTHER READING

Also by Virginia Woolf

Novels

The Voyage Out
Night and Day
Jacob's Room
Mrs Dalloway
To the Lighthouse
Orlando
The Waves
Flush
The Years
Between the Acts

Shorter Fiction

The Haunted House

Non-Fiction

Roger Fry
A Room of One's Own and
    Three Guineas
The Common Reader Vols 1 and 2

Also by Vita Sackville-West

Novels

Heritage
The Dragon in Shallow Waters
The Heir
Challenge

Seducers in Ecuador
The Edwardians
All Passion Spent
Family History
Grand Canyon

Non-Fiction

Passenger to Teheran

Saint Joan of Arc

English Country Houses

Pepita

The Eagle and the Dove

Sissinghurst: The Creation of a Garden

Additional letters and diaries

Congenial Spirits: Selected Letters, Virginia Woolf, edited by Joanne Trautmann Banks

Selected Diaries, Virginia Woolf, edited by Anne Olivier Bell and Quentin Bell

The Letters of Vita Sackville-West to Virginia Woolf, edited by Louise DeSalvo and Mitchell A. Leaska

Vita & Harold: The Letters of Vita Sackville-West & Harold Nicolson 1910–1962, edited by Nigel Nicolson

Letters of Virginia Woolf (6 vols), edited by Nigel Nicolson and Joanne Trautmann

Vita Sackville-West: Selected Writings, edited by Mary Ann Caws

Biographies

Portrait of a Marriage, Nigel Nicolson

Vita: The Life of Vita Sackville-West, Victoria Glendinning

Virginia Woolf: A Biography, Quentin Bell

Vita & Virginia: The lives and love of Virginia Woolf and Vita Sackville-West, Sarah Gristwood

INDEX

penguin.co.uk/vintage-classics